Managerial Economics and Financial Analysis

Managerial Economics and Financial Analysis

Prof. M.S. BHAT

Professor and Chairman, Board of Studies (Management),
School of Management Studies,
JNT University, Hyderabad - 500 072

A.V. RAU

Teaching Associate
Department of Management Studies
A. U. Campus, Vijayanagaram, A.P.

BSP **BS Publications**
A unit of **BSP Books Pvt., Ltd.**

4-4-309/316, Giriraj Lane, Sultan Bazar,
Hyderabad - 500 095.
Phone : 040 - 23445605, 23445688

Published by :

BSP BS Publications
A unit of **BSP Books Pvt., Ltd.**

4-4-309/316, Giriraj Lane, Sultan Bazar,
Hyderabad - 500 095
Phone : 040 - 23445605, 23445688
e-mail : info@bspbooks.net

ISBN : 978-93-52300-21-1 (HB)

Dedicated to

Our Beloved Parents

Preface

Ships are made in the harbour but not used for, books are prepared with the help of Library but not stored for, to grab by readers for acquiring knowledge. This book is written with the aim of introducing **Management Economics and Financial Analysis (MEFA)** to **B.Tech.** students of all branches at undergraduate level and other Postgraduates of M.B.A. and M.C.A. This addition will create more interest as it covers the whole syllabus in precise and systematic way and meets all the needs and requirements of students.

Special features of this book are the fairly detailed study of various topics of **MEFA,** the summary at the end of each chapter, short questions, essay questions and multiple choice questions at the end of the book.

This book contains 8 chapters covering all the topics as per the **JNTU**'s revised syllabus.

Chapter 1 Introduction to Managerial Economics covers the following topics:

1. Nature, Scope and Importance of Managerial Economics
2. Demand Analysis, determinants, Law of demand and its exceptions

Chapter 2 Elasticity of Demand covers the following topics:

1. Types, Measurments and significance if Elasticity of demand
2. Demand forecasting and its factors
3. Demand forecasting methods

Chapter 3 Theory of Production and Cost Analysis covers the following topics:

1. Production function – Isoquants and Isocosts
2. Cobb – Douglass Production Function and Law of Returns
3. Cost Analysis and Break even Analysis

Chapter 4 Introduction to Markets and Pricing Policies covers the following topics:

1. Market Structures
2. Objectives and Policies of Pricing methods

Chapter 5 Business and New Economic Environment covers the following topics:

1. Forms of Business organisations
2. Public Enterprises and Changing Business environment in LPG

Chapter 6 Capital and Capital Budgeting covers the following topics:

1 Working Capital Management

2. Capital Budgeting

Chapter 7 Introduction to Financial Accounting covers the following topics:

1. Double-entry Book Keeping, Journal, ledger and Trial Balance
2. Preparation of Trading Account, Profit and Loss Account and Balance sheet

Chapter 8 Financial Analysis Through Ratios covers the following topics:

1. Meaning, Importance and Classification of Ratios
2. Balance Sheet and Profit and loss Account Ratios

We are very happy to place this book, before the academic fraternity and students. Now it will be our pleasure to receive the reader's feedback for improving the quality of this book and, thereby achieving its purpose.

Finally, we thank wholeheartedly BS Publications, Hyderabad, especially Mr. Nikhil Shah and Mr. Anil Shah for publishing this book. Mr. K.S. Raju and Mr. Naresh and Ms. Kalpana for their valuable suggestions for completing this book.

- Authors

Contents

Chapter 2

Elasticity of Demand

Chapter 3

Theory of Production Function and Cost Analysis

Chapter 4

Market Structures

Chapter 5

Business and New Economic Environment

Chapter 6

Capital and Capital Budgeting

Chapter 7

Introduction to Financial Accounting

Chapter 8

Financial Analysis Through Ratios

CHAPTER 1

Introduction to Managerial Economics

1.1 Introduction

Managerial Economics is the youngest of all social sciences and has great importance in business organization. The prime function of a manager in a business organization is decision-making and forward planning. Managerial economics is an offshoot of two disciplines – economics and management. Therefore, it is necessary to understand what these disciplines are, to understand the nature and scope of managerial economics. The two disciplines are vast. So let us have a brief note about these two disciplines.

According to Adam Smith, the father of modern economics, economics is the subject which studies as to how the wealth is produced and consumed as the wealth is the main objective and purpose of every human activity. He considered economics as the study of nature and uses of national wealth. This is true because if we look around the world of business enterprises, we find that every individual business represents activity transforming a set of inputs into a set of output. Such transformation is the essence of economic activity. In the process of transformation we have men, materials, machines, management, etc. on the input side and various types of goods and services on the output side. The purpose of any economic activity is to create 'surplus' or what is popularly known as 'profit' to satisfy maximum possible wants by sacrificing minimum possible resources.

The purpose of economic activities is so defined because of the peculiar characteristics of human wants, which are unlimited and the resources to satisfy the wants, which are limited. The essence of any economic problem is 'scarcity of resources'. If the resources were not scarce, the unlimited wants could have been easily satisfied by using them. But the resources at our disposal are limited and therefore we are always concerned with remuneration, mobilization, allocation and optimum utilization. This gives rise to economics problem. Economics is mainly concerned with the description and analysis of economic problems faced by individuals, organizations, nations and the world. Economics aims at giving a solution to this problem by teaching us how to 'minimise' the use of resources and/or how to 'maximise' the level of output. Management of an organization uses the tools and techniques from economics to find out the correct solution to the problem in its organizations.

1.2 Definition of Economics

Economics is defined on the basis of four major concepts:

1. Wealth concept 2. Welfare concept 3. Scarcity concept and 4. Growth concept.

1. ***Wealth – definition/concept:*** Adam Smith defines economics as 'an enquiry into the nature and causes of wealth'. This view is vigorously criticized on the ground that it was too materialistic as it completely ignored the welfare of an ordinary man and the society. According to this view wealth is the ultimate goal of a man. But in our real life procurement of wealth is not the ultimate objective. We work hard to make our life comfortable and to earn money. Thus, our ultimate objective is not wealth. Dr. Alfred Marshall for the first time defined economics in which the focus of economics was shifted from wealth to human welfare.

2. ***Welfare – definition/concept:*** According to Alfred Marshall, "Economics is a study of man's actions in the ordinary business of life; it enquires how he gets his income and how he uses it". He strongly believes that the ultimate purpose or objective of economics is to promote the well-being of mankind and thus welfare of society. Thus according to him economics is a study of wealth, on the one hand. However, the more important side, on the other hand, is that it is the study of man and his welfare.

3. ***Scarcity – definition/concept:*** Prof. Lionel Robbins in his book, "An Essay on the Nature and Significance of Economic Science" put forward a more precise definition of the economics. According to him economics is, "the science, which studies human behavior as a relationship between ends and scarce means, which have alternative, uses". The essential features of this definition are :

   Unlimited human wants: We have unlimited number of wants and moreover they are ever recurring.

   Limited or scarce resources: The resources like money, materials and time which are required to satisfy the needs are limited and scarce. Unlimited ends (wants) and limited means (resources) give rise to economic problem.

   Alternative uses: The resources which are scarce can be put to alternative uses. They can be used for more than one purpose, uses of resources can also be graded in the order of priority.

   Choice: Choice has to be exercised in selecting the ends to be satisfied and the uses of means to an end.

4. ***Growth – definition/concept:*** The growth concept of economics is given by the modern Economists. It does not condemn the scarcity concept; rather it is a modification to it. According to this concept, there are three types of economic activities. They are production, consumption and exchange.

   Production deals with the activities where by the resources are transformed into products or services to satisfy human desires or wants.

   Consumption is the process of using the goods and services for getting these desires or wants satisfied.

   Exchange deals with the process of buying and selling of goods and services.

   Prof. Boulding supports this concept. According to him exchange not only includes exchange of goods and services or money but also includes the determination of price and determination of commodities in the market.

   The nature of managerial economics can be understood by understanding its relation with other displines such as micro and macro economics.

1.3 Microeconomics

This is also known as Price Theory or Theory of Firm Microeconomics. It evaluates the performance of a business unit. It deals with behavior and problems of single individual and of organization. It provides various concepts for the determination of prices of commodities, services and factors of production. It uses the technique of indifference curves for studying individual behavior. This technique is used in macro economics for studying consumer preferences.

Macroeconomics evaluates the business environment, i.e. the total level of economic activity in a country. It deals with total aggregates, for instance, total national income and local employment. Micro economics plays an important role especially in forecasting demand as the general economic environment is taken into account. It studies the inter-relations among various aggregates and examines their nature and behavior, their determination and causes of fluctuations in them.

Managerial economics has its roots in microeconomics and it deals with the micro or individual enterprises. Micro economics, on the other hand, provides the necessary framework for the firm to act upon but it has less direct relevance in the study of the theory of firm.

Management: Management is the art of getting the work done through and with the people. It entails the co-ordination of human efforts and material resources towards the achievement of organizational objectives. It embraces all duties and functions that pertain to the initiation of an enterprise, its financials, the establishment of all major policies, the provision of all necessary equipment, the outlining of the general form of organization under which the enterprise is to operate and the selection of the principal officers.

Manager: The manager directs the resources such as men, materials, machine, money and technology. He is responsible for achieving the objective of wealth maximisation. In this process he faces a range of decision-problems in the context of planning any business enterprise and its range of activities. Each decision-problem represents an area of choice. But before coming to a decision, it is very essential to analyse the pros and cons of the decision-environment ignoring which a business unit can neither survive nor grow. It may be suggested that an analysis of a business unit and its environment can be attempted through economics. Decision-science is, therefore, based on the foundation of economics.

What is Business Economics all about?

From the preceding paragraphs, we understand that economics is a discipline that provides a set of concepts and precepts which together furnish to us the tools and techniques of analysis. These techniques serve as an aid to understand business practices and business environment, which further facilitate business decision-making. As already said managerial economics provides tools and techniques from economics and other related disciplines and then applies them in business. These tools and techniques help the manager to conceptualise the problem faced by management of a business firm in decision-making. These concepts and techniques aid logical reasoning and precise thinking, typical of a professional manager. Thus we can say that managerial economics is the application of economic principles and analysis to the problem of formulating rational managerial decision.

Definition: According to Edurin Mansfield, "Managerial Economics is concerned with the application of economic concepts and economic analysis to the problem of formulating rational managerial decisions".

According to Spencer and Siegelman, "Business economics is the integration of economics theory with business practice for the purpose of facilitating decision-making and forward planning for management".

1.4 Nature of Managerial Economics

From the above definition we understand that managerial economics is a special discipline, which integrates economic theory with business practice for the purpose of decision-making and forward planning. Economics provides a strange mixture of various faults and fallacies of analysis and application. Therefore, an indiscriminate application of economics to business analysis may sometimes create confusing paradoxes. For example, economic problems encountered by an individual differ from those economic problems encountered by a national corporate unit of an international organisation. These problems can be analysed variedly depending upon the nature and context of the problem. Thus it is said that a successful business economics will try to integrate the concepts and methods from other disciplines such as micro and macro economics, nominative and descriptive economics, the theory of decision-making, operations research and statistics. Business decisions, if they are to be effective, must be based on a critical awareness and understanding of the environment variables as well as the economic relationships which underlie all business operations.

Managerial economics uses micro economic analysis of the business unit and macro economic analysis of the business environment. Micro economics is used to evaluate the performance of a business unit and business manager's position therein. It foresees its attention mainly on individual units like a consumer, a producer, a firm or a single commodity. It helps us to understand the behavior of a single thing. In macro economic analysis, we study the system as a whole, not the individuals but the total.

The micro economics environment deals with the operation of the firm in an industry and a market. The firm, as a corporate unit, is an element of the industry. Each firm has a position in the industry and its position and operation is affected by demand and supply conditions in the market, price and cost considerations and so on. Thus to understand the position of the firm it is also required to understand the microscopic environment. This means that managerial economics is micro economics in nature working in the backdrop of macro economics.

Most of the business polices of an economic unit, like a firm, are based on micro economic principles. Most of the national or international economic policies are based on macro economic principles. However, neither the business sector can overlook the impact of national and global economic policies of the government, nor the economy can overlook the impact of business policies framed by a particular management. In other words, micro and macro approaches are supplementary and interdependent.

1.5 Characteristics of Managerial Economics

(i) ***Micro-economics in character:*** As managerial economics concentrates only on the study of a firm, it is micro economics in character.

(ii) ***Limited by macro economics:*** The firm's operations are limited by the macro-economic conditions such as government, inflation etc. So it works against the backdrop of macro economics.

(iii) ***Prescriptive actions:*** Managerial economics is concerned only with those decisions, which are made to attain the objectives of the firm. It provides various alternatives so that the best choice can be made to achieve the objective of the firm. Thus it is goal-oriented.

(iv) ***Part of normative economics:*** It indicates only the possible consequences based on certain relations but it does not give the best choice.

(v) ***Multidisciplinary:*** The concepts, tools and techniques of managerial economics are drawn from different subjects such as economics, management, statistics, organizational behavior, etc.

(vi) ***Application in decision-making:*** Managerial economics is judged by its ability to help the managers to make better decisions. 'Models' are built to reflect the real-life complex business situations and case study methods are also employed to conceptualise the problem, identify the alternative and determine the best choice in decision-making.

(vii) ***Evaluates every alternative:*** Managerial economics makes use of quantitative techniques to evaluate each alternative in terms of its costs and revenues. This helps the manager to decide the best alternative to achieve his objective of profit maximation.

(viii) ***Limitations:*** The assumption on which managerial economics is based is not universally valid. The theory fails when there is a change in assumptions.

1.6 Scope of Managerial Economics

Managerial economics suggests the course of action from the available alternatives for optimal solution to a given managerial problem. The problem may be related to any of the managerial decision areas such as production, inventory, accountancy, capital management or human resources management. Different authors have given different views regarding the scope of managerial economics. However, the following aspects generally fall under managerial economics.

1. ***Demand decision:*** Economists use the term 'demand' to mean the desire to have possession and willingness to pay for that possession. In other words, demand is the amount the consumers are willing to buy at a given price over a given period of time. For a firm or an industry consisting of several firms, the extent of demand determines the size of market. The analysis and forecasting of demand for a given product is very important for the successful running of a business firm. Without a clear understanding of consumer's behavior and a clear knowledge of the market demand conditions, the firm is handicapped in its attempt towards profit planning or any other business strategy planning. For example, estimating present demand and forecasting future demand.

   Present demand and forecasting future demand constitute the first step towards the objective of profit maximization. The stability and growth of business is linked to the size and structure of demand. It helps in identifying various factors influencing demand. The objective of demand analysis is to know consumer's behavior. The chief topics include determinants of demand, elasticity of demand and demand forecasting.

2. ***Cost and production decision:*** Production is the process of creating 'utilities'. Production decisions have many facets. It is linked with several other decisions like the decision to supply to the market, choice of technique and technology, product mix decision, etc. It is true that some of the basic concepts of managerial economics are directly helpful in arriving at optimum decisions concerning production, materials purchase and handling. However, production decisions cannot be resolved through considerations of only 'Physical efficiency' but also 'cost efficiency', in fact, production maximizing decisions are invariably cost minimizing decisions. The major topics include cost concepts and classification, production functions and cost control.

3. ***Pricing decisions:*** Price is the expression of value of an item in terms of a monetary unit. Pricing is a very important area of managerial economics as it is the genesis of the revenue of a firm. Also, the success of a business firm largely depends on the correctness of price decisions taken by it. As blades of a pair of scissors are required to cut a piece of paper, twin market forces– demand and supply – are required to determine a price. At any price, if demand exceeds supply, their excess demand pushes up the prevailing price. At any price, if supply exceeds demand, this excess supply pulls down the price, thus price is determined at a point where demand is equal to the supply. The important topics of this area are – pricing methods, price determination, differential pricing, product line pricing and price forecasting.

4. ***Profit decisions:*** Profit is the tool of generating internal funds. The primary focus of any business firm is profit maximization. Profit is the tool of generating internal funds. A firm which wants to grow in near future and would not like to depend on external funds, may like to generate its own internal resources through reserves and surpluses created by way of accumulated retained earnings, i.e., profit. Profit analysis would be very easy if the knowledge of future were perfect. But in a world of uncertainty there occurs a great difference between the expectations and happenings. This constitutes the difficult area of managerial economics. Profit maximization is assumed as a strategy and in that context pricing, product variation, costing, quality control, etc., are all treated as tactical and practical operations towards achieving it. Profit decisions include profit policies, nature and measurement of profit, techniques of profit planning. Profit is a residual earning to the entrepreneur for shouldering non-calculable rises.

   The firm tries to create as much 'surplus values' as possible; it is this surplus, which constitute the profits of the firm. The firm aims at maximizing profit either by maximising revenue, which it earns by sales of its product in the commodity market, or by minimizing costs of productions by cutting down the expenditure on the factors which it purchases in the sector market or by both.

5. ***Capital decision:*** Capital is the foundation of a business. The amount of capital utilized and its relative importance determines the financial structure of a company. An effective financial management would ensure that the capital structure of the company is tailor-made. Therefore, while deciding about the capital structure of the company, the management should bear the following factors in mind.

   (i) The use to be made of the capital,

   (ii) The cost of capital, and

   (iii) Most efficient allocation of capital.

   In short, capital management implies planning and control of capital expenditure. Capital decision includes cost of capital, rate of return and selection of projects.

   In brief the various aspects outlined above represent the major uncertainties, which a business firm has to reckon with. The managerial economics applies economic principles and concepts towards adjusting various uncertainties faced by a business firm.

1.7 Managerial Economics and Other Subjects

As already said, managerial economics is multidisciplinary. There are many sophisticated techniques, which are drawn from disciplines like applied mathematics, statistics, accountancy, operations research and psychology. The use of such methods and measures makes managerial economics a highly technical subject. Managerial economics uses these techniques for the measurement and optimization of economic decision variable.

Managerial economics and economics: Major concept of managerial economics is the application of economics in decision-making. Economics deals with theoretical concepts. Managerial economics deals with the practical application of the concepts. Economics has two main divisions – micro economics and macro economics. Micro economics is the source of various concepts such as elasticity of demand, various market forms etc. Macro economics plays a significant role in the area of forecasting. Economics helps the managerial economist in decision-making and understanding the general economic environment within which the firm operates.

Managerial economics and statistics: Managerial economics also uses statistical techniques for decision-making. A decision-maker first of all has to gather information in the form of statistical figures for the demand of the product, production levels, inputs used, advertisement expenditure etc. Census method and sampling methods can be used to collect the information. The information collected has to be tabulated in the form of statistical tables called frequency distribution and then it has to be analysed by working out various 'constants' to make influences out of it. Some of the important statistical techniques such as averages, measures of dispersion, correlation, regression, time series, probability etc., are used by the managers to deal with the situations of risk and uncertainty.

Managerial economics and mathematics: In managerial economics, we deal with variables, like consumption, demand, supply, income. The knowledge of algebra is highly useful to find out the relationship of various variables. Other important tools and techniques of mathematics like graphs, calculus, vector, matrices, etc. are also extensively used to arrive at appropriate decisions. In managerial economics, the economic concepts can be quantified by the use of mathematical figures. Therefore, the knowledge of mathematics is essential for a business economist.

Managerial economics and operations research: Operations research is also known as linear programming model. It may be defined as a method of optimizing in view of available resources to maximize or minimize an objective function. It is an activity-oriented analysis of a business situation by a group of persons drawn from different disciplines. There are many methods to solve linear programming problems but graphical method is the most extensively used technique in managerial economics.

It includes concepts such as game theory, inventory model etc. Game theory can be treated as optimum action technique guiding decisions. In other words, when there is inter-dependence in decision-making optional decision may be arrived at through the use of game theory.

The use of models is also a very popular technique in economic analysis. In technical sense, a model is a system or relations which has both analytical and predictive value and which helps us in understanding the reality.

Managerial economics and econometrics: Econometrics is a discipline, which combines the statistical method with mathematical precision. This discipline helps us to predict the impact of a change in known terms on the unknown variables. Econometrics is especially helpful in studying those cases where the factors influencing the dependent variables are mutually unrelated and where the variables are mutually related.

Managerial economics and accountancy: Accountancy is defined as the science of recording and classifying business transactions and events, primarily of a financial character and the art of making significant summaries, analysis and interpretations of those transactions and events and communicating the results to persons who must make decisions or firm judgments. The basic objective of accountancy is to provide information to the interested parties to enable them to make business decisions. In managerial economics, it deals with the preparation of summary, analytical and critical statements of financial work. It also aids the top management in reviewing policies and taking vital management decisions.

Managerial economics and decision-making: It is the most important aspect of managerial economics. Decision-making is a task of co-ordination along the timescale–past, present and future. Wherever a manager confronts a decision environment, he must analyse his present problem with the past data of facts to arrive at a decision in future. This means that the manager while taking a decision must always consider the economic concept of time like temporary run, short run or long run. Awareness of risk and uncertainty in the business also helps in correct decision-making.

Finally managerial economics is interdisciplinary adopting tools and techniques from economics and other related disciplines to achieve better business decisions and to achieve the objective of the firms accomplishing a social purpose towards social obligations.

1.8 Demand Analysis

The stability and growth of business is linked to the size and structure of demand. Without a clear understanding of consumer's behavior and a clear knowledge of the forces behind demand, the firm is handicapped in its attempt towards profit planning, sales forecasting or any other business strategy planning. Demand, therefore, is one of the crucial requirements for the production of a product. For example, if there is no demand for a product, its production is unwarranted and, on the other hand if the demand is high for the product, it can charge a high price.

In this chapter we shall discuss the meaning of demand, types of demand, determinants of demand, demand function. Finally, we shall discuss the concept of elasticity.

1.9 Meaning of Demand

According to economists, the term 'demand' refers to (a) the desire to have possession and (b) the willingness to pay for that possession.

Thus demand in the economists' new does not mean the wants, desire or need for people since these may not be backed up by the ability to pay. But it is the amount the consumers are willing to pay at a given price over a given period of time. To understand the meaning of demand better let us consider the willingness to possess a car. Everyone has a desire to own a car but it does not create a demand. A miser's desire to possess a car is not demand; for he does not have the necessary will to pay for a car. Similarly, a poor man's will to possess a car is not a demand for he lacks the ability to purchase the car. We can also consider a person who possess both will and purchasing power to pay for the car but it does not create demand for that commodity if he does not desire to have a car.

Thus demand for any commodity is the desire for that commodity backed by willingness as well as ability to pay for it and is always defined with reference to a particular time and given values of variables on which it depends.

1.10 Types of Demand

It is important to note that demand reflects consumer's behavior. Therefore to analyse the consumer's behavior we have to understand a list of some contrasting types of demand.

(i) Individual vs Market demand.
(ii) Market segments vs Total market demand.
(iii) Company vs Industry demand.
(iv) Domestic vs National demand.
(v) Direct vs Derived demand.
(vi) Autonomous vs Induced demand.
(vii) New vs Replacement demand.
(viii) Short run vs Long run demand.
(ix) Household vs Corporate vs Government demand.

Let us now discuss some important types of demand.

(i) ***Individual demand vs market demand:*** The consumer's choice to buy a product that maximises their personal satisfaction reflects the individual demand. The market demand for goods or service is the sum of all individual demands.

(ii) ***Market demand vs Total market demand:*** An aggregate of individual's demand from high income, middle income and low-income group yields the market demand. An aggregate of various market segments yields the total market demand.

(iii) ***Company vs Industry demand:*** The demand of an individual company is the company's demand and the aggregate of various company's demand yields the industry's demand.

(iv) ***Direct demand vs Derived demand:*** The demand for an item in response to its own price is called 'direct demand' whereas the demand for an item is called 'derived demand'.

(v) ***Autonomous vs Induced demand:*** The demand for an item or service in response to explicit factors like price, income etc., is induced demand, whereas the same demand where the impact of implicit factors is not stated is called autonomous demand. In other words, autonomous demand is the demand for the products and services directly, whereas derived demand arises out of the purchase of a parent product.

Explanation of the Law: The law of demand as presented in the form of the following table represents demand schedule and the same represented in the form of a graph is called demand curve.

Demand schedule

Price of good X (Px) Rs.	Demand for commodity (Dx) Units.
8	40
7	60
6	80
5	100
4	120

Fig. 1.1 Demand curve.

In the above table when the price of the product is Rs.8, the demand is only 40 units. But when the price has fallen to Rs. 4 the demand for the product has gone up to 120 units. This shows that a fall in the price leads to extension of demand. On the other hand, we find a contraction of demand with an increase in price from Rs. 4 to Rs. 8. This can be represented as follows.

On X-axis **(Fig. 1.2)** the quantity of product demanded is represented and on Y-axis the price of the product is represented. Demand of the Product x represents the demand curve.

The intra marginal consumers visually vary inversely with the price of that commodity. The marginal buyers of a commodity disappear from the market when there is a rise in the price and enter the market when there is a fall in the price of the commodity. From this we can say that demand for a commodity always varies inversely with the price of that commodity.

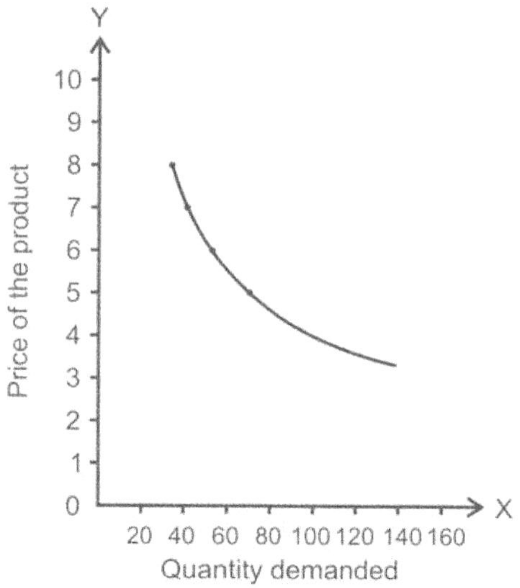

Fig. 1.2 Demand increase.

Assumptions of Law of demand: This law is based on certain assumptions, which are as follows :

1. This law assumes the income of the consumer to be constant.
2. Preference of the consumer is constant and he is ready to spend for it even if it is expensive.
3. A change in government policies will influence demand for the product hence this law assumes a constant government policy.
4. No change in size, composition and sex ratio of population.
5. Change in weather conditions is also likely to affect the demand for a product. Therefore this law assumes a stable weather condition.

Exceptions to the law of demand:

1. ***Giffen's goods:*** An exception to the law of demand arises in the case of Giffen's goods. These goods can be only those which are inferior and on whom consumers spend a significant portion of their income. In this case the demand varies directly with their prices.
2. ***Symbol of luxury:*** There are certain goods, which are purchased by rich people (e.g. diamonds, crystal etc.) in large amounts in spite of their higher prices. They increase such purchase in the face of rising prices as a symbol of luxury to distinguish them from common people who cannot afford them.
3. ***Consumer's psychology:*** In some cases we find the consumer judging the quality of the product by its price; the higher the price the better the quality according to this view.
4. ***Sale during off-season:*** We find reduction offers on certain products like refrigerators during off-reasons; yet demand is low.
5. ***Uncertain future:*** When the availability of the product is uncertain in future, people may buy more of it even in the face of rising prices.

6. ***Expectations of consumers:*** When prices fall, people expect it to fall further and vice-versa. Under such conditions, the purchase of the product may be postponed. Similarly when prices rise, people may expect it to rise further and purchase the product in advance.
7. ***Necessity:*** People tend to adjust their consumption on other goods if there is a change in the price as they consider them to be most urgent.

1.11 Determinants of Demand

1. Consumer's income.
2. Price of the product.
3. Consumer's preferences.
4. Prices of related goods.
5. Population and its distribution.
6. Consumer's expectations about the prices and incomes.

1. ***Consumer's income and demand :*** Consumer's income plays an important role as a constraint variable in demand functions. It determines the quantity and quality of the product. A consumer with an average income spends to buy some commodities. As he becomes richer and richer he spends his money to buy adequate quantities so that he becomes satisfied quantitatively. Once he is satisfied quantitatively he spends his increased income to improve quality consumption. Thus he substitutes poor quality items by good quality items. The former type of goods are called inferior goods and latter are called superior goods. A hypothetical income-demand curve called Engel curve for a normal commodity is as follows.

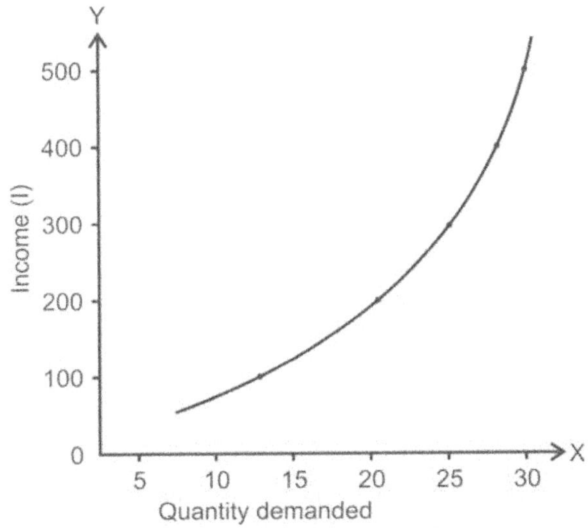

Fig. 1.3 Demand decrease.

2. ***Price of the product:*** The demand for a product varies inversely with its own price. If there is a fall in the price of the product, there is a rise in the demand for that product and vice-versa. This consumption is also called the law of demand. The buyer of a product can be classified into two types – intra marginal and marginal buyers. The intra marginal buyers are those who increase or decrease their consumption of a product but do not give up or start their consumption when faced with changed conditions such as price variation and the marginal consumers are those who will start their consumption of the product if there is a fall in the price or stop the consumption if there is an increase in the price.
3. ***Consumer's preferences:*** An important determinant of demand is the preference of consumers, which exert a great influence on the demand of all goods and services. If a consumer develops a taste for a particular good and that commodity comes up in his preferred terms, his demand for that commodity increases. On the other hand, if the preference of the consumer for a commodity goes down, his demand for it will fall.
4. ***Prices of related goods:*** Goods and services have two kinds of relationships – substitute goods or complementary goods. Substitute goods are goods that have essentially the same use. Complementary goods are often used together. A good may be a substitute or a complementary or may not have any relationship with other goods. According to law of demand, demand for a commodity varies inversely with its own price, other things remaining the same. When there is a fall in the price of a commodity x, the demand for it (x) goes up. This further leads to a fall in the demand for its substitute goods and vice versa. On the other hand, a fall in the price of x, increases the demand for its complementary goods. Thus the demand for a product varies inversely with the prices of its complementary goods.
5. ***Population and distribution:*** As the consumption habits vary from region to region the demand for a product depends positively upon the size of population and its distribution. Furthermore, the needs of children and adults are not identical and also with reference to male and female groups, and rich and poor. Thus demand is affected by various sections of a community.
6. ***Consumer's expectations:*** The consumer's expectations about the prices and availability of goods also affect the demand for a product. If the consumers expect a fall in the price then there will be a fall in the demand for that product and vice-versa. Similarly, if consumer expect shortage of a commodity then there will be an increase in the demand for that product as they think of its non-availability in future and also as the price may go high in future than now.

All these are only the important ones which act as determinants of demand. It may be noted that the role which each of the determinant plays varies from product to product. Some are important in determining the demand for one type of good and unimportant for others.

1.12 Law of Demand

A demand function describes the relationship between the demand for a commodity or service and its determinants. Mathematically the demand function for commodity x can be expressed as follows:

Dx = f (I, Px, Ps, Pc, T, Sp, Dc, A, O),

where

Dx = Demand for x.

I = Consumer's income.

Px = Price of product x.

Ps = Price of substitute of x.

Pc = Price of complements of x.

T = Measure of consumer's tastes.

Sp = Size of population.

Dc = Distribution of consumers.

A = Advertising efforts.

O = Other factors.

Change in demand : The demand function yields an Engel curve if income is allowed to vary while all other variables are held constant. Thus a change in the factors other than price leads to an increase or decrease in demand and this is called change in demand.

Increase in demand : This is caused due to own-price variations. This results in shifting of the curve towards right.

The graph shows increase in demand from DD to D1D1

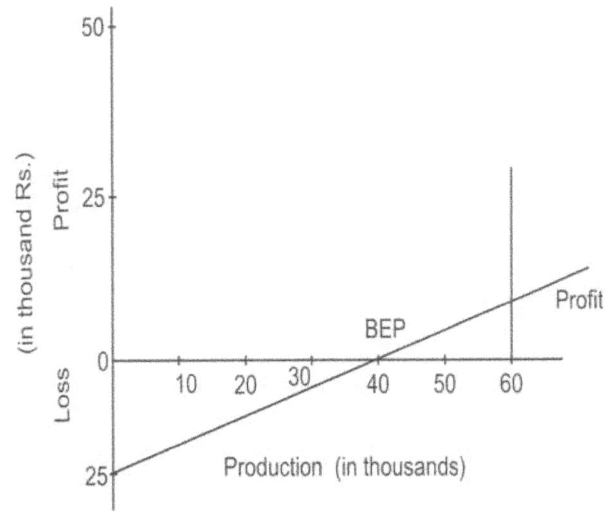

Fig. 1.4 Quality demanded.

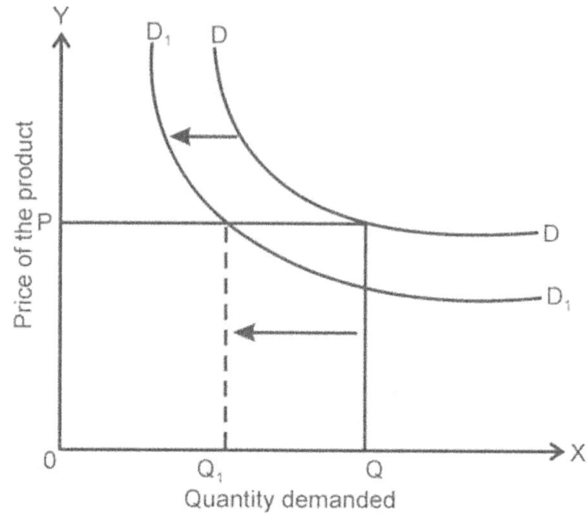

Fig. 1.5 Increase in demand.

Decrease in demand : This is caused due to variations in non-own price variables. This causes the demand curve to shift to left as shown in the figure.

The **Fig** shows decrease in demand from DD to D1D1 thus it is evident that increase or decrease in demand involves a shift in demand curve.

Extension in demand:

Demand variations along a demand curve with the change in price of the commodity are referred to as extensions and contractions in demand. An extension is the downward movement

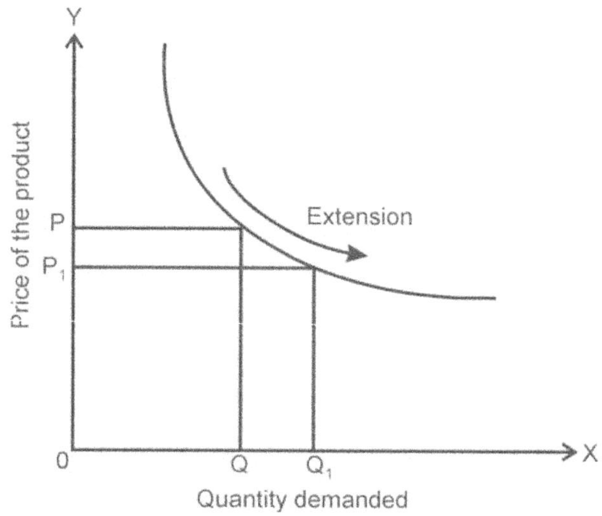

Fig. 1.6 Extenstion in demand.

along the demand curve, which indicates that a higher quantity is demanded for a given fall in the price of the good.

From the graph we can understand that at OP the quantity demanded is OQ. When the price decreases from OP to OP1 the quantity demanded extends form OQ to Q1 along the same demand curve. This is called extension in demand.

Contraction in demand

This refers to an upward movement along the demand curve, indicating a lowering in the quantity demand for a given increase in the price of the commodity.

When the price increases from OP to OP1 the demand contracts from OQ to OQ1 along the same demand curve.

Thus extension and contraction refers to downward or upward movement along the same demand curve.

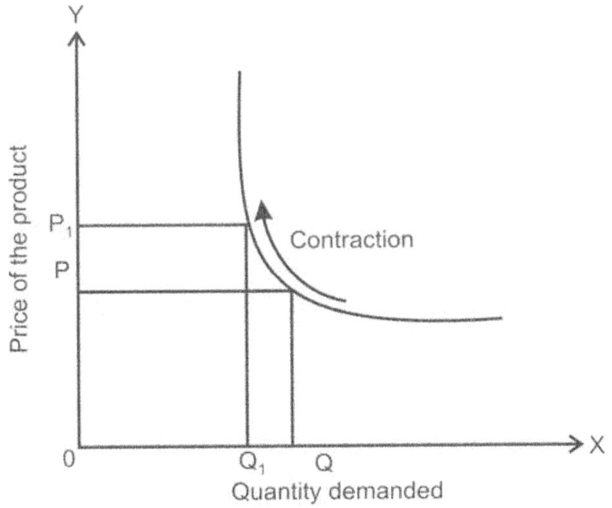

Fig. 1.7 Contraction in demand.

Summary

1. *Adam Smith*, the father of modern economics told that economics is the study of wealth.
2. Economist associated with welfare concept is *Alfred Marshall.*
3. The two major concepts of managerial economics are *decision-making* and *forward Planning.*
4. *James Bates* and *J.R. Parkinson* defined business economics as a study of the behavior of the firm in theory and practice.
5. Price theory is the other name for *micro economic theory.*
6. Managerial economics is applied microeconomics to business.
7. The contents of ME are based mainly on the *theory of firm.*
8. *Prof. Amartya Sen* won the Nobel prize for economics in 1998.
9. The objective of demand analysis is to know *consumer behavior.*
10. The objective of production theory is to know *cost behavior.*
11. *Capital* is the foundation of business.
12. In ME, the role of government interference is by means of *tax policy, trade policy, industry policy etc.*
13. According to *A.C. Pigou,* economic welfare is part of social welfare.
14. Scarcity of Definition is given by *Prof. Lionel Robbins.*
15. Managerial economics is also known as *economics of firm.*
16. *Managerial* economics is considered as a part of normative economics.
17. *Production* theory explains the relation between output and cost.
18. Managerial economics is *prescriptive* in nature.
19. Management is a function of following areas of *POSDCORB.*
20. Management is an art of getting things done through people formally organized groups.

Essay Questions

1. Explain nature and scope of Managerial Economics.
2. What is Demand Analysis? Explain the factors influencing the demand for a project.
3. What is meant by Demand? Every one desires for an ambassador car. Does this mean that the demand for ambassador car is large?
4. Explain the various factors that influence the demand for a computer.
5. (a) Define "Law of Demand", what are its exceptions.

   (b) Define and Explain the law of Diminishing Marginal utility with example.
6. Managerial Economics is an integration of economic theory with business practice for the purpose of facilitating decision-making and forward planning by management. Explain.
7. Define Managerial Economics and point out its chief characteristics. How is Macro-Economics useful to Managerial Economics ?
8. Explain how Managerial Economics is related to Economics, Statistics, Mathematics and Accounting.
9. Explain nature of the problems studied in Managerial Economics. What is the importance of the study of such problems in Business Management ?
10. What is managerial economics? What type of issues come under the preview of managerial economics?
11. Managerial economics is the study of the allocation of resources available to the firm or other unit of management among the activities of the unit. Explain.

Short Questions

1. What is the importance of Managerial Economics ?
2. What are the concepts of Managerial Economis ?
3. What are the concepts of Economics ?
4. What is meant by Demand Analysis ?
5. Define Law of Demand.
6. Define the law of Deminishing Marginal Utility.
7. Define Demand Schedule.
8. What are the exceptions to the law of Demand ?
9. Define determinants of Demand.
10. Define Extension in Demand.
11. Define Contraction in Demand.
12. Define assumptions of Law of Demand ?

CHAPTER 2

Elasticity of Demand

2.1 Elasticity of Demand

The demand function is useful for managers as it identifies the causal variables for and the direction of their effects on the demand for their products. However, this knowledge is not enough. The manager must know the quantitative relationship between the demand for his product and its determinants for taking certain managerial decisions. This leads to the concept of 'elasticity of demand'.

2.2 Types of Elasticity

There are four important kinds of elasticity namely:

1. Price elasticity of demand.
2. Income elasticity of demand.
3. Cross elasticity of demand.
4. Advertising elasticity of demand.

1. *Price Elasticity*

It refers to the quantity demanded of a commodity in response to a given change in the price of the commodity. It can be computed with formula.

$$Ep = eDp = \frac{\text{Proportiante change in quality demand}}{\text{Porportinate change in price}} = \frac{(Q_2 - Q_1)/Q_1}{(P_2 - P_1)/P_1},$$

Where Q1 = quantity demanded before change.

Q2 = Quantity demanded after change.

P1 = price before change.

P2 = price after change.

The demand is said to be elastic with respect to price if the change in quantity demanded is more than the change in price. This implies that the elasticity is more than one (e >1).

The demand is said to be inelastic with respect to price when the change in quantity demanded is less than the proportionate change in price. This implies that the elasticity is less than one (e < 1).

The demand is said to be unity with respect to price when the change in quantity demanded is equal to the change in price (e = 1).

The demand elasticity is zero when a change in price causes no change in quantity demanded and the demand elasticity is said to be infinity when no reduction in price is needed to cause an increase in demand.

Importance of Price Elasticity

(i) A knowledge of price elasticity helps to guide a firm whether its sales proceeds, decrease or remain invariable under conditions of price variations.

(ii) It also helps the firm to estimate the likely demand for its product at different prices.

2. *Income elasticity*

Income elasticity refers to the quantity demanded to the commodity in response to a given change in income of the consumer. It can be computed from the following formula.

$$E_I = ePi$$

The same is expressed as

$$eDi = \frac{(Q_2 - Q_1)/Q_1}{(I_2 - I_1)/I_1}$$

Q_1 = Quantity demanded before change.

Q_2 = Quantity demanded after change.

I_1 = Income before change.

I_2 = Income after change.

The income elasticity of demand is positive for superior goods and negative for inferior goods. Positive income elasticity of demand can be of three kinds – more than unity elasticity, unity elasticity and less than unity elasticity.

(i) The income elasticity of demand is positive and more than unity when change in income leads to a direct and more than proportionate change in quantity demanded. Eg : Luxury articles.

(ii) The income elasticity of demand is positive and unity when a change in income results into a direct and proportionate change in quantity demanded.

Eg: semi-luxury.

(iii) Income elasticity of demand is positive and less than unity when an increase in consumer's income causes a less than proportionate increase in quantity demanded and vice-versa.

Eg: food, clothing etc.

The income elasticity of demand is negative, when an increase in income leads to decrease in quantity demanded.

Importance of income elasticity :

(i) A knowledge of income elasticity of demand helps to estimate the likely changes in demand for a product as a result of changes in national income.

(ii) It also helps us to know whether a commodity is a superior good, normal or an inferior good.

3. *Cross elasticity :*

It refers to the quantity demanded for a commodity in response to a change in the price of a related good, which may be a substitute or a complement.

$$Ec = eDc = \frac{\text{Productionate change in quantity demanded product A}}{\text{Proportionate change in price of product B}}$$

$$Ec = eDc = \frac{(Q_2 - Q_1)/Q_1}{(P_B - P_A)/P_A}$$

where Q_1 = Quantity demanded before change.

Q_2 = Quantity demanded after change.

P_A = Price of product A.

P_B = Price of related product B.

Cross elasticity is always positive for substitute and negative for complements. It should be noted that greater the cross elasticity, the more related the two goods are. The cross elasticity will be zero, if the two goods have no relationship.

Importance of cross elasticity :

(i) It is useful in measuring the inter dependence of demand for a commodity and the prices of its related commodities.

(ii) It helps to estimate the likely effect on its sales of pricing decisions , its competitors and helpers.

4. *Advertising elasticity :*

It refers to the measurement of proportionate change in demand in response to the proportionate change in promotional efforts . Advertising elasticity is always positive.

$$E_A = edA = \frac{\text{Proportionate change in quantity demanded}}{\text{Proportionate change in advertisement costs}}$$

$$= \frac{(Q_2 - Q_1)/Q_1}{(A_2 - A_1)/A_1}$$

where Q_1 = quantity demanded before change.

Q_2 = quantity demanded after change.

A_1 = amount spent on advertisement before change.

A_2 = amount spent on advertisement after change.

Advertising elasticity of demand is high when even a small percentage change in advertising expenditure results in a large percentage of change in the level of quantity demanded.

Importance :

It helps a decision maker to determine his advertisement outlay and necessary amount to be invested for the advertisement.

2.3 Factors Governing Elasticity of Demand

A number of factors govern the elasticity of demand, the important factors are:

(i) *Nature of the product :* The products based on their market can be classified into necessities, comforts and luxuries. The nature of product has a significant impact on the elasticity of demand.

(ii) *Tastes and preferences of the consumer :* The customer who is particular about his taste and preferences tend to buy the product in spite of the changes in price. Hence the product is said to be inelastic.

(iii) *Time period :* When the consumer has enough time then product may be elastic and vice-versa.

(iv) *Level of price :* If the price is too high or too low then the product is likely to have an inelastic demand because a further decrease will not increase more demand.

(v) *Government policy :* A liberal government policy provides an elastic demand and vice-versa.

Importance of elasticity of demand :

It helps:

(a) to fix the prices of factors of production,

(b) to fix the prices of goods or services,

(c) to formulate government policies,

(d) to forecast demand, and

(e) to plan the level of output and price.

Point elasticity :

Elasticity is defined with reference to two observations on two variables and thus there is a problem as to which observation's values, if any to use in the formula. If we use two points A and B on a demand curve, the problem is whether to use A or point B or some other values in elasticity calculation. When the elasticities are calculated the two elasticities are different. Both these are called point elasticities.

The point elasticity is defined as the proportionate change in quantity demanded resulting from a very small change in price of that commodity. It is expressed as:

$$Po = \frac{\Delta Q}{\Delta P} X \frac{P}{Q}$$

The point elasticity is used to find out a change in one variable corresponding to a small change in the other variable.

Arc Elasticity :

The elasticity between two separate points of demand curve is called 'arc elasticity'. It measures the average responsiveness to price change over a finite stretch on the demand curve. Its calculation uses the mid-point values of the two variables under question. Thus, the arc elasticity value lies between the two-point elasticity's. The formula for the arc elasticity of X with reference to Y is:

$$\text{arc elasticity} = \frac{\Delta X/\Delta Y2(X1+X2)}{\Delta Y/\Delta X2(Y1+Y2)}$$

When X1 & Y1 refer to values of X & Y at point A while X2 & Y2 refer to the values at B. This is used to find out a change in one variable resulting from a lower change in the other variable.

2.4 Demand Forecasting

Introduction: The business environment is dynamic and flexible allowing number of changes to occur in it. The marketing managers therefore have to operate under conditions of uncertainty and should take decisions relating to pricing and production. Under the conditions of uncertainity the marketing managers depend upon techniques like demand estimation and demand forecasting.

Demand forecasting is essentially a judgement of future probabilities of the future demand. Since the future is uncertain, no forecast can be cent percent correct. Several methods of demand forecasting are available to business decision-makers and there is no unique method which always guarantees the best result. Therefore, it is important to get acquainted with the whole range of techniques of forecasting.

Demand Estimation

Demand estimation is an integral part of demand analysis and tries to find out expected present sales level for a short period. The marketing manager before taking a decision has to analyse a number of business problems relating the pricing, production and marketing. Therefore, the manager should have a clear understanding of the variables affecting the demand and their inter relationships. Thus, demand estimation is very important and the managers use two important methods viz market research and statistical method for this purpose.

The marketing managers have to operate under conditions of uncertainty and should take decisions relating to pricing and production. Under such conditions of uncertainty, they resort to demand estimation and demand forecasting. Several methods of demand forecasting are available to business decision-makers from which they have to choose the appropriate method suitable to the product and the purpose.

Demand estimation is an integral part of demand analysis. Business managers should depend heavily upon their subjective judgment for analyzing a number of business problems relating to pricing, production and marketing. In this context they should have clear understanding of the variables affecting the demand and their inter relationships. Therefore, demand estimations occupy importance. They use two important methods, viz., market research and statistical methods for estimating demand.

2.5 Market Research Methods

When statistical data is not available or for launching a new product or changes in consumer tastes and preferences suspected, Market research methods are used.

The market research methods most commonly used are consumer's opinion survey method.

Consumer clinics and test marketing (controlled experimentation). Consumer opinion surveys are conducted by contacting all or a representative group of consumers to ascertain their reactions to the hypothetical changes in price, income, advertising, and other determinants of demand. Consumer clinics are organized to manipulate demand and consumer reactions observed under controlled laboratory conditions. Test marketing method is applied in which prices or other variables will be manipulated in a single or multiple markets in order to observe consumer reactions.

2.6 Statistical Methods

When adequate data is available, statistical methods of demand estimation will be useful. The relevant statistical data may be either time series data or cross section data.

Time series data provides information about the variables fairly over long periods of time and cross section data provides information about the variable at a point of time. Since time data is available from published information, business firms use it with some modifications.

An important step in demand estimation is that the selection of appropriate form of the demand function, i.e., choosing a linear or non-linear demand functions. Fitting a curve to the observed data obviously will make the choice. If the trend of observed data is linear then the demand function is a + bx. In case the data is non-linear the choice demand function may be a cubic or quadratic. The non-linear demand functions are converted into a linear relation using logarithms.

The commonly used statistical method of demand estimation is the regression technique. Simple regression applies when the demand depends on one independent variable. When the demand is influenced by more than one variable, multiple regressions are applied.

The important steps involved in demand estimation :

1. ***Selecting the causal variables :***

   The omission of important variable or the omission of less important variables will generate adverse results.

2. ***Collection of data :***

   Collection of past data relating to the chosen variables is the next important step in demand estimation. The data should be accurate, relevant and reliable lest demand estimates go wrong.

3. ***Demand function :***

   As stated earlier the manager has to choose the appropriate form demand function i.e. linear, quadratic, cubic, log or semi-log etc.

The estimated demand function gives information on elastic ties. This is useful for planning and policy decision-making. It also helps in forecasting demand by setting the values of independent variables in the forecast period.

2.7 Demand Estimation and Demand Forecasting

Demand estimation differs from demand forecasting. Demand estimation tries to find out the present level of sales given the present state of demand determinants. Demand forecasting on the other hand tries to predict the future trend of sales.

Demand forecasting

Demand forecasting is an attempt to predict the future demand based on past data under conditions of uncertainty. In this context, the various methods of demand forecasting will come to the rescue of the decision maker. Demand forecasting occupies importance for production, planning, product scheduling, and inventory planning and so on.

Classification of demand forecasts

1. ***Active vs passive forecasting***

   Active forecasting is a method of forecasting the demand on the consideration that a firm is likely to initiate some action like changes in product quality, size, price etc.

   Passive forecasting is based on the assumption that the same product is being offered without any changes.

2. ***Short-run vs long-run forecasting***

   Short-run forecasting normally extends up to one year. These forecasts are useful for product scheduling, inventory planning, and mobilization of working capital etc.

   Long-run forecasts extend beyond one year. They are helpful in capital budgeting, product diversification, personnel recruitment etc.

3. ***Company forecasting vs Industry forecasting***

   Forecasting the demand for the products of a particular firm is company forecasting. These are firm specific and designed to serve the individual firms in planning their policies.

   Industry forecasting forecasts the demand for the products of the industry as a whole. The association of manufacturers or trade associations undertake them and serve the needs of all the firms in the industry.

4. ***Micro level forecasting vs Macro level forecasting***

   Micro level forecasting may take the form of company forecasting or industry forecasting.

   Macro level forecasting on the other hand is concerned with forecasting general economic environment and business conditions in the country as a whole. The national income growth rates, production indices, price indices provide useful insights into the future demand for most of the commodities. Governmental organizations provide the base data to forecast the demand.

2.8 Importance of Demand Forecasting

1. ***Production Planning and product scheduling***

   A business firm cannot function in wilderness. It has to take crucial decisions about what to produce and how much to produce. This in turn depends upon its estimates of future demand for the product. If the forecasted demand is likely to rise, the firm can plan expansion of its production capabilities to meet the growing demand at the right point of time. In the eventuality of declining demand it should resort to product improvement, diversification, design changes or even pursue an aggressive sales promotion strategy

2. ***Inventory planning***

   Demand forecasting is useful for the firm to acquire the right quantum of inventory at the right point of time, to meet the needs of the production department and at the same time without unnecessarily locking up the finances of the firm in inventory accumulation.

3. ***Capital planning***

   Increased production requires increased capital resources fixed as well as working capital. Availability of demand forecasts helps the firm to mobilize the capital resources in time.

4. ***Marketing strategy***

   Demand forecasting will be useful in devising appropriate sales promotion or marketing strategies. If the demand forecasts indicate a declining trend in sales, it should resort to intensive sales promotion campaign to sustain its sales. Demand forecasting will also help the firm in setting sales targets to the sales personnel.

5. ***Manpower planning***

   A firm has to recruit and train the appropriate level of work force. This calls for forecasting the demand well in advance so that the required contingent of the labour resources could be obtained.

6. ***Pricing strategies***

   Devising and setting the optimum pricing depends upon the forecasted demand. If the forecasts indicates a declining share in the market demand then it has to slash the prices to sustain demand. Conversely, if the forecasts indicate increased demand for the product over a longer period it can charge higher prices subject to the other considerations.

2.9 Steps in Demand Forecasting

Demand forecasting is an intricate exercise and conducted in a systematic and meticulous manner. Demand forecasting involves the following steps.

1. ***Identification of the objective***

   The first step in Demand forecasting is the identification of the objective or purpose for which Demand forecasting is undertaken. Based on the objective the type, level and the method of forecasting will be selected.

2. ***Nature of the product***

   Before proceeding towards Demand forecasting, the forecaster should be clear about the nature of the product whether a consumer good or capital good, Durable good or an intermediate product. This is essential since the factors affecting the demand and the decision variables widely differ from one product to the other.

3. ***Determination of demand***

   Demand for different products depends on different variables. Therefore, a forecaster should identify the relevant determinants of the demand for a commodity before he proceeds with demand forecasting.

4. ***Choice of appropriate method***

   The forecaster should select an appropriate method of forecasting based on the nature of the product. There is nothing like a universal method of Demand forecasting. The techniques used for forecasting demand for an existing product may not be suitable for a new product. Hence, choice of the correct method of demand forecasting is an essential prerequisite for forecasting accuracy.

5. *Analysis*

When once the demand is forecasted, the forecaster has to apply his analytical powers to properly understand and interpret the results. If necessary he should subject the results to the available statistical tests like coefficient of variation, percentage absolute tests etc.

2.10 Methods of Demand Forecasting

The methods of demand forecasting are opinion survey methods and statistical methods.

Opinion survey methods

- Consumer's opinion survey
- Expert opinion survey
- Collective opinion survey
- Test marketing or controlled experimentation method
- End use method

2.10.1 Consumers' opinion survey

The consumer opinion survey can be either census or sample survey. Where the numbers of buyers are limited, census survey methods hold. In this case, the opinion of the entire universe is obtained. On the other hand, where the number of buyers is large, universal survey is not feasible; hence, sample survey methods are used. The sample survey can be either purposive sampling or random sampling based on the nature of the product or the objectives of the survey. The results obtained through the sample surveys are blown up to the entire universe to obtain the forecasted demand.

However, it should be borne in mind that consumer opinion surveys are not perfectly reliable as there are consumers biases and based on the likely hood of some future changes that may or may not materialize. Further, consumer opinion surveys are expensive and time-taking.

2.10.2 Expert opinion method or Delphi method

Expert opinion method is a variant of the consumer's opinion survey method. It was also popular as Delphi method and first used by Rand Corporation in USA for predicting the demand under conditions of intractable technological changes. It is used under conditions of non-existence of data or when a new product is being launched.

The fairest step in this method is the identification of experts and eliciting their opinions about the likely demand for the product. The experts may differ in their views in which case the firm has to pass on the opinions of one expert to the other, of course under strict anonymity and seek their reactions. This exercise should go on until a common line of thinking emerges. This method will be an useful tool of demand forecasting provided the experts did not have biased opinions.

2.10.3 Collective opinion survey or sales force opinion survey method

In this method, the firm will extract the opinions of the sales team, which is on the payrolls of the company about the future demand for the product. The sales personnel are very close to the consumers and dealers. They express their opinions about the future demand for the product. The opinions so gathered are tabulated and the demand forecasts will be arrived at. However, care be taken before forming an opinion about the future demand. The opinions of the sales team should not be taken on the face value as an ambitious sales man gives an over estimate of the demand for the product while a sceptic fearing the fixation of higher sales targets always quotes a lesser figure. This can resolved by maintaining a track record of accomplishment of the previous targets and achievements of each member of the sales team and make necessary adjustments in the forecasted sales and arrive at a conclusion. This method is an inexpensive but more reliable method of demand forecasting.

2.10.4 Test marketing or controlled experimentation

Firms resort to test marketing while launching a new product or likely to change the design or model of the existing products. This is also known as controlled experimentation method as the product is likely to be launched in a segmented market to identify its demand potential.

The essential prerequisites of test marketing are that the product price, its design, quality, level of advertisement and sales promotion campaign should be equal in promotion to that of what the firm is likely to incur had it been released in the national market. Test marketing should be continued until the repurchase cycle commences. The geographical, economic, sociological and even the demographic features of the test marketing region should represent all the features of the national market.

Test marketing can be under taken in a single market or different markets with different features of the product. Test marketing will no doubt be useful method as it ventilates the consumer preferences and facilitates the model or design changes if necessary but at the same time, it is an expensive proposition. The forecasted sales in the test marketing area should not be taken on their face values.

2.10.5 End-use or input-output method

The end-use method applies for forecasting the demand for intermediate products. These are products used in the manufacture of some other final goods. The demand for the final product is an indicator of the demand for intermediate product, subject to the availability of the input-output coefficients. Once the demand for the final goods estimated, the demand for the intermediate product can be easily arrived at using the input-output coefficients. The major problem of using this method is that one product is an intermediate product for producing not one commodity but several other commodities as in the case of iron and steel. In such cases, the input-output coefficient in all the uses and the estimated demand for all those products should be available, failing which the demand forecasts become useless.

2.11 Statistical Methods

- Trend projection
- Moving average method
- Regression technique
- Leading indicators method

2.11.1 Trend projection or mechanical exploration method

When time series data is available relating to the sales of a product, trend projection method is applied. Time series data of sales includes cyclic changes in sales (c), seasonal variations(s), trend (t) and irregular movements (l).

$$\therefore \qquad \text{sales} = f(T, C, S, I)$$

Trend shows the long time tendency of the data. It is the result of changes in population. Level of income, competitive conditions, changes in capital technology etc.

Cyclic changes in sales arise due to the periodical swings in the level of economic activity such as prosperity or recessionary forces operating in the economy. These changes are longer in duration and studying these variables is necessary for identifying the turning points. Understanding cyclical changes is rather difficult, as these fluctuations do not follow a regular course.

Seasonal variations in sales occur at particular points of time in a year. The seasonal changes may take the form of climatic variations, festival seasons, holidays, marriage season etc. Seasonal indices help in estimating seasonal fluctuations.

Irregular variations are non-measurable. Who can predict when an earthquake, cyclone, war, or an epidemic breaks out? After deducting the estimated sales attributable to the other three variables, the residue is irregular changes.

Table 2.1 Trend projection

Year	Sales in 'ooo units
1995	25
1996	23
1997	30
1998	35
1999	43
2000	54
2001	49
2002	58

By fitting a trend line to the time series data demand forecast are obtained. Several methods are available to analyze the time series data. The simplest method is assumed that the four components of the time series data are related in an additive or multiplicative function.

In an additive function

$$\text{Sales} = T + C + S + I$$

In a multiplicative function

$$\text{Sales} = T \times C \times S \times I$$

Note that in a multiplicative function if the value of any one variable is zero the sum of the product would be zero. Therefore, it is assumed that the value of each variable is greater than zero.

By using logarithms the multiplicative function is converted into an additive function

∴ Log of sales = Log T + Log C + Log S + Log I

Whether one uses the additive or multiplicative function the trend value will be the same but the seasonal and irregular variable values of sales data varies in both the functions.

Free hand method of trend projection

This is the easiest way of forecasting the demand. In this method, Time series data is plotted on a diagram and a free hand trend line will be fitted in such a way that it passes through the closest points on the scatter diagram as illustrated through the Table 2.2 and Figure 2.1.

Table 2.2 Sales data

Year	Sales in Rs. (000)	X	X²	X×Y
1995	25	1	1	25
1996	23	2	4	46
1997	30	3	9	90
1998	35	4	16	140
1999	43	5	25	215
2000	54	6	36	324
2001	49	7	49	343
2002	58	8	64	464
N = 8	$\Sigma y = 317$	$\Sigma x = 36$	$\Sigma x^2 = 204$	$\Sigma xy = 1647$

The yearly sales data is represented on a graph and then by simple observation a trend line fitted. By extending the trend line to 2003 or 2004 the sales forecasts for the two subsequent years can be obtained. Though, this method is easy and simple to forecast the sales yet it lacks scientific approach.

The scientific approach of forecasting sales is to adopt the method of least squares or a simple to regression approach.

2.11.2 Regression technique or method of least squares

The regression technique is popular as the method of best fit. In this case sales forecasts are made assuming: (i) that there is single determining variables that is sales or function of time and (ii) it is also assumed that there is a linear relationship between the variables.

$$Y = a + bx$$

where

Y = sales

a = Y axis intercept i.e. constant

b = Coefficient of the determining variable x

x = time.

The normal equations for obtaining the values of a and b are :

$$\Sigma Y = Na + b\Sigma x$$

$$\Sigma xy = \Sigma a + b\Sigma x^2$$

Given sales data over a period of time the sales forecast can be made by applying the above equation and solving it to obtain the values of a and b respectively. The sales data in Table 2.1 is used to forecast the demand by applying linear regression equation as illustrated in Table 2.2

Substituting these values in the normal equations

$$317 = 8a + 36b \quad ......(1)$$

$$1647 = 36a + 204b \quad ....(2)$$

Multiplying the equation (1) by 4.5 and subtracting it from equation(2)

$$1426.5 = 36a + 162b$$

$$1647 = 36a + 204b$$

$$\mathbf{220.5 = 0 + 42b}$$

$$b = \frac{220.5}{42} = 5.25$$

Substituting the values of b in equation (1)

$$1426.5 = 36a + 162 \times 5.26$$

$$1426.5 = 36a + 850.5$$

$$576 = 36a$$

$$a = 16$$

Thus the trend equation is

$$Y = a+bx$$

$$Y=16 + 5.25x$$

Applying these values the sales for the years 2003 and 2004 forecasted

Sales in 2003 $Y=16 + 5.25 \times 9 = 16 + 47.25 = 63.25$

Sales in 2004 $Y=16 + 5.25 \times 10 =16 + 52.5 = 68.5$

Note that 9 and 10 are the 9th and 10th years, respectively.

In case the Time Series data takes the form of non-linear trend it can be Parabolic Exponential or Geometric etc.

The following equations forecast the demand where the trend is non-linear.

Second degree or Quadratic trend $Y=a-bx+cx^2$

For solving the second degree are quadratic trend function the normal estimating equations are

$$\Sigma Y = a + b\Sigma x + c\Sigma x^2$$

$$\Sigma Yx = a\Sigma x + b\Sigma x^2 + c\Sigma x^3$$

$$\Sigma yx^2 = a\Sigma x^2 + b\Sigma x^3 + c\Sigma x^4$$

By solving these equations, it is possible to forecast the demand for a commodity.

1. Third degree or cubic trend

$$Y = a - bx + cx^2 - dx^3$$

2. Exponential or Semi-log trend

Table 2.3 Sales data

Month	Sales	Total 3 months	3 months average
JAN	10		
FEB	12	37	12.3
MAR	15	30	10.0
APR	13	46	15.3
MAY	18	46	15.3
JUN	15	49	16.3
JUL	16	51	17.0
AUG	20	61	20.3
SEP	25	67	22.3
OCT	22	71	23.6
NOV	24	74	24.6
DEC	28	84	

$$Y = ae^{bx}$$

or $\log y = \log a + bx$

Here the trend equations assume a constant growth rate in sales over time

3. Double log trend

$$Y = ax \quad \text{or} \quad \log y = \log a + \log x$$

The Double log function assumes the value of elasticity of y over time.

The non-linear trend equation is converted in to the linear form by the use of logarithms.

Multiple regression technique holds when there is more than one independent variable affecting the demand. Advanced statistical packages are available to forecast the demand by the use of multiple regression techniques.

2.11.3 Moving Average Method

This method of demand forecasting can be used for those products whose demand fluctuates mostly due to seasonal disturbances. Moving Average Method is also known as smoothing method as it tries to estimate the extremities by averages.

When sales data is available continuously for a long time, the moving average method is applied. While applying moving averages one can take odd or even number of periods (months or years). Generally odd number of periods is preferable to even number of periods for calculating moving averages. When a three-month (or year) moving average is calculated, it is placed against the second month and the next three months moving average is placed against the third month and so on. The data so obtained is plotted in a diagram and the sales can be forecasted by extending the trend line for the future as illustrated through Table 2.3 and Figure. 2.2.

A close observation of Table 2.3 shows that there are large variations in the demand for the product over a year. In some months, the sales are dripping to low levels while in the other months the sales are very high. Pronounced seasonal variations can cause errors in forecasts. Moving average method minimizes or eliminates these errors. By fitting a trend line to the average sales and extending it, the future sales can be forecasted.

Observe that in Figure 2.2 the average sales are increasing with the passage of time and by extending the moving average line for the future months the future sales forecasted. Note that here a three monthly moving average is taken. In case the average of even months is taken, then the averages are placed in between the months. For example if a four months average is calculated, the averages are placed in the middle of the 2nd and 3rd months. The next quarter average will be placed in the middle of the 3rd and 4th months and so on. This is called as centered averaging method.

2.11.4 Leading indicators method

If proper time series data is not available and the available data does not show particular trend, the forecaster has to rely upon secondary sources of data for forecasting. Some times changes in demand for one product occurs before an increase in the demand for another then the demand for the first acts as an indicator for the likely demand for the second. Increased availability of bank loans indicates the likely increase in the demand for commodities like steel and cement. Similarly increased farm incomes may act as an indicator for increased demand for farm machinery and farm inputs.

Precautions to apply the leading indicators method:

1. The leading indicator should be accurate.
2. The indicator should provide adequate lead-time.
3. The lead-time should be constant, i.e., the increase in demand for one should affect the demand for another within a fixed interval.
4. There should be a logical reason why the demand for one affects the demand for another. There shall be some correlation between the two.

Despite the availability of leading indicators, there is the problem that time series variations in the demand for the indicators itself consists of random or irregular variations. To overcome these problems econometricians use composite or diffusion indices. The leading indicators method is also popular as the barometric method.

Summary

1. The relation between demand for commodity and its price is *inverse relation.*
2. The sole purpose of any production is *consumption.*
3. Methods of demand forecasting are : *Survey method and statistical method.*
4. Trend projection method is divided into *5* types.
5. *Expert's opinion* method is cheap and fast.
6. *Delphi* technique is an example of Expert's opinion method.
7. Defects of sales – force opinion method are *congenital optimism or congenital pessimism.*
8. Goods can be classified into *necessities, comforts* and *luxuries.*
9. Income Elasticity of demand,

$$Ei = \frac{\%\text{ change in quantity demand}}{\%\text{ change in income}}$$

10. If Ei = 0 then that elasticity is Zero income elasticity of demand.
11. Cross elasticity of demand,

$$Ec = \frac{\%\text{ change in demand of given good (A)}}{\%\text{ change in price of related good (B)}}$$

12. *Demand forecasting* refers to an estimate of future demand for the product.
13. Demand means desire to have possession and willingness to pay for that possession.
14. Hospitals, colleges, libraries are examples of *autonomous* demand.
15. *Derived* demand is created by parent company.
16. The quantity of demanded goods by a single firm is called *firm* demand.
17. The demand with its immediate reaction because of price changes or income fluctuations etc is *short run* demand.
18. The demand which will ultimately exist as a result of changing prices or promotions etc., is long run demand.
19. *Replacement* demand is the demand due to the resulting act of replacing the existing assets with new ones.

20. Define Law of demand.

    It states the relationship between the price and the quantity demanded. The relationship is an inverse relationship assuming other things remain constant.

21. Demand for prestige goods will actually be demanded more with a rise in price. These goods are called *velben goods.*
22. Diamond is an example for *velben good.*
23. *Segment market* demand is that demand for a product in terms of location, area etc.
24. *Demand function* describes a relationship between one variable and its determinants.
25. Assumption of law of demand is also called as limitation of law of demand.
26. Price Elasticity of Demand:

$$Ep = \frac{\%\text{ Change in Quantity demand}}{\%\text{ Change in price}}$$

Essay Questions

1. Calculate the price elasticity of demand

   $Q_1 = 4000$ $P_1 = \text{Rs } 20.$

   $Q_2 = 5000$ $P_2 = \text{Rs } 19.$

   How do you interpret the result?
2. What is the cross elasticity of demand ? Explain.
3. Define the price elasticity of demand. What are the various degrees of price Elasticity? Illustrate graphically.
4. What is meant by elasticity of demand ? Explain giving a suitable illustration, how elasticity of demand determines the price policy of a firm.
5. Define income-elasticity of demand and distinguish its various types. How does income-elasticity differ from price – elasticity of demand ?
6. (a) Explain the various factors that influence the demand for a computer.

   (b) What is cross elasticity of Demand ? Explain.
7. Illustrate the difference between change in demand and shift in demand.
8. What do you mean by elasticity ? What are the factors governing it ?
9. Concept of elasticity is of much practical importance – discuss.

10. Explain the concept of income elasticity of demand and also its role in business – discuss.
11. What is demand forecasting? Explain briefly various methods of forecasting ?
12. What is the criteria for choice of good forecasting method ?
13. What is impact of substitutes and complements on demand of a product ?
14. Explain briefly
    (a) Sales force opinion method
    (b) Least square method
    (c) End use method
    (d) Experts opinion method.
15. Explain briefly statistical methods of forecasting.
    (a) Moving average method
    (b) Leading indicators method
    (c) Regression method
    (d) Trend projection method

Short Questions

1. Define Elasticity of demand.
2. What are the types of Elasticity of demand?
3. Define Price Elasticity of demand.
4. Define Income Elasticity of demand.
5. Define Cross Elasticity of demand.
6. Define Advertisement Elasticity of demand.
7. What is the importance of Elasticity of demand ?
8. What are the factors governing Elasticity of demand ?
9. Define point Elasticity.
10. Define Arc Elasticity.
11. Define Demand Forecasting.
12. Define Demand Estimation.
13. Brief explain Market Research Method.
14. Define Statistical Methods.
15. Explain importance of Demand Forecasting.

CHAPTER 3

Theory of Production Function and Cost Analysis

3.1 Production Function

Production function is really an engineering concept that establishes relationship between the output of a commodity and its inputs. In the traditional terms, economic theory speaks of four factors of production, land, labour, capital and organization or management. But in the modern world technology also contributes to output growth and it is now regarded as an additional determinant. Thus, the output of an industry is a positive function of the quantities of land, labour, capital, and quality of management and level of technology that is employed in production. It can be represented symbolically as,

$$X = f(Ld, Lb, K, M, T)$$

where X = output of commodity X

Ld = land employed in the production of X

Lb = Labour employed in the production X

K = capital employed in the production of X

M = management employed in the production of X

T = technology employed in the production of X

f = unspecified function.

Importance :

1. When inputs are specified in physical units, production function helps to estimate the level of production.

2. It becomes isoquants when different combinations of inputs yield the same level of output.
3. When price is taken into the consideration, the production function helps to select the least combination of inputs for the desired output.
4. It indicates the manner in which the firm can substitute one input for another with altering to total output.
5. It considers the two types of input – output relationships namely law of variable proportions and law of returns to scale.

In general, production function may be fixed and variable production functions. In a fixed production function, each level of output requires a unique combinations of inputs. In a variable production function is one in which the same level of output may be produced by two or more combination of inputs.

Production function can be fitted to a particular firm or industry or for the economy as a whole. Production function provides the maximum quality of output which can be produced from the minimum quantities of various inputs that are revised to produce a given quantity of output. Production function will change with an improvement in technology. The new production function due to change in technology has a greater flow of output from the original inputs or the same flow of output for a lesser input.

The above expression describes a general production function. Under some specific conditions, one or the other of these various factor inputs may not be important and the relative importance of a factor of production varies from one type of product to another. For example, Land is the most important input factor in the production of wheat where as it is of least importance in the production of a manufacturing product. For good exposition of production decision problems, it is convenient to work with two input factors for an output. If labour and capital are the only two inputs, the above expression reduces to,

$$X = f(L, K)$$

where X = output of commodity X

L = unit of labour

K = units of capital

f = unspecified function

According to Michael R. Baye production function is "that function which defines the maximum amount of output that can be produced with a set of inputs".

Productions function is defined as "the technical relationship, which reveals the maximum amount of output capable of being produced by each and every set of inputs".

3.2 Cobb-Douglas Producton Function

As already stated, the production function denotes an energy relationship. However, it can be estimated by statistical techniques using historical data on inputs and output. One can hypothesis several alternative forms for this function, but the most appropriate form of the empirical studies on the subject has been given by Cobb and Douglas.

The production function is for American manufacturing industry using annual Time Series data for the period 1899 to 1922 by Cobb and Douglas. It is represented as

$$Q = A K \alpha L$$

where K = capital Q = output L = labour

A, α = positive constants.

This function is widely used in economics because it has properties representative of many production processes.

3.2.1 Properties of Cobb-Douglas Production function

1. This function assumes the returns to scale to be constant.
2. The constant and a and 1 – a in the Cobb-Douglass production function are the output elasticities of capital and labour respectively.
3. If one of the input is zero, output also will be zero.
4. The value of (a) and (1 – a) is the return to scale.

   If (a) + (1 – a) = 1, then constant returns to scale will operate.

   If (a) + (1 – a) > 1, then increasing returns to scale will operate.

   If (a) + (1 – a) < 1, then decreasing returns to scale will operate.
5. Elasticity of substitution in the Cobb-Douglass production function is equal to one.
6. Cobb-Douglass production function satisfies Euler's theorem.
7. Expansion path generated by the Cobb-Douglas production function is linear and passes through the origin.
8. a represents the capital and 1 – a represents the labour share of the output.
9. Cobb-Douglas production function becomes linear in logarithm, i.e.,

$$\log Y = \text{Log } A + a \log K + (1 - a) \log L$$

3.2.2 Managerial uses of production function

There are several managerial uses of the production function.

1. It can be used to compute the least-cost input combination for a given output or the maximum output-input combination for a given cost.
2. Knowledge of production function is useful to decide the value of the variable input employed.
3. It aids in long run decision-making.
4. It is highly useful for decision-makers to find out the most appropriate combination of input factors.
5. It shows the maximum output obtainable from any and all, input conditions.

Law of Returns: Production function explains the relationship between the quantity of inputs and the possible output. But the law of production deals with the relationship between additional input and additional output. They explains the relationship in the form of (i) Law of variable proportion (ii) Law of returns to scale.

3.3 Law of Deminishing Returns or Law of Variable Proportions

The law of returns is also called the law of diminishing returns. According to this law there will be an increase in the total output in the initial stages with one factor fixed and other factors being varied. This continues until a certain point and after reaching a certain level of output the total will increase at decelerating rate. If the variable input factors are added further to the fixed input factor, the total output will decline. This law is universal in nature.

As per the Fig.3.1 the desire quantity of output increased at State-I hence reached optimum at stage to and finally declined at stage-III it indicates that one variable proportion (labour) increases, the output will increase at optimum level and finally it decreases.

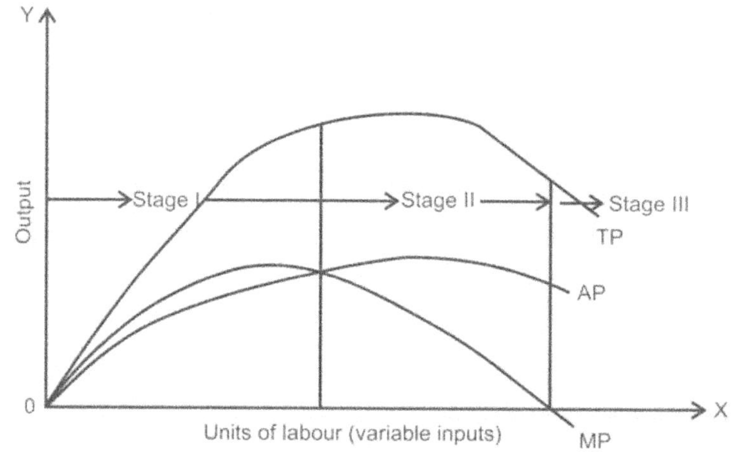

Fig. 3.1

The following hypotehtical numerical table explains the operation of the law of variable proportions in Table 3.1.

Table 3.1

Units of labour	Total product (TP)	Marginal product (MP)	Average product (AP)	Stages
0	0	0	0	Stage I
1	10	10	10	
2	22	12	11	
3	33	11	11	Stage II
4	40	7	10	
5	45	5	9	
6	48	3	8	
7	48	0	6.85	Stage III
8	45	–3	5.62	

This law states that when increasing amounts of the variable inputs are combined with a fixed level of another input, a point will be reached where the marginal product of the variable input will decline. This law is not based on theoretical argument but is based on actual observation of many production processes.

3.4 Production Function with Two Variable Inputs

If both K & L inputs are variable, a different set of analytical techniques can be applied to determine optional input rates. The firm has three ways to approach the problem of efficient resource allocation in production. They are: (i) maximize predictions for a given cost outlay on capital and labour (ii) minimize the cost outlay on labour and capital inputs necessary to produce a specified rate of output (iii) produce the output rate that maximizes the profit.

The first two problems are called constrained optimization problems. In the first case the problem is the constraint, which is a fixed-cost outlay of capital and labour. In the second case, the constraint is a specified rate of output that must be produced. However, in the third case the firm seeks that output level which will maximize profit. Here the constraint is not either the budget available for production or the output level to be produced. Firm is only constrained by the limits set by the production function itself.

A standard managerial economics technique called the concept of production isoquants and production isocosts is used to solve each of the problems mentioned above.

3.5 Isoquants

A production function with two variable inputs can be represented by a family of isoquants or isoproduct curves. The term isoquant is derived from the words 'iso' and 'quant', 'iso' means equal and 'quant' implies quantity. Isoquant, therefore means equal quantity.

Isoquant are the curves, which represent the different combinations of inputs producing quantity of output. Any combination on isoquant represents the same level of output. This is also known as production indifference curves.

For a given output level, firm's production becomes

$$X^o = F(a_1, a_2)$$

where X^o, the units of output is a function of the quantity of two inputs a_1, a_2

Thus an isoquant shows all possible combinations of the two inputs which are capable of producing equal or a given level of output. Since each combination yields equal output, the producer becomes indifferent towards these combinations.

The family of isoquants makes up all the possible combinations of labour and capital that can be employed to produce different outputs of a commodity. Thus, they are a geometric representation of a production function.

The characteristic features of isoquants :

1. They are falling. They can neither be raising nor constant.
2. An isoquant never intersects another isoquant.

3. Isoquants are convexes from origin.
4. The higher the isoquant, the larger the output represented by it.
5. Isoquants do not touch either of the ordinates.

Combinations	Capital (Rs. in lakh)	No.of labourers
A	1	20
B	2	15
C	3	12
D	4	8
E	5	6
F	6	5

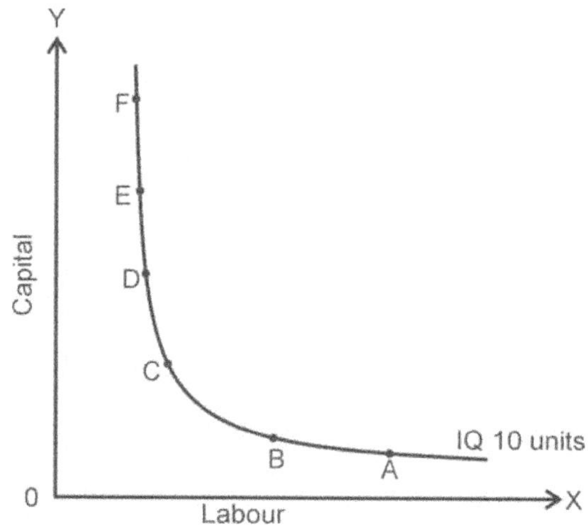

Fig. 3.2 Isoquant yielding 10,000 units of production

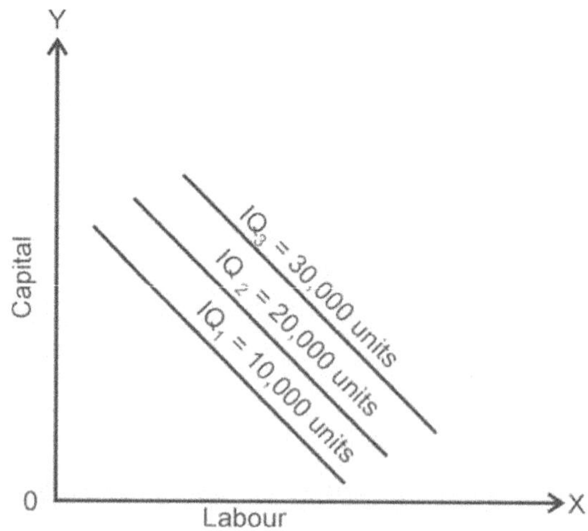

Fig. 3.2 (a) Isoquant where input factors are perfect substitutes.

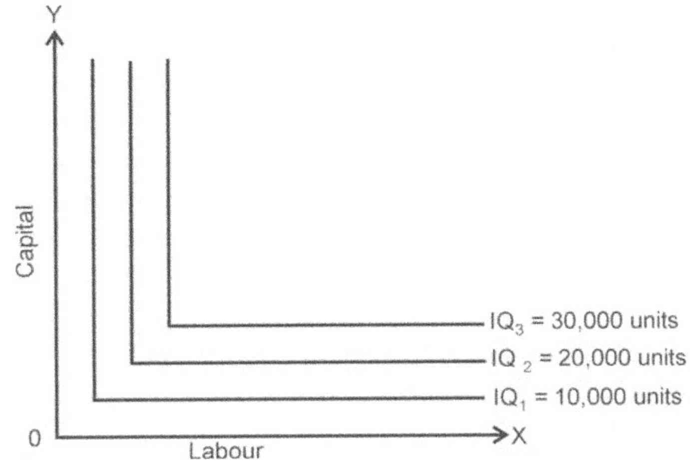

Fig. 3.2 (b) Isoquants where input factors are not perfect substitutes.

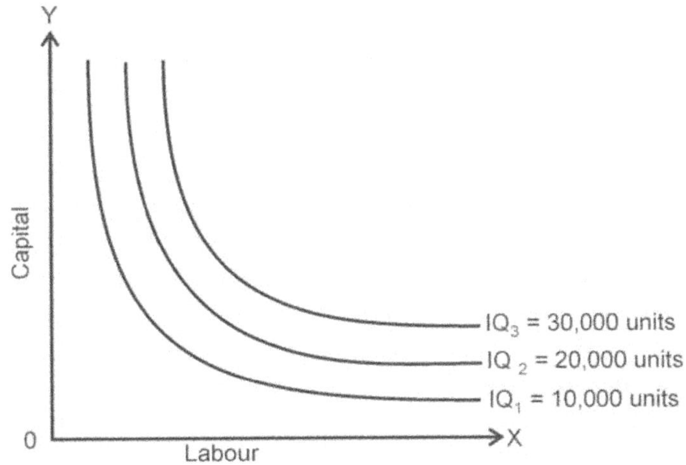

Fig. 3.2 (c) Isoquants each showing different volumes of output.

3.6 Iso-cost or Least-cost Combination of Inputs

The isoquant is a physical relationship that denotes different ways to produce a given rate of output whereas isocost function is the set of all combinations of capital and labour that can be purchased for a specified total cost. They help to determine the least-cost combination of inputs for a given output.

3.7 Economies and Diseconomies

The term 'economies' refers to cost advantages, which will be from either extending the scale of production or exploring the scope of production. The term 'diseconomies' refers to cost disadvantages. These may result when the economics are over-exploited. In general, the cost of producing and marketing products depends both on the scale (the amount of labor and capital employed) of the firms operations. They are referred to as economies of scale and economies of scope. However, in this chapter, we shall discuss only economies of scale.

Internal economies and diseconomies of scale :

The expansion of a firm in size by increasing the scale of its output results in certain cost advantages to the firm referred to as internal economies. The internal economies may be of various types.

(a) Technical (b) Labour (c) Commercial (d) Financial (e) Managerial (f) Risk spending.

(a) ***Technical economies :***

As the firm expands it can adopt and implement new and latest technology, which help in reduction in cost of manufacturing process, check the capacity under utilization and to turn out the volume of by-product. In this way the firm can manage a continuous production process without any loss of time thereby saving in time and transportation cost. These are technical economies.

(b) ***Labour economies :***

The most efficient labour will increase the productivity resulting to a decrease in the labour cost per output.

(c) ***Commercial economies :***

An expanding firm purchases the material in bulk and sell product in bulk. This reduces the transport cost, distribution costs and procurement costs. These are called commercial economies.

(d) ***Financial economies :***

A growing firm can raise their float funds easily from internal as well as external sources of economies. These are financial economies.

(e) ***Managerial economies :***

When a firm expands its business, the recruitment of managerial personnel need not be increased in the same proportion. The manager cost per unit will decrease due to increased production, as the salary remains constant whether the output is high or low.

(f) ***Risk-bearing economies :***

The expansion of a firm can minimize the business risk of the availability of a large variety of products. The loss in one product line can be balanced by the profit in other product line.

3.8 Cost Analysis

There are various expenditures that are incurred in meeting of various business transactions. Managerial economist's responsibility is to know about the nature and type of expenditure which can better be analysed by understanding the cost function and various cost concepts.

3.9 Cost Function

Cost functions express the relationships between cost and its determinants, like the size of plant. Level of output, prices, technology, etc. In a mathematical form it can be expressed as

$$C = f(S, O, P, T, M)$$

where C = Cost (unit cost or total cost)
S = Size of plant
O = Level of Output
P = Price of inputs used in production
T = Nature of Technology
M = Managerial efficiency
f = Function.

3.10 Determinanats of Cost

(i) ***Size of Plant :*** Plant size is an important variable influencing cost. The relation between scale of operations or size of plant to the unit cost is negative in the sense that, as the former increases, per unit cost decreases and vice versa.

(ii) ***Output level :*** Level of output and total cost are obviously related. Total cost increasing with increase in output. But average total cost or marginal cost function are derived by the increase in the output. The average total cost or marginal cost function are derived by relating the relevant costs with the level of capacity utilization of given plant size. Since such a cost function forms:

(a) *U-shaped curve quadratic* or cubic function is more appropriate to use.

(b) *Price of inputs :* Changes in input prices influence costs. Depending on the selective usage of the inputs and relative changes in the prices. When a factor which is a major component in production becomes relatively costly it rises the cost significantly.

(iii) ***Technology :*** Technology is often qualified as capital-output ratio. Modern and efficient technology is certainly cost saving. Generally this is found to have higher capital-output ratio.

(iv) ***Managerial Efficiency :*** Generally cost is influenced by a managerial efficiency and it is difficult to quantify it. However, a change in cost at two points of time may explain how organizational or marginal changes with in the form have brought labour cost efficiency. Sometimes it is possible to exclude the effect of other factors.

3.11 Classification of Cost

The different bases of cost classification are :

1. By time (historical, pre-determined).
2. By nature of elements (material, labour and overhead).

3. By degree of traceability to the the product (direct, indirect).
4. Association with the product (product, period).
5. Change in the activity or volume (fixed variable, semi-variable).
6. By function (manufacturing, administrative, selling, research and development, pre-production).
7. Relationship with accounting period (capital, revenue).
8. Controllability (controllable, noncontrollable).
9. Cost of analytical and decision-making purposes (opportunity, sunk, differential joint, common, imputed, out-of-pocket, marginal, uniform, replacement).

3.11.1 Classification on the Basis of Time

(a) ***Historical cost :*** These costs are ascertained after they have incurred. Such costs are available only when the production of a particular thing has already been done. They are objective in nature and can be verified with reference to actual operations.

(b) ***Pre-determined costs :*** These costs are calculated before they are incurred on the basis of a specification of all factors affecting cost. Such costs may be :

- **(i)** ***Estimated costs :*** Costs are estimated before goods are produced; these are naturally less accurate than standards.
- **(ii)** ***Standards costs :*** This is a particular concept and technique. This method involves:
  - (a) Setting up pre-determined standards for each element of cost and each product;
  - (b) comparison for actual with standard; and
  - (c) pin pointing the causes of such variances and taking remedial action.

Obviously, standard costs, though pre-determined, are arrived with much greater care than estimated costs.

3.11.2 By Nature of Elements

There are three broad elements of costs :

1. ***Material :*** The substance from which the product is made is known as material. It can be direct as well as indirect.

   (a) ***Direct material :*** It refers to those materials which become a major part of the finished product and can be easily traceable to the units. Direct materials include:

   - (i) All material specially purchased for a particular job/process.
   - (ii) All material acquired and later requisitioned from stores.
   - (iii) Components purchased or produced.
   - (iv) Primary packing materials.
   - (v) Materials passing from one process to another.

(b) ***Indirect materials :*** All materials which are used for purposes ancillary to production and which can be conveniently assigned to specific physical units are termed as indirect materials.

E.g., oils, grease, printing and stationary materials, consumable stores etc.

2. ***Labour :*** Labour cost can be classified into direct labour and indirect labour.

   Direct Labour : It is defined as the wages paid to workers who are engaged in the production process whose time can be conveniently and economically traceable to units to products. For example, wages paid to compositors in a printing press, to workers in the foundry in cast iron works etc.

   Indirect Labour : Labour employed for the purpose of carrying on tasks incidental to goods or services provided, is indirect labour. It cannot be practically traced to specific units of output. Examples, wages of store keepers, foreman, time - keepers, supervisors, inspectors etc.

3. ***Expenses :*** Expenses may be direct or indirect.

   Direct expenses : These expenses are incurred on a specific cost unit and identifiable with the cost unit. E.g. cost of design, layout or drawings, hiring of a particular tool or equipment for a job, fees paid to consultant etc.

   Indirect expenses : These are expenses which can not be directly, conveniently and wholly allocated to cost centre or cost unit. Examples are rent, rates and taxes, insurance, power, lighting and heating, depreciation etc.

3.11.3 By degree of Traceability to the Products

Cost can be distinguished as direct and indirect. Costs which can be easily traceable to a product or some specific activity are called direct costs; indirect costs are difficult to trace to a single product or it is uneconomic to do so. They are common to several products, i.e. E.g. salary of a factory manager.

Indirect costs have to be apportioned to different products, if appropriate measurement techniques are not available. These may involve some formula or base which may not be totally correct or exact.

3.11.4 Association with the Product

Cost can be classified as product costs and period costs.

Product costs :

Product costs are those costs which are traceable to the product and included in inventory values. In a manufacturing concern it comprises the cost of direct materials, direct labour and manufacturing overheads. Product cost is a fully factory cost. Product costs are used for valuing inventories which are shown in the balance sheet as asset till they are sold. The product cost of goods sold is transferred to the cost of goods sold account.

Period cost :

Period costs are incurred on the basis of time such as rent, salaries etc., include many selling and administrative costs essential to keep the business running though they are necessary to generate revenue. They are not associated with production, therefore, they can not be assigned to a product. They are charged to the period in which they are incurred and are treated as expenses.

Selling and administrative costs are treated as period costs for the following reasons:

(i) Most of these expenses are fixed in nature.

(ii) It is difficult to apportion these costs to products equitably.

(iii) It is difficult to determine the relationship between such cost and the product.

(iv) The benefits accruing from these expenses cannot be easily established.

3.11.5 By changes in Activity or Volume

Costs can be classified as fixed, variable and semi-variable cost.

Fixed costs :

Fixed cost as "The cost which is incurred for a period, and which within certain output and turnover limits, tends to be unaffected by fluctuations in the levels of activity (output or turnover)".

These costs are incurred so that physical and human facilities necessary for business operations, can be provided. These costs arise due to contractual obligations and management decisions. They arise with the passage of time and not with production and are expressed in terms of a time. Examples are rent, property taxes, insurance, supervisors' salaries etc.

Variable cost :

Variable costs are those costs that vary directly and proportionately with the output e.g., direct labour. It should be kept in mind that the variable cost per unit is constant but the total cost changes corresponding the levels of output. It is always expressed in terms of units, not in terms of time.

Semi-fixed (or semi-variable) costs :

Such costs contain fixed and variable elements. Because of the variable element, they fluctuate with volume and because of the fixed element, they do not change in direct portion to output. Semi-variable costs change in the same direction as that of the output but not in the same proportion. Depreciation is an example; for two shift working the total depreciation may be only 50% more than that for single shift working. They may change with comparatively small changes in output but not in the same proportion.

3.11.6 Functional Classification of Costs

A company performs a number of functions. Functional costs may be classified as follows:

(a) ***Manufacturing/Production costs :*** It is the cost of operating the manufacturing division of an undertaking. It includes the cost of direct materials, direct labour, direct expenses, packing (primary) cost and all overhead expenses relating to production.

(b) ***Administration costs :*** They are indirect and covers all expenditure incurred in formulating the policy, directing the organization and controlling the operation of a concern, which is not related to research, development, production, distribution or selling functions.

(c) ***Selling and distribution costs :*** Selling cost is the cost of seeking to create stimulate demand e.g. advertisements, market research etc. Distribution cost is the expenditure incurred which begins with making the reconditioned packages available for reuse e.g. warehousing, cartage etc. It includes expenditure incurred in transporting articles to central or local storage. Expenditure incurred in moving articles to and from prospective customers as in the case of goods on sale or return basis is also distribution cost.

(d) ***Research and development costs :*** They include the cost of discovering new ideas, processes, products by experiment and implementing such results on a commercial basis.

(e) ***Reproduction costs :*** When a new factory is started or when a new product is introduced, certain expenses incurred. There are trial runs. Such costs are termed as reproduction costs and treated as differed revenue expenditure. They are charged to the cost of future production.

3.11.7 Relationships with Accounting Period

Costs can be capital and revenue.

Capital expenditure provides benefits to future period and is classified as an asset and revenue expenditure benefits only the current period and is treated as an expenditure. As and when an asset is returned off, capital expenses to that extent becomes cost. Only when capital and revenue is properly differentiated, the income of a particular period can be correctly determined. It is not possible to distinguish between two under all circumstances.

3.11.8 Controllability

Cost can be controllable and non-controllable.

Controllable cost : Controllable cost is which can be influenced by the budget holder.

Non-Controllable cost : It is the cost which is not subject to control at any level of managerial supervision.

The difference between the terms is very important for the purpose of the cost accounting, cost control and responsibility accounting.

A controllable cost can be controlled by a person at a given organizational level. Controllable costs are not totally controllable. Some costs are partly controllable by one person and partly by another. Example maintenance cost can be controllable by both the production, maintenance manager. The term "controllable cost" is often used to mean variable cost and non-controllable cost as fixed.

3.11.9 Cost of Analytical and Decision-Making Purposes

(a) ***Opportunity cost :*** It is the cost of selecting one cost of action and losing of their opportunities to carry out that course of action. It is the amount that can be received if the asset is utilized in its next best alternative.

(b) ***Sunk Cost :*** It is the one which has already been incurred and cannot be avoided by decision taken in the future. As it refers to past costs, it is called an unavoidable cost. Sunk cost is defined as an expenditure for equipment or productive resources which has an economic relevance to the present decision-making process. This cost is not essential for decision-making as all past costs are irrelevant. It has also been defined as the difference between the purchase price of an asset and its salvage value.

(c) ***Differential cost :*** It has been defined as the difference in total cost between alternatives, calculated to assist decision making. Differential cost is the increase or decrease in total cost resulting out of :

    (i) producing and distributing a few more or a few less of products,
    (ii) a change in the method of production or distribution,
    (iii) an addition or deletion of a product or a territory, and
    (iv) the selection of an additional sales channel.

    The differential cost between any two levels of production is the difference between the marginal cost at these two levels and the increase or decrease in fixed cost. These costs are usually specific purpose cost as they are determined for a particular purpose under specific circumstances.

    Incremental cost measures the addition in unit cost for an addition in output. This cost need not be the same at all levels of production. It is usually expressed as a cost per unit whereas the differential cost is measured in total. The former applies increase in production and is restricted to the cost only. Whereas the differential cost has comprehensive meaning and application in the sense that it denotes both increase or decrease.

    The differential cost is useful in planning and decision making and helps to choose the best alternative. It helps the management to know the additional profit that would be earned if ideal capacity used or when additional investments are made.

(d) ***Joint Cost :*** The processing of a single raw material results in two or more products simultaneously. The joint products are not identifiable as different types of products until a certain stage of production known as the split off point is reached. Joint costs are the costs incurred up to the point of separation. One product may be of major importance and others of minor importance which are called by products.

(e) ***Common Cost :*** Common costs are those costs which are incurred for more than one product, job, territory or any other specific costing object. They are not easily related with individual products and hence are generally apportioned. It should be kept in mind that management decisions influence the incurrence of common costs. Example : Rent of a factory is common cost to all department located in factory.

(f) ***Imputed cost :*** Some costs are not incurred and are useful while taking decision pertaining to a particular situation. These costs are known as imputed or notional costs and they do not enter into traditional accounting systems.

Examples : Interest on internally generated funds, salaries of owners of proprietorship or partnership, notional rent etc.

(g) ***Out- of- pocket costs :*** Out-of-pocket costs signifies the such outlay required for an activity. The management would like to know that the income from a particular project will at least cover the expenditure for the project. Acceptance of a special order requires to be considered as additional costs need not be incurred if the special order is not accepted. Hence the importance of out-of-pocket costs.

(h) ***Uniform costs :*** They are not distinct costs as such. Uniform costing signifies common costing principles and procedures adopted by a number of firms. They are useful in inter-firm-comparison.

(i) ***Marginal costs :*** It is the aggregate of variable costs, i.e., prime cost plus variable overheads. Thus costs are classified as fixed and variable.

(j) ***Replacement costs :*** This is the cost of replacing an asset at current market values e.g., when the cost of replacing an asset is considered, it means the cost of purchasing the asset at the current market price is important and not the cost at which it was purchased.

3.11.10 Other Costs

(i) ***Conversion cost :*** It is the cost of a finished product or work-in- progress comprising direct labour and manufacturing overhead. It is production cost less the cost of raw material but including the gains and losses in weight or volume of direct material arising due to production.

(ii) ***Normal Cost :*** This is the cost which is normally incurred at a given level of output in the conditions in which that level of output is achieved.

(iii) ***Traceable cost :*** It is the cost which can be easily associated with a product, process or department.

(iv) ***Avoidable costs :*** Avoidable costs are those costs which under the present conditions need not have been incurred.

(v) ***Total cost :*** This is the sum of variable and fixed costs.

(vi) ***Value added cost :*** Strictly, it is not cost. It means the selling price of the product / service less the cost of materials used in the product or the service. Often depreciation is also deducted for ascertaining "value added".

(vii) **Long run cost :** It is defined as period of adequate length during which a company with all factors of production is at high degree of flexibility.

(viii) ***Short run cost :*** It is defined as the period of relatively shorter duration when at least some of the factors of production are fixed. It refers to what are recorded as expenses in the books of accounting records. The accountant recognizes the cost only when it is incurred and recorded, as this necessarily forms the legal point of view. In accounting system, the assets are valued at the book value. Book value means the cost of acquisition less depreciation.

(ix) ***Accounting cost :*** It is the sum of all cost associated to a particular unit, or process or department or batch or the entire concern. It may also mean the sum total of material, labour and overhead. The term accounting cost however, is not precise, if needs to be made precise by using terms that indicated the elements of cost included.

(x) ***Economic cost :*** The economic cost looks beyond the accounting cost. Economists and mangers recognize that there are other implicit cost that are never recorded in the books. However, these must be considered in managerial decision making. The Economist or manager tries to ascertain the costs much before they are incurred and trials to explain how the managerial decision can be made based on this; for example, an economist would like to see the value of these assets in terms of replacement costs.

3.12 Cost-Output Relationship

The cost and output are interrelated. The cost of product depends upon several factors such as volume of production, relationship between the cost and output, prices and productivity of inputs such as land, capital, labour, time scale.

The cost-output relationship mainly differs in short-run and the long-run. In short-run, the cost can be classified into fixed cost and variable cost. The cost-output relationship in short-run is governed by certain restrictions in terms of fixed costs. Whereas in the long run, the cost output relationship is governed by the effect of varying size of plant upon its cost.

Cost-output relationship facilitates many managerial relationships such as :

(a) Formulating the standards of operations.

(b) Formulating the rational policy on plant size.

(c) Formulating a policy of profit prediction.

(d) Formulating a policy of pricing fixation.

(e) Formulating a policy of promotion methods.

(f) Formulating a policy of expenses control.

3.13 Cost in short-run

Cost in the short-run can be classified into fixed cost and variable cost. The fixed cost may ascertained in terms of total fixed cost and average fixed cost per unit. The variable cost can be determined in terms of average variable cost, total variable cost. The following Table 3.2 gives information about the behaviour of costs in the short-run.

Table 3.2 Cost-Output Relation under short- run.

Output	TVC	TVC	TC	AFC	AVC	ATC	MC
0	50	0	50	-	-	-	-
1	50	25	75	50	25	75	25
2	50	55	105	25	27.5	52.5	20
3	50	60	110	16.6	20	36.6	15
4	50	75	125	12.5	18.7	31.2	15
5	50	90	140	10	18	28	25
6	50	145	195	8.3	24.1	32.4	45
7	50	225	275	7.1	32.1	39.2	80
8	50	355	405	6.2	44.3	50.5	130
9	50	555	605	5.5	61.6	67.1	200

From the above table, it is clear that :

1. Total fixed cost remained fixed irrespective of increase or decrease in production of activity.
2. The total variable cost increases proportionately with production. Here the rate of increase is not constant.
3. The total cost increases with volume of production. The average fixed cost per unit decreases as the volume of production increases; whenever production increases, the fixed costs are shared to a greater number of units, thus, fixed cost of unit variable declines.
4. The averge total cost decreases upto a certain level of production. After this level it rises slowly. If this is represented graphically, it results in a flat U-shaped curve. The lowest point of the average total cost curve denotes the ideal level of production.
5. Marginal cost is the change in total cost resulting from unit change in output.
6. The marginal cost also decreases up to a certain level of production, later it rises slowly.

From the above table, we find as the output goes on increasing, average fixed cost curve (AFC) will continue to decrease. AFC curve indicates downwards slope and it appears to meet the X-axis but will never meet the X-axis for several reasons. The average variable cost (AVC) is a U-shaped curve denoting that the AVC tends to fall in the beginning when the output is increasing but for a particular level output, it rises because of the application Law of Returns or Law of Variables Proportions or Law of Diminishing Returns. Average total cost (ATC) is the sum of the AVC and AFC. It is to be noted that it will be nearer to the AFC curve in the initial stages because the higher AFC at the initial level of output has greater influence on ATC. As output increases and AFC decreases, the influence of AFC on ATC also will decline. It indicates with the increasing output, the ATC curve will be distancing itself from the AFC curve. In the final stages the ATC curve will be nearer the AVC curve because the influence of AVC on ATC is greater at higher levels of output. It is to be noted the ATC curve never touches the AVC curve or AFC curve for several reasons.

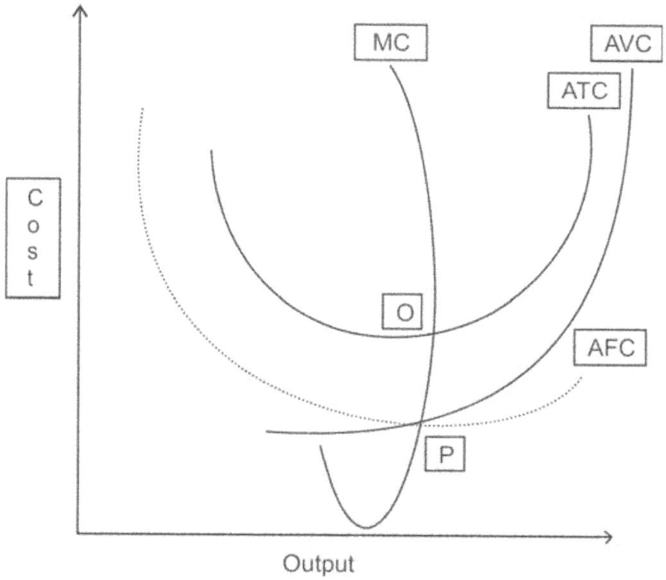

Fig. 3.3 Behaviour of costs in the Short-run.

The marginal cost curve is also a U-shaped curve. It falls in the beginning and rises sharply. The rising marginal cost curve will pass through the minimum point of the AVC and the minimum point on ATC at P and Q respectively.

Marginal Cost :

Marginal cost is less than the average cost when the average cost is falling. The Fig. 3.4 shows marginal cost where MC < AC.

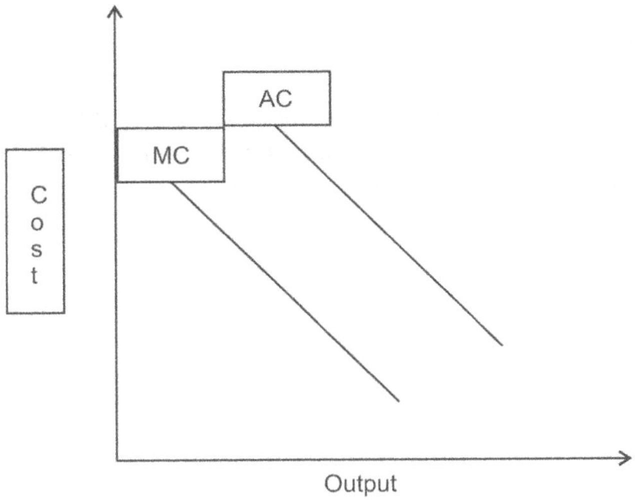

Fig. 3.4 Where MC < AC.

Average cost :

When the average cost is rising, the marginal cost is more than the average cost. The Fig. 3.5 shows average cost where MC > AC.

If average cost is constant, the marginal cost is also constant, the Fig. 3.6 presents when AC constant, MC coincides with the AC.

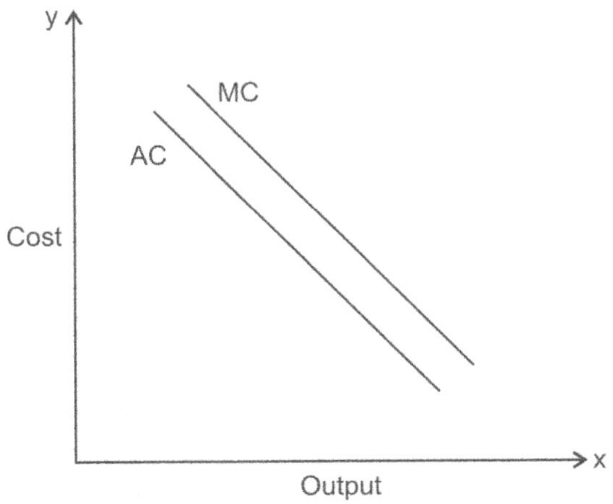

Fig. 3.5 Where MC > AC

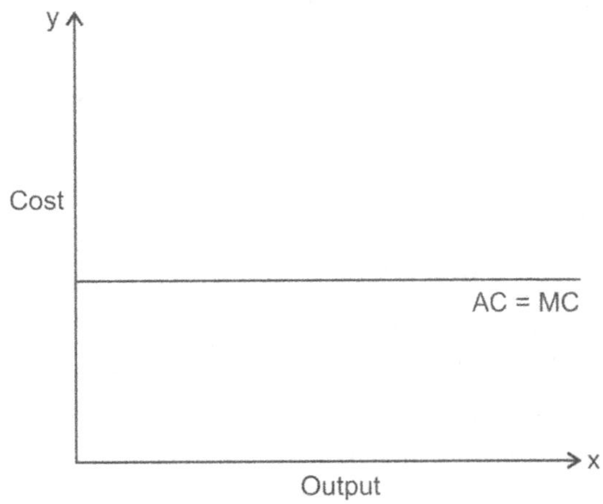

Fig. 3.6 Where MC = AC

3.14 Cost in Long-run

Long-run refers to the period of time over which all factors are variable. The firm has more time at its disposal to make any change in the production depending on its requirements. The firm can expand its production, upgrade its production facilities, enter into new markets, initiate necessary changes in the labour force, import technology, or undertake research and development. The firm can plan and organize every strategy to reduce its cost of production or maximize the volume of production. It has no constraints in terms of resources. It has no fixed costs. All costs are variable. So, the long-run costs refer to the costs of producing different levels of output by changing the scale of production.

A long-run is also expressed as a series of short- runs. It is already expressed that every short-run average cost curve is associated with a short-run. This further explains that the long-run is associated with series of short-run of average cost curves. The long-run average cost curve (LAC) is flat U-shaped curve enveloping a series of short- run average cost curves, (SACs). It is tangential to all the SACs. The points of tangency represent minimum average cost in the long run, and not in the short run.

The long-run and short-run average cost are equal to each other only at particular points of tangency. Each of the SAC curves is an operating curve, which decides the current production level. The LAC curve is planning curve as the long-run demand of the product is to be taken into consideration before deciding upon the right size of the plant.

The U-shape implies that the cost of production continues to be low till the firm reaches the optimum scale (Marginal cost = Average cost). Beyond this level the cost of production increases. In the beginning stages, when the firm unleashes all its potential, that is, releases all its inputs proportionately and simultaneously, it enjoys increasing returns to scale, for some time. The cost of production for unit decreases. It is, at the stage, that the firm enjoys the economies of scale. This benefit continues for some time and after reaching a particular level of output, the long-run average cost reaches minimum beyond which the output increases less than proportionately. This indicates that diseconomies of scale creep in.

Fig. 3.7 shows how LAC curve envelopes several short-run average cost (SAC) curves. Suppose the firm is producing an output of OX_1 units on a plant of SAC_1. If it wants to produce OX_2 units of output, either it can operate on SAC_1 by over utilizing SAC_1 plant or by acquiring a bigger size plant SAC_2 and operating on it. It will be less costly to operate on SAC_2. If it wants to produce OX_3 units of output, it can operate on the bigger size plant SAC_3 at least cost. X_3A_3 is the least cost at the output OX_3 and the firm attains optimum output in the long- run at OX_3 level of output. If it operates on SAC_2 to produce OX_3 units of output, the cost will be prohibitively high being X_3A_{33} as shown in Fig. 3.7.

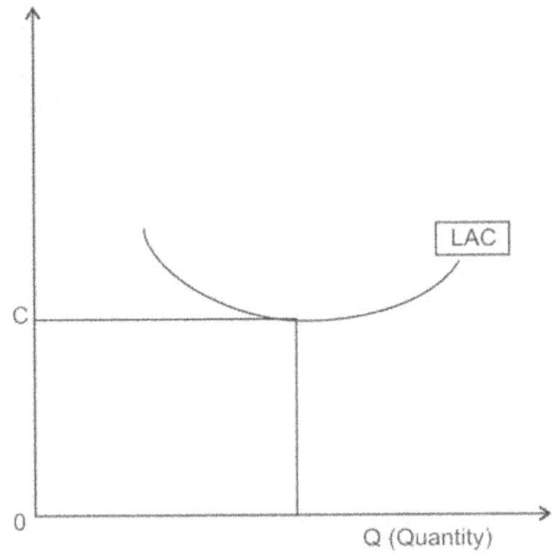

Fig. 3.7 Long-run Average output cost (LAC) curve envolping series of SACs.

It is to be noted that there is only one short-run average cost curve SAC_3 which is tangential to the long-run average cost curve at its minimum point. All other SAC curves are tangential to the LAC curves at higher than their minimum average cost points.

Long-run average cost curve is of great utility for the entrepreneur to make decisions relating to expansion of the size of the firm. It helps to minimize the costs to the advantage of the firm. However, it is to be noted that the U- shaped LAC curve assumes away the technological progress. One deficiency of economic theories is that technology is assumed to be constant but whereas it is not really so and we find rapid technological changes taking place very frequently making economic theories less relevant.

3.15 Optimum Size of the Firm

The term 'optimum' literally means the conditions that produce the best result wherein the firm the maximum profits per unit at minimum average cost. Optimum size is defined by several experts. For instance, Robinson defines an optimum firm as follows:

"We must mean that firm which in existing conditions of technique and organizing ability has the lowest average cost of production per unit when all those costs which must be covered in the long-run are included".

It is clear that a firm is said to be in optimum size when it is in a position to utilize its resources, including technology, most efficiently. As a result of this, the cost of production is the minimal and the productivity is very high. Many a time, we find a business unit of a particular size operating efficiently than a unit of slightly bigger than a smaller size, this size is called the "optimum size". The size of the firms depends on the nature of industry.

An understanding of optimum size of the firm will enable the entrepreneur or promoter to choose the right size of the firm in the setting up of project. Generally, in every industry, there is an 'economic size' of the firm. If a business is started with a larger than the economic size, there is every possibility of suffering losses and hence it is necessary to understand the concept of optimum size before venturing into business.

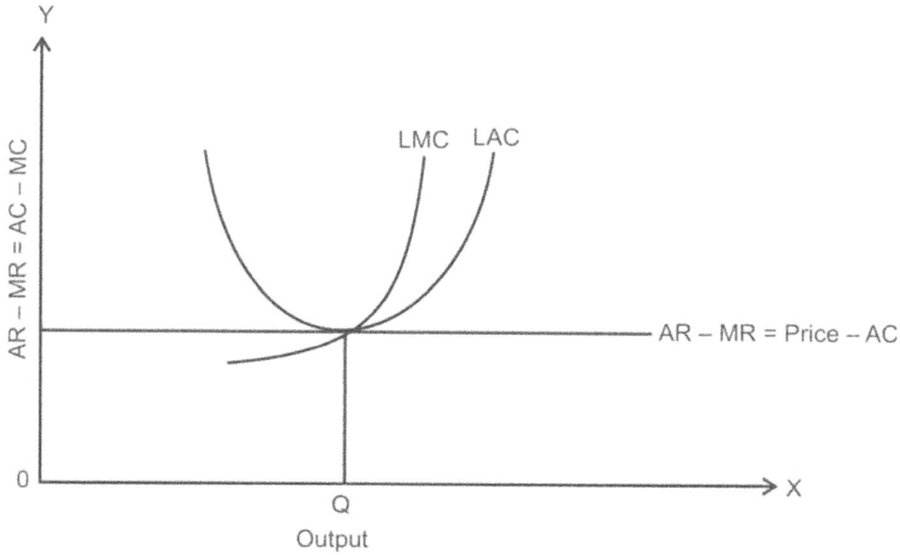

Fig. 3.8 Long-run equilibrium position.

Fig. 3.8 shows the long-run equilibrium position of the firm under perfect competition. Two conditions are to be fulfilled in the long-run : (a) MR = MC, (b) AR = AC, and AC must be tangential to AR at is lowest point. QE is the price and also the long-run average cost (LAC). Long-run marginal cost (LMC) curve passes through the minimum point of the long-run average cost curve (LAC) at E_1 while passing through the marginal revenue curve. E is the equilibrium point and the firm produces OQ units of output. It can be noted that normal profits are not visible to the naked eye since normal profits are included in the average cost. Long-run average cost includes the opportunity cost of staying in business. If the market price is below long-run average cost of the firm. The firm will have to quit the industry since in the long-run the firms have ot recover average cost.

The output does not always increase commensurate with increase in inputs. The production is governed by certain laws of returns to scale, which are popularly known as **Scale economics.** These are governed by certain economies the firm enjoys because of the scale of its operations. Growth beyond the manageable size may lead to diseconomies also, unless it is strategically managed.

3.16 Break-Even Analysis

The 'Break-even point' may be defined as that point of sales volume where total revenue is equal to total cost, i.e., point of no profit or no loss. At this point contribution is equal to the fixed cost. If sales are higher than this point, it means the business is earning profit.

On the other hand, if sales are below this point it means it is in losses, i.e., break-even point is equilibrium point or balancing point of no-profit no-loss.

Break-Even Analysis – In the broader sense : When it is used in the broader sense it means it is a system of analysis that can be used to determine the probable profit or loss at any given level of output. Under this sense, break-even analysis refers to the study of relationship between cost, volume and profit at different levels of production or output.

Assumption of Break-Even Analysis :

The following are the important assumptions of Break-Even Analysis.

1. The costs can be segregated into fixed cost and variable cost.
2. Total fixed cost remains the same.
3. Variable cost per unit remains constant.
4. The selling price does not change.
5. There will be no change in the general price level.
6. There is one product or in the case of multiple products, the present sales mix continues.
7. There is a constant demand for the product, it means, whatever is produced can be sold out.
8. Volume of the production is the only factor that influences the cost.

Limitations of Break-even Analysis :

1. Theoretically segregation of expenses into fixed and variable cost is easy, but in proactive it is a difficult job. Some of the expenses depend upon the policies of the government and the management, e.g., bonus to staff and welfare amenities to the workers etc.
2. Selling price may not remain as a constant. If the output is more then there is a possibility for an increase in supply, decrease in demand and resulting into a fall in the selling price.
3. Marginal cost ignores fixed cost but it is an important element in the total cost, which cannot be ignored.
4. Cost, volume and profits are governed by the external factors like availability of capital for increased output, government policy etc.
5. Stocks are not valued properly; the marginal cost takes only variable cost into consideration. The BEP analysis assumes whatever is produced is sold out, this assumption may not hold in many cases.

The study of cost- volume-profit analysis is often referred to as break-even analysis. Break-even analysis is an extension of the marginal costing principles. It is interpreted in broad as well as narrow sense. In this narrow sense, break-even analysis is concerned with finding out the break-even point, i.e. the point of no profit and no loss. When used in broad sense, it is a system of analysis that can be used to determine probable profit/loss at any given level of output.

Break-even point (BEP) to be determined as follows :

This is that level of sales where there is no profit and no loss. At this point total cost is equal to total sales. This is also the point after which there will be profit and before which there will be loss.

$$\text{B.E. Point (in Units)} = \frac{\text{Normal Fixed Cost}}{\text{Contribution per unit}}$$

$$\text{Or} \quad = \frac{F}{S - V}$$

$$\text{B.E. Point (in Rs.)} = \frac{\text{Total Fixed Cost}}{\text{Contribution}} \times \text{Sales}$$

$$\text{Or} \quad = \frac{\text{Total Fixed cost}}{\text{P/V ratio}}$$

Example

Total Fixed cost = Rs. 12,000

Selling Price = Rs. 12 per unit

Variable cost = Rs. 9 per unit

Calculate break even point, (i) in units and (ii) in rupees.

Solution

Contribution = Sales – Variable cost

= Rs. 12 – 9 = Rs. 3

$$\text{P/V ratio} = \frac{C}{s} \times 100$$

$$\text{B.E. Point (in units)} = \frac{\text{Total Fixed Cost}}{\text{Contribution per unit}}$$

$$= \frac{12000}{3} = 4000$$

$$\text{B.E. Point (in Rs.)} = \frac{\text{Total Fixed Cost}}{\text{P / V ratio}}$$

$$= \frac{12000 \times 100}{25} = 48000$$

P/V ratio

This term is important for studying the profitability of operations of a business. Profit volume ratio establishes relationship between the contribution and the sale value. The formula can be expressed thus :

$$P/V\ Ratio = \frac{Contribution}{Sales} = \frac{Sales - Variable\ Costs}{Sales}$$

$$\text{Or} \qquad \frac{C}{S} = \frac{S-V}{S} \qquad \text{Or} \qquad 1 - \frac{Variable\ Costs}{Sales}$$

This ratio can also be called as 'Contribution/Sales' ratio. This ratio can also be known by comparing the change in contribution to change in sales or change in profit to change in sales. Any increase in contribution would mean increase in profit only because fixed costs are assumed to be constant at all levels of production. Thus.

$$P/V\ Ratio = \frac{Change\ in\ Contribution}{Change\ in\ Sales} = \frac{Change\ in\ Profits}{Change\ in\ Sales}$$

This ratio would remain constant at different levels of production since variable costs as a proportion to sales remain constant at various levels.

Example : Sales Rs. 2,00,000

Variable costs 1,20,000

Fixed Costs 40,000

$$P/V\ Ratio = \frac{200000 - 120000}{200000} = 0.4 \text{ or } 40\%$$

The ratio is useful for the determination of the desired level of output or profit and for the calculation of variable costs for any volume of sales. The variable costs can be expressed as under.

$$VC = S\ (1\text{-}P/V\ ratio)$$

In the above example :

If we know the P/V ratio and sales before hand, the variable costs can be computed as follows:

Variable costs = 1– 0.4 = 0.6, i.e. 60% of sales

= Rs. 120000 (60% of Rs. 200000)

Alternatively, by the formula

$$\text{Since} \qquad P/V\ Ratio = \frac{S-V}{S}\ A$$

S – V = S × P/V ratio

Or V = S – S × P/V ratio or S(1– P/V ratio).

Comparison of different P/V Ratios is usually made by the management to find out which product is more profitable. Management tries to increase the value of the ratio by reducing the variable cost or by increasing the selling prices.

Contribution :

Contribution is the difference between sales and variable cost or marginal cost of sales. It may also be defined as the excess of selling price over variable cost per unit. Contribution is also known as Contribution margin or Gross margin. Contribution being the excess of sales over variable cost is the amount that is contributed towards fixed expenses and profit.

If the selling price of a product is Rs. 20/- per unit and its variable cost is Rs. 15/- per unit, contribution per unit is Rs. 5/- (i.e. Rs. 20 – 15). Further, let us say that the fixed expenses are 50,000 and the total number of units sold is 8,000. This means that the total contribution is 8000 × 5 or Rs. 40,000 which is not sufficient even to meet the fixed expenses and the result is a loss of Rs. 10,000 units, then total contribution of Rs. 50,000 equals the fixed cost, and no amount of contribution exceeds the fixed costs. Hence, any output beyond 10000 units, will give some profit e.g. at a level of output of 15,000 units, the total contribution is 15000 × 5 = Rs. 75,000 while the fixed costs remain Rs. 50,000, thus making a profit of Rs. 25,000.

Contribution can be represented as :

Contribution = Sales – Variable (Marginal) Cost

or Contribution (per unit) = Selling price – Variable (or marginal) cost per unit

or Contribution = Fixed costs + Profit (– Loss)

Advantages of Contribution :

The concept of contribution is a valuable aid to management in making managerial decisions. A few benefits resulting from the concept of contribution margin are given below.

1. It helps the management in the fixation of selling prices.
2. It assists in determining the break-even point.
3. It helps management in the selection of a suitable product mix for profit maximization.
4. It helps in choosing from among alternative methods production; the method which gives highest contribution per limiting factor.
5. It helps the management in deciding whether to purchase or manufacture a product or a component.
6. It helps in taking a decision as regards to adding a new product in the market.

3.17 Break-Even Chart

Break-even chart is nothing but graphical representation of Break-even analysis. The relationship between costs, sales and profits can be shown in the form, of a chart. Such a chart not only represents the level of activity in a graphical manner where there will be neither profit nor loss but also shows the profit or loss at various levels of activity. According to the CIMA (Chartered Institute of Management Accountants, London), " the break even chart means, a chart which shows profit or loss at various levels of activity, the level at which neither profit not loss is shown being termed the break even point."

Thus, it is a graphical presentation of cost and revenue data so as to show their inter-relationship at different levels of activity.

Assumptions underlying Break-even charts

The following are the assumptions of the Break-even charts:

(a) Fixed costs remain constant at every level and they do not increase or decrease with change in output or production.

(b) Variable cost fluctuates per unit of output. In other words, they vary in the same proportion in which the volume of output or sales varies.

(c) All costs are capable of being segregated into fixed and variable costs.

(d) Cost and revenue depend only on volume and not on any other factor.

(e) Selling price remains constant even when the volume of production or sales changes.

(f) Production and sales figures are either identical or changes in the inventory at the beginning and at the end of the accounting period are not significant.

(g) Either the sales mix is constant or only one product is manufactured.

Advantages of Break-even Chart

1. Provides visualized, detailed and clearly understandable information.

   It provides the different elements of cost-direct materials, direct labour, overheads (factory, office and selling etc.) can be presented through an analytical Break-even chart.

2. Profitability of products and business can be known. The profitability of different products can be known with the help of Break-even charts, besides the level of no-profit or no-loss.

3. Effect of changes in cost and selling price can be demonstrated.

   The effect of changes in fixed and variable costs at different levels of production or profits can be demonstrated by the graph legible. The relationship of cost, volume and profit at different levels of activity and varying selling price is shown through the chart.

4. Cost control can be excercised.

   This chart shows the relative importance of the fixed cost in the total cost of a product. If the costs are high, it induces management to take proper steps to control such costs.

5. Economy and efficiency can be effected.

   The capacity can be utilized to the fullest possible extent and the economics of scale and capacity utilization can be effected.

6. Forecasting and planning possible.

   Break-even analysis is very helpful for forecasting, long term planning, growth and stability.

3.18 CVP Anlysis

Meaning of Cost Volume Profit analysis :

Cost volume profit analysis is very useful for management of planning and control. It may be applied for profit planning, cost control and decision making. CVP analysis is used to establish and illustrate the inter relationship between cost and profit at various levels of output. The higher the volume of output the lower will be the unit of cost of the production and vice versa. This is due to the presence of fixed overhead cost in the total cost which does not rise or fall due to changes in the volume of output. Therefore by separating fixed cost from the total cost a direct relationship between variable cost and volume of output can be established.

Profit is the surplus of revenue left after a acquiring the total cost. If the sales price remain the same profitable desire. If the volume of output is lower the Total unit cost and therefore the profit is also higher in cost volume profit analysis This fact is illustrated by means of marginal cost analysis and is represented by break even chart. All items of costs are analysed and classified into fixed cost and variable cost. The fixed cost remains fixed whatever may be the volume of output and variable cost is assumed to vary with the output. Therefore the total cost for any project projected output would be the aggregate of the fixed cost and the variable cost and the variable cost is applicable to the output.

Objectives of CVP analysis : This analysis may be applied for profit planning at cost control and decision making. The following are the main objectives of such an analysis.

1. In order to forecast profit fairly and accurately. It is essential to know the relationship between profit and cost on the one hand and volume on other hand.
2. Sales and cost vary with the volume of output while establishing budgets per sales variable cost, it is necessary to budget the volume first (CVP analysis is useful in setting up flexible budgets which indicate costs at various levels of activity).

3.19 Graphical Presentation of Break-Even Analysis (Break Even Chart)

A. Break-even chart can be presented in three forms.

   (a) Simple Break-even chart

   (b) Contribution Break-even chart

   (c) Profit Break-even chart.

3.20 Simple Break even chart

This can be presented in tabular form as well as graphical form. This is also known as traditional or orthodox Break-even chart. This can be presented by any of the following two methods.

First Method : On the X-axis of the graph is plotted the scale of production or the volume the quantities of sales and on the Y-axis costs and sales revenues are represented. The fixed cost line is drawn parallel to the X-axis because cost increases with increase in volume of production.

3.20.1 Break-even Analysis through Tabular Form

Selling price per unit Rs.3.00

Variable cost per unit Rs.2.00

Total Fixed costs Rs. 40,000

As explained earlier, Break even point is 'Point of no profit or no loss.' The point will therefore, be there where total costs are equal to total sales. This tabular form presents different levels of output and sales, as shown below:

Table 3.3

Output (Unit)	Variable Costs Rs.	Fixed Costs Rs.	Total Costs Rs.	Sales Rs.
10,000	20,000	40,000	60,000	30,000
20,000	40,000	40,000	80,000	60,000
30,000	60,000	40,000	1,00,000	90,000
40,000	80,000	40,000	1,20,000	1,20,000
50,000	1,00,000	40,000	1,40,000	1,50,000
60,000	1,20,000	40,000	1,60,000	1,80,000

Break even point (Rs) where Total cost = Total sales

$$1,20,000 = 1,20,000$$

Break even point (units) 40,000 units

The fixed costs shall remain the same. The variable cost line is depicted above fixed cost line, which shows that the cost is increasing with the increase in the volume of output. This line can also be regarded as the total cost line because it starts from the point where variable cost and sales are plotted from the origin and a line is drawn up which goes in the upward direction with the increase of production sales. The two lines – total cost line and sales line shall intersect each other at one point i.e. where the business shall be at no-profit or no-loss, since the total costs are equal to total slaes revenue here i.e. known as Break-even point. This is shown in Fig. 3.9.

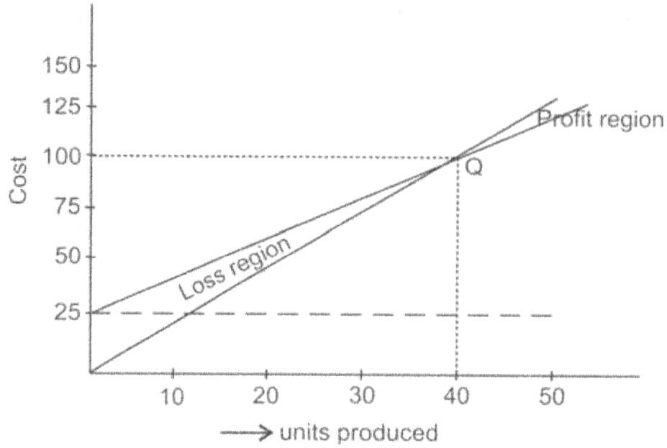

Fig. 3.9 Break-even point

If the business produces less than this point or this level of output, it shall be running at a loss. The portion of loss is shown by the lower sales line and upper total cost line. If the business produces more units than the break-even level, profit shall result and it shall be higher and higher as the production/sales increases. This is indicated by upper sales line and lower total cost line.

3.20.2 Second Method

This method of drawing a break-even chart is showing the variable cost line first and there after drawing the fixed cost line above the variable cost line. The latter, however, will be the total cost line as in the first case. The difference under this method from the first method is that the fixed cost line shown above the variable cost line. It shall be parallel to the latter, whereas under first method the fixed cost line is parallel to the X-axis. The sales line is drawn as usual and therefore the added advantage of this method is that 'Contributions' at varying levels of output are automatically plotted in the chart ('contribution' means the difference of sales revenue and the variable cost). The break even point is indicated by the intersection of the total cost line and the sales line. This is shown in Fig. 3.10.

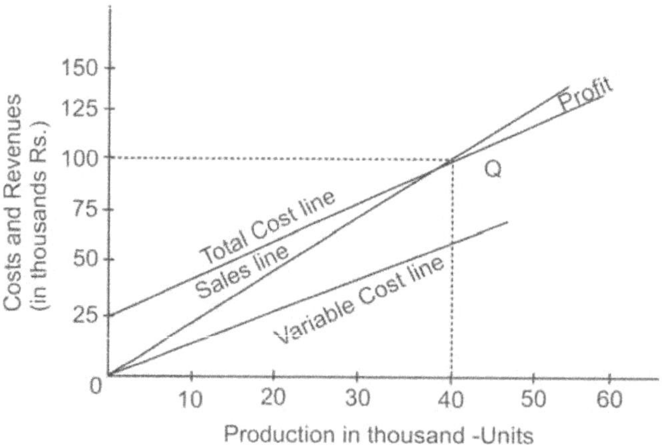

Fig. 3.10 The second method of Break-even chart.

3.21 Contribution Break-Even Chart

The chart helps in estimating the amount of contribution at different levels of activity besides the break even point. In case of this chart, first the fixed cost is drawn parallel to the X-axis. The contribution line is then drawn from the bottom, or the origin, which goes up with the increase of output of production or sales. The sales line is plotted as usual from the 'zero' point but since there is no total cost line, the question of intersection of sales line with it to show the break-even point does not arise. In such a case, the contribution line crosses the fixed cost line and the point of intersection is treated as break-even point. At this level, the fixed cost shall be equal to contribution which means that there shall be no profit and no loss. As the contribution increases to more than the fixed cost, profit shall arise to the business at different levels of output or sales and as the contribution steps down from the level of fixed cost, business shall be operated at a loss of varying levels of production or sales.

3.22 Profit Break-Even Chart

The Chart helps in ascertaining the profit at different levels of activity besides the Break-even point. In case of this chart, the fixed cost line need not be drawn. The profit line is drawn from the Y-axis below the origin. It indicates below the orgin 'O' and as well as negative profit (loss). The output is mentioned on the X-axis. The intersection of profit line with X-axis indicates the Break even point. As the profit crosses the break even point, profit shall arise to the business at different levels of output or sales. The profit Break-even chart will appear as given below. **(Fig. 3.10)**

Problem 1

From the following details compute :

(a) Variable costs (b) P/V Ratio

Sales	:	Rs. 3,00,000
Fixed Costs	:	Rs. 70,000
Profit	:	Rs. 80,000

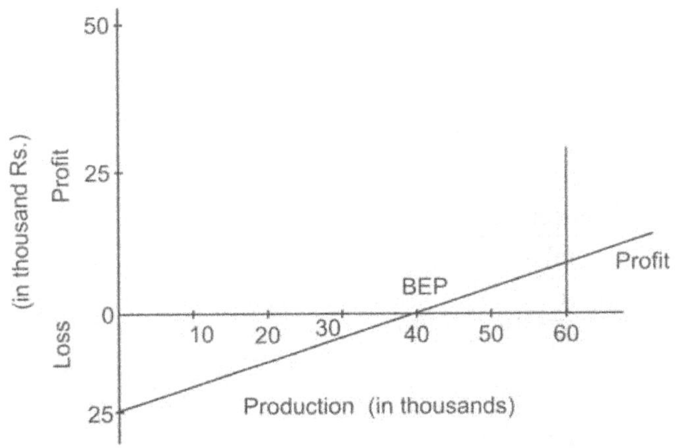

Fig. 3.11

Solution :

(a) *Variable cost :*

Sales – contribution = variable cost

Sales = 3,00,000

Contribuion

Fixed cost = 70,000

Profit = 80,000

= 1,50,000

Variable cost = Sales – Contribution

= 3,00,000 – 1,50,000

= 1,50,000

(b) *P/V Ratio* $= \dfrac{\text{Contribution}}{\text{Sales}}$

$= \dfrac{1{,}50{,}000}{3{,}00{,}000} = \dfrac{1}{2}$

(or) 0.5 (or) 50%

Problem 2

The following figures relating to sales and profits of a company are of two periods.

	Sales (Rs.)	Profit (Rs.)
Year ending 31-12-1990	1,00,000	15,000
Year ending 31-12-1991	1,20,000	23,000

Calculate (a) P.V. ratio, (b) Fixed cost, (C) Break Even Point.

Solution :

Contribution for additional sales in the year 1991 :

Additional sales = 1,20,000 – 1,00,000 : 20,000

Contribution for 20,000 sales = 23,000 – 15,000 = 8,000

(a) P/V ratio $= \dfrac{\text{Contribution}}{\text{Sales}}$

$= \dfrac{8000}{20{,}000}$ 0.4 or 40%

Contribution = P/V ratio × sales

= 0.4 × 100000 = 40,000

(b) *Fixed cost :*

Fixed cost = contribution – Profit

= 40,000 – 15,000 = 25,000

(c) Break even point $= \frac{\text{Fixed cost}}{\text{P/V ratio}} = 25{,}000 \times \frac{5}{2}$ = Rs. 62,500

Problem 3

From the following particulars, find

(i) contribution (ii) P/V ratio

Variable cost per unit Rs. 20; selling price per unit Rs. 40; Fixed expenses Rs. 1,00,000; Output 5000 units.

Solution:

1. Contribution = Sales – Variable cost

   Sales = 5000 units × 40 per unit = 2,00,000

   Variable costs = 5000 units × 20 per unit = 1,00,000

   Contribution = 2,00,000 – 1,00,00 = Rs. 1,00,000

2. P/V ratio $= \frac{\text{Contribution}}{\text{Sales}} = \frac{1{,}00{,}000}{2{,}00{,}000}$

   = 0.5 or 50%

Problem 4

From the following information pertaining to the two years, calculate

(a) P/V ratio

(b) Amount of sales to earn profit of Rs. 40,000

(c) Profit on sales Rs. 1,20,000

Years	Sales	Profit
1996	1,40,000	15,000
1997	1,60,000	20,000

Solution :

(a) Contribution and Sales

	Sales	Profit
1997	1,60,000	20,000
1996	1,40,000	15,000
20,000	5,000	

$$\text{P/V ratio} = \frac{\text{Contribution}}{\text{Sales}} = \frac{5{,}000}{20{,}000} = \frac{1}{4} = \text{(or) } 25\%$$

(b) Amount of sales to earn profit of Rs. 40,000

$$= \frac{\text{Fixed cost + Profit to be earned}}{\text{P/V ratio}}$$

Fixed cost – (based on 1997 sales)

Contribution of 1997 sales = 1,60,000 × = 40,000

Fixed cost = Contribution – Profit

= 40,000 – 20,000 = Rs. 20,000

Profit to be earned = Rs. 40,000

$$\text{P/V ratio} = \frac{1}{4}$$

$$\therefore \text{ Sales to earn profit of } \frac{20{,}000 + 40{,}000}{\frac{1}{4}} = 60{,}000 \times 60{,}000 \times 4 = \text{Rs. } 2{,}40{,}000$$

Contribution = × 1,20,000

(a) Profit on sales of Rs. 1,20,000

Profit = Contribution – Fixed cost

= 30,000 – 20,000 = Rs. 10,000

Problem 5

From the following data, you are required to calculate.

(a) P/V ratio

(b) Break even sales with the help of P/V ratio

(c) Sales required to earn a profit on Rs. 4,50,000

Fixed expenses = Rs. 90,000

Variable cost per unit :

Direct Material	=	Rs. 5
Direct labour	=	Rs. 2
Direct overheads	=	Rs. 100 percent of direct labour
Selling price per unit	=	Rs. 12

Solution :

(a) $P/V\ \text{Ratio} = \dfrac{\text{Contribution}}{\text{Sales}}$

Contribution = Sales – Variable cost

Sales = 12/- per unit

Variable cost :

Direct Material = 5

Direct labour = 2

Variable overheads = 2

= 12 – 9 = 3

P.V. Ratio $= \dfrac{3}{12} = \dfrac{1}{4}$ or 0.25 or 25%

(b) Break even sales with the help of P/V ratio $= \dfrac{\text{Fixed expenses}}{\text{P/V ratio}}$

Fixed expenses = 90,000; P/V ratio $= \dfrac{1}{4}$

$$= 90000 \times \frac{4}{1} = \text{Rs } 3{,}60{,}000$$

(c) Sales required to earn a profit of Rs. 4,50,000

$$= \frac{\text{Fixed expenses} + \text{Profit to be earned}}{\text{P/V ratio}}$$

Fixed expenses = 90,000

Profit to be earned = 4,50,000

P/V ratio = 1/4

$$= \frac{90000 + 450000}{\frac{1}{4}} = 540000 \times 4 = \text{ Rs } 21{,}60{,}000$$

Problem 6

M Ltd., is manufacturing and selling industrial boxes. It is proposed to decrease prices due to heavey competition. By decreasing the selling prices by 10% and 15%, how many units to be sold to maintain the current level of profit. The additional information is given.

	Rs.	Rs.
Current sales	30000 units	3,00,000
Variable cost	30000 units	1,80,000
Fixed cost		2,50,000
Net profit		50,000

Solution :

Proposed selling prices –

Decrease in selling price by 10%

Selling price $\dfrac{3,00,000}{30,000} = 10.00$

(-) 10% (10 × 10/100) = 1.00

10.00 – 1.00 = Rs 9.00

Decrease in selling price by 15%

Selling Price : $\dfrac{3,00,000}{30,000} = 10.00$

(-) 15% (10×15/100) = 1.50

10.00 – 1.50 = Rs 8.50

Profit to be maintained = 50,000

Variable cost/unit = $\dfrac{1,80,000}{30,000} = 6.00$

Fixed cost = 70,000

Contribution = Price – Variable cost

No.of units to be sold to maintain Rs. 50,000 profit when there is 10% decrease in selling price:

$$= \frac{\text{Fixed cost + Profit to be maintained}}{\text{Contribution per unit}}$$

$$= \frac{70,000 + 50,000}{9.00 - 6.00} = \frac{1,20,000}{3} = 40,000 \text{ units}$$

When there is 15% decrease in selling price

$$= \frac{70,000 + 50,000}{8.50 - 6.00} = \frac{1,20,000}{2.5} = 48,000 \text{ units}$$

Problem 7

Fixed expenses Rs. 10,000; Selling price per unit Rs.5/-; Variable cost per unit Rs. 3/-

Calculate the break-even point.

Solution :

$$\text{break even point in Units} = \frac{\text{Total fixed expenses}}{\text{Selling price per unit} - \text{Variable cost per unit}}$$

$$= \frac{10,000}{5-3}$$

$$= \text{Rs. } 5,000$$

$$\text{break even point (in Rupees)} = \frac{\text{Total fixed expenses}}{\text{Selling price per unit} - \text{Variable cost per unit}}$$

$$= \frac{10,000}{5-3} \times 5$$

$$= 25,000$$

Problem 8

Calculate break-even point from the following information.

Sales	Rs. 40,000
Fixed expenses	Rs. 20,000
Direct labour	Rs. 2,000
Material	Rs. 5,000
Other variable expenses	Rs. 1,000

Solution :

Variable costs are

Labour = Rs. 2,000

Material = Rs. 5,000

Expenses = Rs. 1,000

$\therefore$ Variable costs = Rs. 8,000

P/V ratio =

$$= \frac{\text{Selling price} - \text{Variable cost}}{\text{Sales}}$$

$$= \frac{40{,}000 - 8{,}000}{40{,}000} \times 100$$

= 80%

$$\text{Break even point in sales} = \frac{\text{Fixed cost}}{\text{P/V ratio}}$$

$$= \frac{20{,}000}{80} \times 100 = 25{,}000$$

Problem 9

Find the number of units to be sold to earn a profit of 2,00,000 per year.

Selling price per unit	Rs. 40
Variable cost per unit	Rs. 15
Fixed cost	Rs. 3,00,000

Solution :

$$\text{No. of Units sold} = \frac{\text{Fixed cost} + \text{Desired profit}}{\text{Selling price per unit} - \text{Variable cost per unit}}$$

$$= \frac{3{,}00{,}000 + 2{,}00{,}000}{40 - 15} = \frac{5{,}00{,}000}{25} = 20{,}000 \text{ units}$$

Problem 10

Calculate margin of safety for the following data.

Sales	Rs. 80,000
Fixed expenses	Rs. 50,000
Direct material	Rs. 18,000
Labour	Rs. 6,000
Variable expenses	Rs. 3,000

Solution :

Material	18,000
(+) Labour	6,000
(+) Variable expenses	3,000
Variable cost	– 27,000

$$\text{P/V ratio} = \frac{\text{Selling price} - \text{Variable cost}}{\text{Sales}} \times 100$$

$$= \frac{80{,}000 - 27{,}000}{80{,}000} \times 100$$

$$= 66.25\%$$

$$\text{Break even point in sales} = \frac{\text{Fixed cost}}{\text{P/V ratio}}$$

$$= \frac{50{,}000}{66.25} \times 100$$

$$= 75.471.69 = 75.472$$

$$\text{Margin of safety (or) M/S ratio} = \frac{\text{Actual Sales} - \text{BEP Sales}}{\text{Actual Sales}} \times 100$$

$$= \frac{80{,}000 - 75472}{80{,}000} \times 100$$

$$= 5.66\%$$

Problem 11

Mohan & Company has supplied you the following information.

No.of units sold 20,000 units

Fixed cost Rs. 2,40,000

Variable cost per unit Rs. 15

Selling price per unit Rs. 30

Find out :

(a) Break even sales in units
(b) P/V ratio
(c) Margin of safety
(d) Sales to get a profit of Rs. 2,00,000
(e) Verify the results in all the above cases

Solution :

Marginal cost statement

Fixed cost	=	2,40,000
Selling price per unit	=	30
Less: variable cost per unit	=	15
Contribution per unit	=	15

(a) B.E.P. (in units) $= \frac{\text{Fixed cost}}{\text{Contribution per unit}} = \frac{2,40,00}{15} = 16,000$ units

B.E.P (in rupees) $= \frac{\text{Fixed cost}}{\text{P/V ratio}} = \frac{2,40,000}{0.50} =$ Rs. 4,80,000

Summary

1. Production is an organised activity of transforming inputs into outputs to satisfy the demand for commodities and services of the community.
2. The production function expresses a functional or technical relationship between physical inputs and physical outputs of a firm at any particular time period. Mathematically, production function can be written as

   $Q = f(A, B, C, D)$ or $f(Ld, L+D, K, M, T)$

   Q = Quantity of output

   A, B, C, D = input factors such as land, labour, capital, management and organisation.
3. Isoquant can be defined as the locus of all those combinations of labour and capital, which yield the same output.
4. The laws of production deal with the relationship between additional inputs and additional output in the form of law of variable proportions and law of returns to scale.
5. The law of variable proportion explains the input output relation, the change in output due to addition of one variable input.
6. The law of variable proportions is also known as the law of diminishing returns as it brings diminishing tendency in production. It is a short run phenomenon.
7. The law of returns to scale explains the relationship between changing scale of inputs and outputs.
8. The law of returns to scale also explains how a simultaneous and proportionate increase in all the inputs affects the total output.
9. When a firm expands its size of production by increasing all the factors, it secures certain advantages known as economies of production.
10. Marshall classified economies of large scale production into internal economies and external economies.
11. Internal economies are those which are opened to a single factory or a single firm independently of the action of other firms.
12. External economies are those benefits, which are shared in by a number of firms or industries when the scale of production in an industry or groups of industries increases.
13. The disadvantages secured by a firm when it is expanded like rise in costs are the diseconomies.
14. Diseconomies both internal and external limit large scale production.
15. Cost function expresses the relationship between cost and its determinants.

16. Cost Function expressed in mathematical firm i.e., C = f(S, O, P, T, M) or f(A, B, C, D, E)

    Where C = Cost (Unit cost or Total cost)

    A, B, C, D, E = Input factors such as size of plant, level of output, price of inputs used in production, nature of Technology and managerial efficiency.

17. Historical cost, pre-determined cost, Estimated costs and Standard costs are prepared on the basis of time.

18. Direct and Indirect material costs, Direct and Indirect labour costs, Direct and Indirect expenses are prepared out the basis of nature of elements.

19. Fixed costs, variable costs and semi-fixed or semi-variable costs are prepared on the basis of volume or changes in activity.

20. Manufacturing production costs, Administration costs, Selling and Distribution costs, Research and development costs and reproduction costs are prepared on the basis of Functional classification.

21. Opportunity cost, Sunk cost, Differential cost, Joint cost, Common cost, Imputed cost, Out of pocket cost, Uniform cost, Marginal cost and Replacement cost are prepared on the basis of decision making purposes.

Essay Questions

1. (a) What are Isocosts and Isoquants? Do they intersect each other?

   (b) Explain Cobb-Douglas production?

2. Explain and illustrate the following.

   (a) The law of constant returns.

   (b) The law of increasing returns.

3. If sales is 10,000 units and selling price is Rs 20 per unit, variable cost Rs. 10 per unit and fixed cost is Rs. 80,000. Find out BEP in units and in sales revenue. What is the profit earned? What should be the sales per earning a profit of Rs. 60,000.?

4. Sales are Rs. 1,10,000 producing a profit of Rs. 4000 in period –1, sales are Rs 1,15,000 producing a profit of Rs. 12,000 in period –2. Determine the BEP and fixed expenses.

5. Explain the following with reference to production functions.

   (a) Marginal rate of technical substitution.

   (b) Variable proportions of factors.

6. The PV ratio of martrix books ltd, is 40% and the margin of safety is 30%. You are required to work out the BEP and netprofit, if sales volume is Rs 14,000.

7. Explain the meaning of Demand. What are its features and determinants?
8. Explain internal and external economies of larger firm.
9. Distinguish between
   (a) Fixed cost and variable cost
   (b) Explicit and implicit cost
   (c) Out of pocket cost and book cost .
10. What do you understand by Production Function . How does a producer achieve least cost combination of factors ?
11. Define and Explain Iso-quants. What are the properties of Iso-quants ? Explain the producer's equilibrium with the help of Iso-quants.
12. "All costs are variable in the long –run". Explain.
13. Define cost. Explain the different cost concepts used in the process of cost analysis.
14. Explain how the short run influences the costs.
15. Explain the features of short – run average cost curve and long - run average cost curve.
16. Explain how cost – output relationship helps the enterprise or entrepreneurs in expansion decisions.
17. Explain Break-Even Analysis through tabular and graphical manner with numerical presentation
18. Define cost, Explain the different cost concepts used in the process of cost analysis.
19. Explain how the short – run influence the costs.
20. "Most of the cost concepts are overlapping and repetitive". Do you agree with this statement? Substantiate you answer.
21. Explain the features of short- run average cost curve and long- run average cost curve.
22. Explain how cost-output relationship helps the entrepreneurs in expansion decisions.
23. (a) What are Isocosts and Isoquants? Do they intersect each other?
    (b) Explain Cobb-Douglas production?
24. Explain and illustrate the following.
    (a) The law of constant returns.
    (b) The law of increasing returns.
25. If sales is 10,000 units and selling price is Rs 20 per unit, variable cost Rs 10 per unit and fixed cost is Rs. 80,000. Find out BEP in units and in sales revenue. What is the profit earned? What should be the sales per earning a profit of Rs. 60,000.?

Short Questions

1. Write a short notes on Opportunity costs.
2. Write a short notes on Semi – variable costs.
3. Write a short notes on Accounting costs and economic costs.
4. Write a short notes on Explicit and implicit costs.
5. Write a short notes on Direct and indirect costs.
6. Write a short notes on Short – run average cost curve.
7. Write a short notes on Long – run average cost curve.
8. Write a short notes on Optimum size.
9. Write short notes on Out of pocket cost.
10. Write a short notes on Replacement cost.
11. Write a short notes on Production Function with two variable inputs.
12. Write a short notes on Iso-cost.
13. Write a short notes on Iso-quant.
14. Write a short notes on Managerial use of production function.
15. Write a short notes on Internal economies.
16. Write a short notes on Diseconomies of scale.
17. Write a short notes on Contribution and P.V. Ratio.
18. Write a short notes on Angle of Insidence and margin of safety.

CHAPTER 4

Market Structures

4.1 Market

Market forms an important phase in the economic activity. It is a place where the seller sells the goods to the buyer, i.e., producer sells the goods to the consumers and thus transfers the ownership. Economists describe a market as a collection of buyers and sellers who deal with a particular product or service. Markets play an important role in the utility of goods and services.

Generally the term market has came to signify a public place in which goods and services are bought and sold. In an economic sense, the term market does not mean shops or establishments. In economics it has no reference to a place, but to a commodity which is being bought and sold.

Prof. Jevons defines market as "any body of persons who are dealing in any commodity". According to Prof. Cournot, a French economist, the term market is "not any particular market place in which things are bought and sold, but the whole of any region in which buyers are in such free intercourse with one another that the price of same goods tends to equalise easily and quickly".

To Prof. Frederict Berhan, market is "any area over which buyers and sellers are in such close touch with one another, either directly or through dealers, that the prices obtainable in one part of the market affect the prices paid in other parts. The existence of market does not require face to face contact between the buyers and sellers. In modern day, buyers and sellers can come into contact through modern means of communications".

Presence of Buyers & Sellers of a Commodity : There should be buyers as well as sellers for the commodity. The instance when a vegetarian passes through a meat market, there is no market in an economic sense for him, as he has no demand for meat. Existence of buyers and sellers of the commodity constitutes the first feature of the market.

Establishment of contact between buyers and sellers : The establishment of contact between buyers and sellers is essential for the market; otherwise there will not be a market. Here the distance is of no consideration, provided buyers and sellers could be in touch through the available communication system.

Similarity of the Product : The buyers and sellers should deal with the same commodity or variety. Since the market in economics is identified on the basis of the commodity, similarity of the product is very essential.

Ex-charge of commodity for a price : There should be a price for the commodity. The price need not be a fair price. It may be high or low. There need not be a large number of buyers and sellers. The number is not the criterion for a market.

According to economics, if there is a contact between buyers and sellers for a commodity, at a price, it is a market. In terms of business, we define market as people or organizations with wants or needs to satisfy, money to spend and the willingness to spend it. Broadly market represents the structure and nature of buyers and sellers for commodity/service and the process by which the price of the commodity/service is established.

4.2 Classification of Markets

Markets can be classified in many ways. In economics, generally the classification is made in the basis of :

(i) Area
(ii) Time
(iii) Nature of transaction
(iv) Regulation
(v) Volume of business
(vi) Position of sellers
(vii) Type of competition.

Area: On the basis of geographical area cornered markets are classified into: (a) Local Markets (b) Regional Markets (c) National Markets (d) International Markets.

A local market for a product exists when buyers and sellers carry on business in a particular locality or village or area where demand and supply conditions are influenced by local conditions only. Generally markets for perishables like butter, milk, eggs, vegetables etc.

will have local markets. Similarly bulky articles like bricks, sand, stones, etc., will have local markets as the transport of these over a long distance will be uneconomic.

Semi-durable goods command a regional market. National market exists for industrial and durable goods. The precious commodities like gold, silver etc., are traded in the international market.

Based on time : Based on the time, the markets are classified into:

(a) ***Very short period market***

Very short period market refers to that type of market in which the commodities are perishable and supply of commodities cannot be changed at all. In this type of market, the market supply is almost fixed and it cannot be increased or decreased; because skilled labor, capital and organizational are fixed. Commodities like vegetables, flowers, fish, eggs, fruits, milk etc., which are perishable & the supply of which cannot be changed in the very short period come under this category. Since the supply of these commodities is fixed the demand factor plays a decisive role in determining the price of the commodity.

(b) ***Short period market***

Short period market refers to that type of market in which the commodities are durable and also reproducible. The supply of the commodity is alterable subject to one condition that the plant and machinery remains unchanged. Any increase or decrease in supple of commodity has to be done with the existing plant and machinery. The price that exists in the market is the short term normal price.

(c) ***Long period market***

Long period market implies that the time available is adequate for altering the supply by altering even the fixed factors of production. The supply of commodities may be increased by installing even a new plant or machinery and the output adjustments can made accordingly.

(d) ***Very long period market or Secular market***

Very long period or secular period is one when secular movements are recorded in certain factors over a period of time. The period is stood long. The factors include the size of the population, capital, supply, supply of raw materials etc. For instance, if 5 years are required to reclaim the barren land denote cultivable land, then period beyond five years is very long or secular period.

Markets on the basis of Nature of Transactions : On the basis of nature of transactions are markets classified as : (a) Sport market (b) Future Market.

Sport transaction or Sport market refers to those markets where goods are physically transacted on the spot, whereas Future Markets are related to those transactions which involve contracts of the future date.

Markets on the basis of Regulation : On the basis of regulation, markets are classified in (a) Regulated Market (b) Unregulated Market.

In the former type of markets transactions are statutorily regulated so as to put an end to unfair practices. Such markets may be established for specific products or group of producers. Produce and stock exchanges are suitable examples of the regulated markets.

Unregulated or free markets are those where there are no restrictions in the transactions.

Markets on the basis of 'volume of Business' : Based on the volume of business transacted, markets are classified into: (a) Wholesale Market and (b) Retail Market.

The wholesale market comes into existence when the commodities are bought and sold in bulk or large quantities. The dealers in this market are known as wholesalers. The wholesaler acts as an intermediary between the producer and the retailer. Retail market, on the other hand, exists when the commodities are bought and sold in small quantities. This is the market for ultimate consumers.

Markets on the basis of 'Position of Sellers' : On the basis of the position of the sellers in the chain of marketing, markets are divided in to primary market, secondary market and the terminal market. Manufacturers of commodities constitute the primary market who sell the products to the wholesalers. The secondary market consists of wholesalers who sell the products in bulk to the retailers. Retailers alone constitute the terminal markets who sell the products to the ultimate consumers.

4.3 Market Structure

This depends on many factors such as nature of products, their demand, time factors, classification of markets and so on.

Market structure refers to the characteristics of a market that influence the behavior and performance of firms and describes the competition environment in the market for any good or services.

The structure of market is based on the following features.

(i) *Seller Concentration :* This refers to the number of sellers and their market share for a particular product or service in the market.

(ii) *Buyer Concentration :* This refers to the extent by which a product is different from the other.

(iii) *Product Differentiation :* This refers to the number of buyers and their market share for a particular product or service the market.

(iv) *Restrictions to enter into a market :* In most cases, there would be certain restrictions to enter into a market. This regulates the number of firms to enter or exit from a market. If there are less restrictions there will be more firms.

Market structures are classified as following.

MARKET STRUCTURES

- Perfect competitions
- Imperfect competition
  - Monopoly
  - Monopolistic competition
  - Oligopoly
  - Duopoly
  - Monopsony
  - Oligopsony

Market Structures or Markets on the basis type of competition : Based on the type of competition, markets are classified into (a) perfectly competitive market and (b) Imperfect market.

Perfect Competition :

Perfect Competition is said to exit when certain conditions are fulfilled. These conditions are ideal and hence only imaginative, not realistic. Financial markets, agricultural products are some of the sectors of perfect competition.

Imperfect Competition :

The broad classification is perfect and imperfect competition. The opposite type of perfect market is imperfect. Under this imperfect markets, there are many types, viz.:

Monopoly
Monopolistic competition
Oligopoly
Duopoly
Monopsony
Duopsony
Oligopsony

Perfect competition refers to a market structure where competition among the sellers and buyers prevails in its most perfect form. In a perfectly competitive market, a single price exists for a particular commodity depending upon the demand and supply of that service or commodity. The market with perfect competition is known as “Perfect Market”.

4.4 Features of Perfect Competition

A perfectly competitive market is characterized by the following features:

(i) *Large Number of buyers and Sellers :* There should be significantly large number of buyers and sellers in the market. The number should be so large so that it should not make any difference in the determination of price even if one enters or exists the market.

(ii) *Homogeneous Product :* The product should be homogeneous. It should be of same quality and same price in all the firms of the market.

(iii) *Freedom to enter or exit :* There should be freedom to enter or exit the market. The consumers can enter or leave the market whenever they want.

(iv) *Perfect Knowledge :* Each buyer and seller has total knowledge of the prices prevailing in the market at every given point of time, quantity supplied, costs, demand etc.

(v) *No existence of transport costs :* There should be no transport costs in a perfect competitive market.

(vi) *Perfect Mobility of factors of Production :* This means that there should be free availability of factors of production, i.e., they should be available whenever they are wanted.

(vii) *Each firm a Price taker :* Each firm should sell its commodity at the prevailing price in the Market. It has no right to sell its good according to its own choice.

Under such a market, no single buyer or seller can play a significant role in price determination. In other words, all of them jointly determine the price i.e., buyers and sellers. Here the industry demand curve represents the total demand from all the consumers at various prices. Similarly, the industry supply curve represents the total quantity supplied by all sellers at various prices. However, the demand curve for an individual firm is horizontal and elastic.

Total Revenue (TR), Average Revenue (AR), and Marginal Revenue(MR)

Total Revenue is refers to the earnings earned by producing and selling ‘n’ number of units.

Total Revenue (TR) = Price unit (p) × No. of units produced & sold (Q)

Thus $TR = P \times Q$

Average revenue is the revenue earned per unit sold.

In other words, $AR = TR / Q$

But $TR = P \times Q = AR = P$

Marginal Revenue (MR) refers to the change in revenue by producing and selling one more unit.

Consider an example. You are selling cars. Each car costs Rs. 5 lakhs. Suppose 5 cars are sold. The Total Revenue (TR) is Rs. 25 lakhs. Average Revenue (AR) is 25/5 lakhs. Suppose you are selling one more car. Then Marginal Revenue (MR) is Rs. 5 lakhs.

Thus under perfect competition,

Price = Average Revenue (AR) = Marginal Revenue (MR)

4.5 Role of Time Factor in determination of Price

The price level depends upon the demand and also supply. A delay in supply may push the prices up and vice versa. Based on how quickly the supply can be arranged to meet a given demand situation, Marshall distinguished the following three periods indicating the price-supply equilibrium.

(a) *Very short period equilibrium :* Here, the supply is limited to the stock on hand. Any addition to the currently available stock is not possible as there is no time to arrange for additional production. The price at which the available stock can be sold is called "Market Price". So a sudden increase in demand may push up the market price significantly.

(b) *Short-run equilibrium :* The short-run is long enough to make adjustment to its product in a limited way. In the short-run, the price will not be as high as the market price. But it may be higher than the price before the increase in demand.

(c) *Long-run equilibrium :* It is a sufficiently long period where in the firm can make all possible adjustments to attain maximum profit. New firms may enter the industry while the old ones may even leave the market. Price in the long run is called "Normal Price".

4.6 Equilibrium Point

It refers to a position where the form enjoys maximum profits and it has no incentive either to reduce or increase its output level. In perfect competition, the form has to satisfy two conditions to attain equilibrium: (a) MR = MC and (b) MC curve should cut the MR curve from below. In Monopoly, the firm attains equilibrium if its MR = MC.

4.7 Imperfect Competition

A competition is said to be imperfect when it is not perfect. That is, when the conditions of perfect competition do not exist in a given market, it is referred to as an imperfect market. Based on the number of buyers and sellers, the imperfect markets are classified as:

(i) Monopoly (ii) Monopolistic Competition (iii) Duopoly

(iv) Oligopoly (v) Monopsony (vi) Duopsony (vii) oligopsony.

Let us explain about each of them in detail.

Generally, "Poly" means seller and "Psony" means Buyer.

Monopoly : It is an extreme version of imperfect market. The word "Monopoly" is made up of two syllables, mono and poly. Mono means single while poly means seller. Thus, Monopoly is a market organization where there is only one seller for a particular commodity and there are no close substitutes for it. That is, there should not be any good substitute for it.

Monopoly exists when there are certain restrictions on the entry of other firms into business or where there are no close substitute for a given product or service. These factors determine the degree of hold for the monopolist in the market in terms of influencing the price and ability to earn supernormal profits.

Monopoly can be interpreted in two ways. When there is a sole supplier, it is a case of a pure monopoly. In this case, the firm and the industry are one and the same. For example, the RBI is the sole supplier of currency notes in India. Another context is where the firm supplying a half of the total market may have a greater market power, if the rest of the market is shared by a number of small firms. When the remaining firms are equally big, it may face fierce competition from the other firms.

4.8 Feature of Monopoly

The following are the features of Monopoly.

1. *Single person or a firm :* Here the total supply of the product is controlled by a single person or a firm.
2. *No close substitutes :* There should be no close substitutes and no competitors.
   Ex: Electric bulb and Railway.
3. *Large Number of Buyers :* There may be large number of buyers under monopoly.
4. *Poly Market :* Since there is only one in the industry he is the Price Maker.
5. *Supply and Price :* the Monopolist can decide either the price or quantity, not both.
6. *Downward Sloping Curve :* the demand curve of monopolist slopes downward from left to right.
7. *Inelastic Demand :* The Products and services provided by the monopolist bear inelastic demand.
8. *Easy Creation :* Monopoly can be created through statutory grant of special privileges such as licenses, permits, patent right and so on.

4.9 Types of Monopoly

Monopoly may be classified into various types. They can be explained as follows:

1. *Legal Monopoly :* If Monopoly arises on account of legal rights, it is called 'Legal Monopoly'.

   Ex: Patent Rights, Copy right, Trade name etc.
2. *Voluntary Monopoly :* To get the advantages of monopoly some private firms come together voluntarily to control the supply of a commodity. These are called country monopolies. Generally, these monopolies arise with industrial combinations. These voluntary monopolies are of three kinds: (a) Cartel (b) Trust (c) Holding Company. It may be called Artificial monopoly.

3. *Government Monopoly :* Sometimes the government will take the responsibility of supplying a commodity and avoid private interference.

   Ex: Water, Electricity.

   These monopolies, created to satisfy social wants, are formed on social consideration. These are also called 'Social Monopolies'.
4. *Private Monopoly :* If the total supply of a good is produced by a single private person or firm it is called Private Monopoly. Hindustan Lever Ltd., is having the monopoly power to produce Lux soap.
5. *Limited Monopoly :* If the monopolist is having limited power in fixing the price of his product, it is called as 'Limited Monopoly'. It may be due to the fear of distant substitutes.
6. *Unlimited Monopoly :* If the monopolist is having unlimited power in fixing the priced of his good or service, it is called unlimited monopoly.

   Ex: A doctor in village.
7. *Single Price Monopoly :* When the monopolist charges same price for all units of his product, it is called Single Price Monopoly.

   Ex: Hero Honda Company charges same price to all its bikes of the same model.
8. *Discriminating Monopoly :* When a monopolist charges different prices to different consumers for the same product, it is called discriminating monopoly.

   Ex: the telephone rent may be more to rich i.e. in urban and less in rural areas.
9. *Natural Monopoly :* Sometimes monopoly may arise due to scarcity of natural resources. Nature provides raw materials in some places only. The owner of the place will work become monopolist. For Ex: Diamond mines in South Africa.

4.10 Is Monopoly Socially Desirable?

A monopolist gains control over a given market over a period of time with his products and services. But is it socially desirable? Many economists still feel that monopoly is socially undesirable as it reduces economic welfare in many ways. The following are some of the reasons that support their view point.

1. *Inefficient allocation of resources :* A monopolist will restrict the output of his product to increase the price and maximize profit, this means, he intentionally reduces the output using fewer resources.
2. *Exploitation of consumers :* The monopolist exploits the consumers by charging a higher price for his product. Because there is no competition, the monopolist is free to charge any price as long as the government does not interfere.
3. *Wide gap between rich and poor :* This may widen gap between the rich and poor. The monopolist makes large profit by charging higher prices. The income in the hands of consumers is taken away by the monopolist in this way. This leads to concentration of economic power and wealth in the hands of a few. Income inequalities widen.

4. *Unfair trade practice :* Gaining control over price or supply, the monopolist may resort to unfair trade practices such as blocking the entry of new firms into the market.
5. *Restricted output :* The monopolist may intentionally restrict the output though he has scope to increase the production. This could be one of the strategies to continue to hold control over price in the market.
6. *Restricted scope to R&D :* Since there is no threat for the monopolist, he may not take serious interest in brining out innovations or creativity in the products or improve the product standard.

4.11 Arguments in Favour of Monopoly

Some economists argue that monopoly is also beneficial to the consumer as large size results in economies of scale and average cost will be considerably lower, resulting in lower price. Because of the larger size and abundant financial resources, the monopoly firms can invest in R&D, and bring out innovative products into the market. Thus, monopoly firms may make available to the consumer's better quality products of new varieties at reasonable prices. With increasing focus on liberalization, globalization and deregulation, governments in several countries including India have been reviewing anti-monopoly laws. For instance, Government of India, in recent years, repealed several provisions in the MRTP Act.

Monopolistic competition : Perfect competition and perfect monopoly are dare phenomena in the deal world. Monopolistic competition is said to exist when there are many firms and each one produces such goods and services that are close substitutes to each other. They are similar but not identical. Edward H. Chamberlain developed the theory of monopolistic competition which presents a more realistic picture of the actual market structure and the nature of competition.

4.12 Characteristics of Monopolistic Competition

The important characteristics of monopolistic competition are:

1. *Existence of Many firms :* Industry consists of many sellers who are independent. A monopolistic competition form follows an independent price policy.
2. *Product Differentiation :* Product differentiation is the essential feature of monopolistic competition. Products can be differentiated by means of unique facilities, advertising, brand loyalty, and so on. Through heavy advertisement budgets, Pepsi and Coco-Cola make it very expensive for a third competitor to enter the cola market on such a big scale.
3. *Large Number of Buyers :* There are a large number of buyers in the market. But the buyers have their own brand preferences. Each seller has to plan various incentive schemes to retain the customers who patronize his products.
4. *Free Entry and Exit of Firms :* There is freedom of entry and exit. That is, there is no barrier as found under monopoly.

5. *Selling costs :* Since the products are close substitutes much efforts is needed to retain the existing consumers and to create new demand. So each firm has to spend a lot on selling cost, which includes cost on advertising and other sales promotion activities.
6. *Imperfect Knowledge :* Imperfect knowledge about the product leads to monopolistic competition. If the buyers are fully aware of the quality of the product they cannot be influenced much by advertisement or other sales promotion techniques. For example, effective dealer service backed by advertisement helped popularization of certain brands though the quality of almost all the cement available in the market remains the same.
7. *The Group :* Under perfect competition the term industry refers to collection of firms producing a homogeneous product. But under monopolistic competition, the products of various firms are not identical though they are close substitutes. Prof. Chamberlain calls these collection of firms producing close substitute products as a group.

4.13 Oligopoly

The term "oligopoly" is derived from two greeck words, "OLIGOS' means a "few" and "pollen" means to "sell". OLIGOPOLY is that form of imperfect competition where there are a few firms in the market, producing either a homogeneous product or producing products which are close but not perfect substitutes of each other.

Chapacteristics of Oligopoly

The main features of oligopoly are:

1. *New firms :* There are only a few firms in the industry. The various firms in the industry compete with each other.
2. *Interdependence :* As there are only very few firms, any steps taken by one firm to increase sales, by reducing price or by changing product design affects the sales of other firms in the industry. So the decisions of all the firms in the industry are interdependent.
3. *Indeterminate demand curve :* The interdependence of the firms makes their demand curve indeterminate. When one firm reduces price other firms also reduces. Thus the demand curve loses its definiteness and thus is indeterminate as it constantly changes due to the reaction of rival firms.
4. *Advertising and selling costs :* Advertising plays a greater role in oligopoly market when compared to other market systems. According to Prof. William J. Baumol " it is only under oligarchy that advertisement comes fully to its own"
5. *Price rigidity :* In the oligopoly market price remains rigid. No firm will be ready to change the prevailing price as there will be loss for themselves.

So, there will be price rigidity in the oligopoly market.

Duopoly : Only two sellers. Ex. Coca-Cola and Pepsi.

Monopsony : Mrs. Joan Robinson was first to use it. Only one single buyer.

Oligopoly : Few buyers and many sellers.

Bilateral Monopoly : Single seller and single buyer.

4.14 Objectives and Policies of Pricing Methods

In a market mix, out of the 4 P's price is the odd one out, because it is the revenue carrier and the other three elements of the marketing mix-product, promotion and place are costs. The price of a product is what the company gets back in return for all the effort that is put into manufacturing and marketing the product. It is therefore essential that managers understand how to set prices, because both undercharging and overcharging can have dramatic effects on profitability.

One of the key factors that marketing managers need to remember is that price should not be set in isolation, it should be blended with product, promotion and place to form a coherent mix that provides superior customer value.

Understanding how to set prices is an important aspect of marketing decision-making. Price is a major determinant of profitability and developing a coherent strategy therefore assumes major significance. Shapiro and Jackson have identified three methods used by the managers generally, to set price.

1. Cost-oriented – based upon costs.
2. Competitor-oriented – based upon competitor activities.
3. Market-oriented – based upon marketing strategy.

Let us now discuss these methods briefly.

1. Cost-oriented pricing

This is the commonly used method in setting prices. It is again of two types.

1. Full cost pricing, and
2. Direct cost pricing.

(a) Full cost pricing

Full cost pricing includes direct costs and fixed costs. This method forces managers to calculate costs and gives an indication of the minimum price necessary to make a profit. Once direct and fixed costs have been measured break-even analysis can be used to estimate the sales volume needed to balance.

Revenue and costs at different price levels. Therefore the procedure calculating full costs is useful. Other pricing methods are used since full costs may act as a constraint.

Disadvantages

1. It leads to an increase in price as sales fall.
2. The procedure is illogical because a sales externate is made before setting the price.

3. It focuses on internal costs rather than customers willingness to pay.
4. There may be technical problem in allocating overheads in multiproduct firms.

(b) Direct cost pricing

This involves the calculation of only those costs, which are likely to rise as output increases. Direct cost pricing is useful for services marketing. Direct costs indicate the lowest price at which it is sensible to take business if the alternative is to let machinery lie idle. It does not suffer from the price up as demand down problem that was found with full cost pricing, as it does not take account of fixed costs in the price calculation.

Disadvantages

1. The obvious problem is that this price does not cover full costs and so the company would be making a less-selling product at the low price.
2. It avoids the problem of allocating overhead charges found with full cost pricing for the same reason.
3. When the business is bought it gives no indication of the correct price because it does not take into account customers willingness to pay.
4. It cannot be used for long term, as at some point fixed costs must be covered to make a profit.

2. Competitor-Oriented Pricing

This approach focuses on competitors rather than costs when setting prices. These are two types and they are 1. Going rate pricing and 2. Competitive bidding.

(a) *Going-rate Pricing*

In situations where there is no product differentiation, a producer may have to take the going-rate for the product. This accords most directly to the economist's notion of perfect competition. To the marketing manager it is fundamental of creation of a differential advantage which enables companies to build monopoly positions around their products. This allows a degree of discretion dependent upon how much customers value the differential advantage.

(b) *Competitive bidding*

The most usual process is the drawing up of detailed specifications for a product and putting the contract out for tender. Potential suppliers quote a price, which is confidential to themselves and the buyer. All other things being equal, the buyer will select the supplier, which quotes the lowest price. The bidder uses the past experience to estimate a probability of each price level being successful.

Demerits

1. It is difficult for managers to express their views on the likelihood of a price being successful in precise statistical probability terms.
2. Use of the expected profit criterion is limited to situations where the bidder can play the percentage game over the medium to long term.

3. Marketing-Oriented Pricing

This method of pricing is more difficult than cost-oriented or competitor-oriented pricing because it takes a much wider range of factors into account. In all, less factors need to be considered when adopting a marketing-oriented approach as shown in **the figure.**

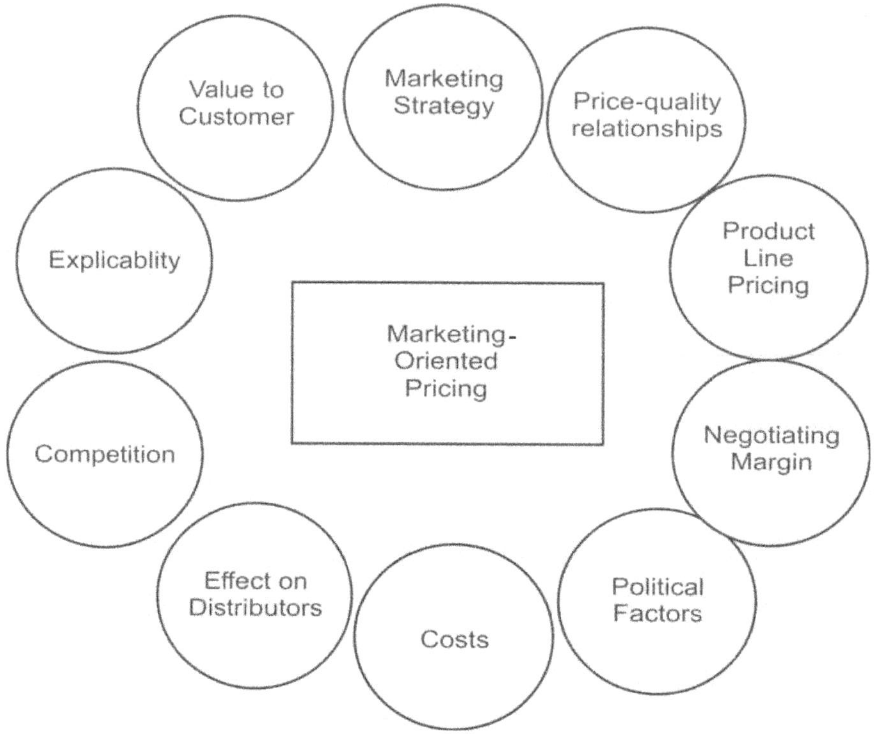

Fig. 4.1 Marketing-oriented prices approach

(i) *Marketing Strategy*

The price of a product should be set in line with the marketing strategy. It is often viewed in isolation with no reference to other marketing decisions such as positioning, strategic objectives, promotion, distribution and product benefits. The result is an inconsistent mess, which makes no sense in the market place and causes customer confusion.

The way out of this problem is to recognise that the pricing decision is dependant on other earliest decisions in the marketing and planning process. For new products, price will depend upon positioning strategies, and for existing products, price will be affected by strategic objectives.

(ii) *Value to the customer*

Price should be accurately keyed to the value of the customer. In brief, more value that a product gives compared to the competition, the higher the price that can be charged.

The buy-response method, trade-off analysis, test-marketing and economic value to the customer analysis are the four methods adopted for analysing the value of the product to the customer.

(iii) *Price quality relationships*

A third considerable factor to marketing-oriented pricing is the relationship between price and perceived quality. Many people use price as an indicator of quality. This is particularly the case of products where objective measurement of quality is not possible such as drinks and perfume. However a study of price and quality perceptions of cars found that higher priced cars were perceived to possess high quality. This clearly indicates that price had influenced quality perceptions.

(iv) *Product-line Pricing*

Marketing-oriented companies have to take into account of where the price of a new product fits into its existing product-line. Some companies prefer to extend their product lines rather than reducing the price of existing brands in the face of price competition. They launch cut-price fighter brands to compete with the low-price rivals. This has the advantage of maintaining the image and profit margins of existing brands.

(v) *Explicability*

The capability of sales people to explain a high price to customers may constrain price flexibility. In markets where customers demand economic justification of prices, the inability to produce costly products when higher prices cannot be set.

(vi) *Competition*

Competition factors are important determinants of price. Care should be taken when defining competition. When asked to name competitors marketing managers list companies who supply technically similar products but products, which are dissimilar but solve the same problem in a similar way and products which solve the problem in a dissimilar way also should be taken into account.

(vii) *Negotiating margins*

In some markets customers except a price reduction. Price paid is therefore is very different from list prices. The difference between the list price and realised price is the price waterfall and the difference can be accounted for by order-size discounts, competitive discounts, a fast payment discount, an annual volume bonus and promotional allowances. Managing the price waterfall is a key element in achieving a satisfactory transaction price.

(viii) *Effect on distributors or retailers*

When products are sold through intermediaries, the list price to the customer must reflect the margins required by them. The implication is that pricing strategy is dependant on understanding not only the ultimate customer but also the needs of the distributors and retailers who form the link between them and the manufacturer. If their needs cannot be accomodated product launch may not be viable, or a different distribution system required.

(ix) *Political factors*

High process can be a continuous public issue, which may invoke government intervention. Companies need to take great care that their pricing strategies are not seen to be against the public interest. Exploitation of a monopoly position may bring short-term profits but incur the backlash of a public inquiry into pricing practices.

(x) *Costs*

The final considerable factor in price setting is cost. It is essential to consider costs alongside all of the other considerations discussed under marketing-oriented price setting rather than in isolation what should be avoided is the blind reference to costs when setting prices. Simply because one product costs less to make than another does not imply its price should be less.

4.15 Strategy-Based Pricing

4.15.1 Market skimming

When the product is introduced for the first time in the market, the company follows this method. Under this method, the company fixes a very high price for the product. The main idea is to charge the customer maximum possible. This strategy is mostly found in case of technology products. When Sony introduces a particular TV model, it fixes a very high price. When new series of Pentium is released into market, it is priced very high. Initially, all cannot afford except a very few. As the time passes by, the price comes down and more people can afford to buy. This method can be followed only when (i) the demand for the product is inelastic, (ii) there is no threat from competitors, (iii) a high price is coupled with high technology or quality.

4.15.2 Market penetration

This is exactly opposite to the market skimming method. Here the price of the product is fixed so low that the company can increase its market share. The company attains profits with increasing volumes and increase in the market share. More often, the companies believe that it is necessary to dominate the market in the long-run than making profits in the short-run. This method is more suitable where market is highly price-sensitive. In such a case, a low price stimulates more rapid growth. It will be more appropriate in cases where the costs are likely to fall with increase in output. A low price may not attract significant degree of competition also.

4.15.3 Two-part pricing

The firms with market power can enhance profits by the strategy of two-part pricing. Under this strategy, a firm charges a fixed fee for the right to purchase its goods, plus a per unit charge for each unit purchased. Entertainment houses such as country clubs, athletic clubs, golf courses, and health clubs usually adopt this strategy. They charge a fixed initiation fee plus a charge, per month or per visit, to use the facilities. There are also organisations that charge membership fee (equivalent to the consumer surplus) and offer their products and services cost-to-cost basis.

The fixed fee generally equals the consumer surplus each consumer receives at this per unit price. The charge per visit or on monthly basis equals the marginal cost. Under this method, if the membership fee is fixed to equal one's consumer surplus, actual profits can even be higher than in case of monopoly.

4.15.4 Block pricing

Block pricing is another way a firm with market power can enhance its profits. We see block pricing in our day-to-day life very frequently. Six Lux soaps in a single pack or five Maggi noodles is a single pack illustrate this pricing method. By selling certain number of units of a product as one package, the firm earns more than by selling unit wise. The block pricing is a profit maximisation price on each package. It is generally the total value the consumer receives for the package, including consumer surplus.

It works out as follows: Suppose six International Lux soaps are offered, as a single unit along with a elegantly looking soap box, at a price of Rs.100. Here the consumer has to make an all-or-none decision between buying eight units or buying nothing. From the customer point of view each international Lux soap costs, say, Rs. 18, and the soap-box is priced at Rs. 25. So the soaps and box together cost the customer $(6 \times 18) + 25 = 108 + 25 =$ Rs 133. As against this, the pack of six International Lux soaps is offered at Rs.100, which is fairly attractive from the customer angle. The consumer surplus is here equal to Rs.33.

Block pricing enhances profits by forcing consumers to make an all-or-none decision to purchase units of a product. This can enhance profits even in situations where consumers have identical demands for a given product.

4.15.5 Commodity bundling

Commodity bundling refers to the practice of bundling two or more different products together and selling them at a single 'bundle price'. The package includes the airfare, hotel, meals, sight seeing and so on at a bundled price instead of pricing each of these service separately. Computer firms offer PCs, assembling as per the customer specifications and offer them at a bundled price. The car companies provide cars with air-conditioning, power steering, automatic transmission, autogear and so forth, and sell them at a special price.

Commodity bundling is a viable pricing strategy to enhance profits when consumers differ with respect to the amounts they are willing to pay for multiple products sold by a firm. It is advantageous for the trader to know how much the consumer is prepared to pay any price for viewing Niagara Falls for longer hours, the tourist company can charge better for this customer by allowing him good time.

4.15.6 Peak load pricing

During seasonal period when demand is likely to be higher, a firm may enhance profits by peak load pricing. The firm's philosophy is to charge a higher price during peak times than is charged during off-peak times. The pricing is done in such a way that the business is not lost to the competitors. The firm following such a strategy covers the likely losses during the off-peak times from the likely profits from the peak times.

Where the demand during the peak times is so high that all customers cannot be accommodated at the same price due to capacity constraints, the profitable alternative for the firm is to follow peak load pricing.

Airlines such as Air India, Indian Airlines, Jet Air and so on, keep revising their fares every three months to charge higher fares during festival/holiday seasons. Toll roads/bridges tend to have more traffic during rush hour than at other times of the day; utility companies tend to have higher demand during the day than during the late-night hours.

Peak load pricing is similar to price discrimination. But due to capacity limitations, the firm is unable to fully equate the marginal revenues of those who purchase at different times.

4.15.7 Cross-subsidisation

In cases where demand for two products produced by a firm is interrelated through demand or costs, the firm may enhance the profitability of its operations through cross subsidisation. Using the profits generated by established products, a firm may expand its activities by financing new product development and diversification into new product markets.

To illustrate, a computer company, selling both hardware and software, may find economies, relating to volume and cost, in selling the two products jointly. There can accrue cost savings as the software is developed as per the requirements of the customer within the company. The demand for the two products is likely to be interdependent. In such circumstances, the company may find it profitable to sell hardware at or below cost and charge a relatively high price for the software. The customer also is happy that the software is customised as per his requirements and compatible with the hardware.

The strategy of cross subsidies facilitates the company to sell multiple products. This may result in cost savings. If the two products are such that they are interdependent in terms of demand, the customer can be shown incentive to buy more of each product than they would otherwise buy.

4.15.8 Transfer pricing

Transfer pricing is an internal pricing technique. It refers to a price at which inputs of one department are transferred to another, in order to maximise the overall profits of the company.

In case of a company having multiple processes the output of one process is the input of the next process. Till the production reaches the last stage, the output of each process is termed as work-in-progress. The price of output of one process affects the price of output of the next process. The engine department of Kinetic Honda makes the scooter engines and forwards these to the assembly department. The assembly department in turn assembles the scooter. Here, the price at which the engine department forwards each engine affects the price of the scooter.

Transfer pricing refers to the method of pricing the work in progress at different levels of processing at which one department forwards their output to the next department for further processing.

4.16 Pricing Strategies in Times of Stiff Price Competition

In markets we find firms selling similar products competing neck-to-neck in price. If the price wars lead to prices close to marginal cost, the firm does not really get any profit. In such a situation, there are three strategies that are valuable for firms:

4.16.1 Price Matching

Price matching is a strategy in which a firm promises to match a lower price offered by any competitor, while announcing it own price. It is necessary that one should be confident, before this strategy is adopted, that the price cannot be lower in the market than one offered. If all the firms maintain the same price, the firms share the market and charge the monopoly price, which results in high profits. The firm that comes out with a similar product at lower price, will gain back its market share.

4.16.2 Promoting Brand Loyalty

This is an advertising strategy where the customers are frequently reminded by the brand value of a given product or service. The conviction here is that the customers, once they are loyal to the given branded product or service, will not slip away when the competitors come out with products at lower prices. Pepsi and Coke spend huge amounts to advertising campaigns to draw the attention of consumers. Brand loyal customers continue to be with the firm despite its higher prices. However, this strategy does not work out where the customer perceives no difference in the quality of products.

4.16.3 Time-to-time Pricing

This is also called randomised pricing strategy where the firm varies from its price from time-to-time, say hour-to-hour or day-to-day. This method offers two advantages: the rival firms can no more play with price cuts. Also the customers cannot learn from experience which firm charges the lowest price in the market. There is no guarantee that one firm continues to offer the best price. The person who has price information often stands to gain. But this gain is short-lived or a one-time benefit. It is because such information needs to be updated from time-to-time. Customers cannot keep one-time benefit. It is because such information needs to be updated from time-to-time. Customers cannot keep on humting for price information every time. So all the firms in the market have their own undisturbed market share. Added to this, the firms can sustain their market share by providing better customer care and service.

This method is frequently in the markets of bullion, currency, and bank deposits. The gold prices vary internationally from time-to-time for various extraneous considerations. The banks keep changing their deposit interest rates from time-to-time. Similarly the exchange rate of US dollar varies from time to time. Different exchange houses vary their buying and selling rates of different currencies.

4.16.4 Promotional Pricing

To promote a particular product, at times, the firm may offer the product at the most competitive price. Sometimes, the price of a particular product is kept intentionally

4.17 Intiating Changes in Price

By taking into account the ten marketing oriented factors, managers can judge the correct level at which to set prices. But in a highly competitive world, pricing is dynamic; managers need to know when and how to raise or lower prices, and whether or not to react to competitors price moves.

Three important issues associated with intiating price changes are the circumstances that may lead a company to raise or lower process, the tactics that can be used and in estimating competitor reaction.

4.17.1 Circumstances

A price increase may be justified as a result of marketing research, which reveals that customers place a higher value on the product than is reflected in its price. Rising costs and hence reduced profit margins also stimulate price rises. Success demand is another factor that increase margins even though the sales may fall.

Correspondingly, price cuts may be provoked by the discovery that price is high compared to the value that customers place on the product, falling costs bring down costs and where there is excess supply leading to excess capacity.

4.17.2 Tactics

Price increases and cuts can be implemented in many ways. The most direct is the price jump or fall that increases or decreases the price by the full amount at one go. Price unbundling is another tactic which allows each element in the offering to be separately priced in such a way that the total price is raised. A final tactic is to maintain the list but lower discounts to customers.

4.17.3 Estimating Competitor Reaction

A key factor in the price change decision is the extent competitor reaction. A price rise that no competitor follows may turn customers away while a price cut that is met by the competition may reduce industry profitability. Competitors strategic objectives, self-interest and past experience are the factors that affect the extent of competitors reaction.

Summary

1. Price = *cost* + *profit*
2. *Market* is a place where the combination of buyers and sellers are available who deal with a particular commodity or service.
3. According to *Marshall*, demand and supply behave like a pair of scissors in cutting cloth.
4. The price at which demand and supply of a commodity is equal is called equilibrium *price*.
5. Market structures are of *two* types.
6. Imperfect competition is divided into *three* types.
7. Define perfect competition.

   A market structure where competition among the sellers and buyers is perfect.
8. Any three features of perfect competition.

   (a) Homogeneous product (b) Free entry and exit (c) Indifference.
9. *Pure* competition is seen in agricultural products.
10. Conditions for attaining equilibrium by a firm
    (a) Marginal cost = Marginal revenue.
    (b) MC curve must cut MR curve from below.
11. Marshall divided time periods on the basis of supply into four types.
12. The price determined in very short period is called market price.
13. During *short* period new firms cannot enter into the industry.
14. The price determined in long period is called normal price.
15. Using market period, goods are classified into two types namely.
    (i) Perishable goods.
    (ii) Non-perishable goods.
16. Normal price is a *hypothetical* price.
17. Reproducible commodities have *normal* price.
18. *Pure monopoly* is a market situation where there is no good substitute to the product being sold by a single firm.
19. Monopoly arising on account of legal support is called *legal monopoly*.
20. Kinds of voluntary monopolies are (i) *Cartel* (ii) *Trust* (iii) *holding company*.

21. Voluntary monopoly is also called as *artificial* monopoly.
22. Monopoly, which arises due to scarcity of natural resources, is called natural monopoly.
23. *Social* monopoly is the other name for government monopoly.
24. ***Oligopoly :***

    It is that form of imperfect competition where there are a few firms in the market producing either homogeneous or close substitute products but not perfect substitutes to each other.
25. *Duopoly* is a market situation where there are only two sellers.
26. A market situation where there is a single seller and a single buyer is called *bilateral* monopoly.
27. *Monophony* refers to market, which has a single buyer.
28. ***Limited monopoly :***

    If the monopolist has limited power of fixing price of the product then it is called as limited monopoly.

    Charging different prices to different consumers by a monopolist is called discriminating monopoly.

Essay Questions

1. How does an individual firm behave under perfect competition. Also explain the firm and the industry equilibrium under perfect competition.?
2. Explain the role of time factor in the determination of price. Also explain price output determination incase of perfect competition.
3. Explain how the price is determined under conditions of perfect competition. Illustrate this with the help of diagrams.
4. Monopoly is disappearing from market. Do you agree with this statement? Do you advocate for the monopoly to continue in the market situations.
5. Compare and contrast between perfect competition and monopoly.
6. Explain how markets can be classified in many ways.
7. Explain how market structures can be classfied.
8. What are the features of perfect competion ?
9. How markets are classified under imperfect competition.
10. How monopoly can be classfied into various types.
11. What are the important characteristics of Monopolistic competition?
12. What are the objectives and policies of making pricing methods ?

Short Questions

1. Define Market.
2. How will you classification of Markets ?
3. Define Market Structures briefly.
4. What are the features on which Market structure is based ?
5. Explain perfect competition.
6. Explain imperfect competition.
7. Define Oligopoly.
8. Define Oligopsony.
9. Define Market Skimming.
10. Define Market Penetration.
11. Explain briefly:
    (i) Two-part pricing (ii) Block pricing
    (iii) Commodity bundling (iv) Transfer pricing

CHAPTER 5

Business and New Economic Environment

5.1 Introduction

Business creates not only profits or losses. The business economic environment influences the control of the business as well as profits. In India the following are the different types of formation of business organisations.

1. Sole Proprietorship
2. Partnership firm
3. Joint Stock Company
4. Joint Hindu Family firm
5. Co-operative society.

Factors affecting the choice of the new economic environment of business organisation. The following are the factors affecting the choice of business organisation.

1. ***Easy to start and easy to close :*** The form of business organisation should be such that it should be easy to start and easy to close. There should not be hassles or long procedures in the process of setting up business or closing the same.
2. ***Division of labour :*** There should be possibility to divide the work among the available owners. The idea is to pool the expertise of all the people in business and run the business most efficiently.
3. ***Large amount of resources :*** Large volume of business requires large volume of resources. Some forms of business organisations do not permit to raise larger resources. Select the one which permits to mobilise the large resources.

4. ***Liability :*** The liability of the owners should be limited to the extent of money invested in business. It is better if their personal properties are not brought into business to make up the losses of the business.
5. ***Secrecy :*** The form of business organisation you select should be such that it should permit to take care of the business secrets. We know that century old business units are still surviving only because they could successfully guard their business secrets.
6. ***Transfer of ownership :*** There should be simple procedures to transfer the ownership to the next legal heir.
7. ***Ownership, management and control :*** If ownership, management and control are in the hands of one or a small group of persons, communication will be effective and coordination will be easier. Where ownership, management and control are widely distributed, it calls for a high degree of professional skills to monitor the performance of the business.
8. ***Continuity :*** The business should continue forever and ever irrespective of the uncertainities in future.
9. ***Quick decision-making :*** Select such a form of business organisation which permits you to take decisions quickly and promptly. Delay in decisions may invalidate the relevance of the decisions.
10. ***Personal contact with customers :*** Most of the times, customers give us clues to improve business. So choose such a form which keeps you close to the customers.
11. ***Flexibility :*** In times of rough weather, there should be enough flexibility to shift from one business to the other. The lesser the funds commited in a particular business, the better it is.
12. ***Taxation :*** More profit means more tax. Choose wuch a form which permits to pay low tax.

These are the parameters against which we can evaluate each of the available forms of busines organisation.

5.2 Sole Proprietorship

A sole proprietorship concern is the oldest, simplest and the most familiar forms of business organization. In this form of organization, a single individual takes the initiative to start a business all by himself by supplying the entire capital, uses his own skill and intelligence in the management of its affairs and is solely responsible for the results of its operations. The individual may run the business alone or may obtain the assistance of employees or his family members. It is the first form in the evolution of the forms of organization and is the oldest among them.

Even today, sole proprietorship concerns constitute the single largest class of business establishments in all countries of the world. Most often, business units are started on a sole proprietorship basis because of simplicity of operation, easy of formation, freedom of action etc.

Features :

1. In this form of sole proprietorship organization, a single individual takes the initiative of starting a business, supplies the entire capital and manages the business all by himself.
2. He shoulders the entire responsibility of the business activities.
3. He performs all the duties in connection with the business activities. Some time, he is assisted by paid employees or his family members.
4. The sole proprietorship carries on the business for his exclusive gain and bears all the risks incidental to the conduct of his business.
5. The liability of the sole proprietorship is unlimited. It means that the sole trader has to make good the business losses out of his private property.
6. The sole proprietorship concern does not have a separate legal existence separate from that of the proprietor. It is the proprietor who can sue others and can be sued.

5.2.1 Merits of sole proprietorship

1. ***Ease of formation :*** A sole proprietorship concern can be very easily formed. No legal formalities such as registration are necessary. Any person having the required capital can set up any business ventures, except those prohibited by law.
2. ***Ease of dissolution :*** Dissolution or closure of business is equally simple in case of a sole proprietorship concern. There are no legal formalities in this matter. All that he has to do is to arrange for the satisfaction of creditors' claims.
3. ***Direct motivation :*** The direct relationship between effort and reward that exists in a sole proprietorship concern serves as a powerful incentive to the proprietor to manage the concern efficiently. It encourages him to put forth all his efforts in the management of the business.
4. ***Promptness in taking decisions :*** Another advantage is that decisions can be taken quickly and promptly in the case of a sole proprietorship concern. This is because, the sole proprietorship, being the only and final authority in all business matters need not consult others or take the approval of others while deciding on any business matters.
5. ***Secrecy :*** Secrecy of the production processes can be maintained under this form of organization. This enables him to take full advantage of the new ideas or innovations that the may make regarding production etc.
6. ***Social utility of sole trading concerns :*** A sole proprietorship concern is useful to the society.

   It is a source of independent way of living. As the sole proprietorship requires one man to be all in all of the business, it is very suitable to those members of the society who want to be self-dependent and utilise their skills.

Demerits :

The sole proprietorship form of organization suffers from the following drawbacks :

1. ***Limited finance :*** The capital that can be secured by a single individual limited. It is neither easy nor safe for him to procure funds from banks or other financial institutions. As a result the size of the business should remain small.
2. ***Unlimited liability :*** The liability of a sole proprietorship is unlimited. Not only the assets of the business, but also his private assets will be used to pay off the debts.
3. ***Limited managerial skills :*** The managerial ability of the sole proprietorship is limited. Modern business is full of complications especially due to ever changing nature of the market and the various laws that are being enacted. An individual may not be an expert in all matters and therefore, his decisions may be unbalanced.
4. ***Limited growth :*** The sole proprietorship concern can be successful only on a small scale. If the scale of operations increases, the sole proprietorship faces such problems as supervisory problem, financial problem etc. So the sole proprietorship concern will have only a limited growth.
5. ***Uncertainty of duration :*** The life of the business is based on the life of the sole proprietorship. The business can continue after the death or the sole proprietorship only by inheritance. But the successors may not be willing to continue the business activities.
6. ***Secrecy :*** The secrecy of a sole proprietorship concern is a social disadvantage. A new innovation made by the proprietor, if kept as a secret, is a social loss, because its use is restricted.

5.2.2 Importance of the sole proprietorship form of organization

Despite its weaknesses, the Sole Proprietorship concerns still hold an important place against the other forms of organization. This is because they are best-suited under the following circumstances :

1. ***Local market :*** It is suitable when the business or market is local and requires simple organization, ordinary skill and limited amount of capital. Such conditions are usually fulfilled in the retail proprietorship. Hence the bulk of the retail trade is carried on by sole proprietorship concerns.
2. ***Personal contact :*** When the business requires personal element and qualities e.g., doctors, medicals etc., the sole trading concern is the best form of organization. In some businesses for example garment industry, tastes and fashions of the customers play an important role. Under such circumstances, this form of organization is the best, because the sole trader can establish contacts with the customers and satisfy their peculiar needs and demands.
3. ***Speculative business :*** The sole proprietorship concern is also suitable for a business which is speculative and where there are sudden changes in demand price. For example, in case of precious metals such as Gold, Silver etc. In such cases, the proprietor has to take quick decisions and prompt action to take advantage of a particular business opportunity.

5.3 Partnership Firm

A partnership firm of organization is defined as "the relation between two or more persons who have agreed to share profits of a business carried on by all or any of them acting for all". Persons who have entered into partnership with one another are individually called "partners" and collectively as a "firm". The name under which the business is carried on is called the "firm's name".

1. ***Agreement :*** A partnership is the result of an agreement and not of status. It is created by mutual consent between the partners. There must be an oral or a written agreement to form a partnership.
2. ***Presence of business :*** A partnership is a form of Business organization. The association of a few individuals is for conducting a certain business.
3. ***Sharing of profits :*** The object of starting a partnership should be the sharing of profits.
4. ***Unlimited liability :*** Each partner has an unlimited liability in respect of the debts of the firm. The creditors can recover their dues from the property of any or all the partners of the firm.
5. ***Dual role of principal and agent :*** Every partner can act simultaneously as a principal and agent of the firm. As an agent, he can bind the other partners by his acts. As a principal he is bound by the acts of the others.
6. ***Number of members :*** A partnership firm can be formed with a minimum of two members. The maximum number of members to conduct a general business is twenty and in case of banking business, the maximum is ten.

Restriction on transfer of Shares : A partner cannot transfer his share in a firm, to an outsider without the consent of the other partners.

5.3.1 Types of Partners and Partnership Firms

In partnership firms there are different kinds of partners. They are as follows :

1. ***Active or actual or ostensible partner :*** A person who becomes a partner by an agreement and is actively engaged in the conduct of the business of partnership is known as an actual partner. He is the agent of the other partners and binds himself and the other parties by his acts in the ordinary course of the business.
2. ***Sleeping or dormant partner :*** A partner who does not take active part in the conduct of the business is known as a sleeping or a dormant partner. He invests capital and shares in the profits and losses of the firm and having an unlimited liability.
3. ***Nominal partner :*** A partner, who lends his name to the firm without having any interest in it, is called a nominal partner. He does not invest in the business of the firm, nor does he share in the profits or take part in the management of the business. But, he is liable to the outsiders for all the debts of the firm.

4. ***Partner in profits only :*** If a partner is entitled to a certain share of profits in the firm without being liable for the losses, he is known as partner in profits only. He will not be allowed to take part in management of the business, but he will be liable to the third parties for all the acts of the partnership.
5. ***Partner by estoppels :*** Such a partner is not a partner of the firm. If a person by words spoken or written or by his conduct, represents himself to be a partner of a firm, although he is not a partner in real terms, he will be liable to the third parties for all the debts of the firm, as if he a partner. He is liable to the third parties, because by his representation, the third party was misled and lent finance to the firm, on the assumption that he is a partner. Such a partner is not entitled to a share in the profits of the firm.
6. ***Partner by holding out :*** A partner by holding out is a person who is not in fact the partner of a firm. He is a person who is represented as a partner of a firm, although he is not a partner. On knowing the fact, that he is represented as a partner, such a person should deny the fact. If he fails to deny, he will be liable to those third parties who extend loans to the firm on the basis of his being a partner.
7. ***Sub-partner :*** A partner may enter into an agreement with a third party of the sharing of partnership profits. The third party is termed as a "sub-partner". But such a partner cannot enforce his claims against the other partners.
8. ***Minor partner :*** A minor cannot enter into a contract since partnership is the result of an agreement, But he can be admitted to the benefits of partnership. On his attaining majority age the minor can decide whether or not to continue in the firm as a partner within six months and give a public notice of his intention in case he opts to discontinue.

5.3.2 Kinds of partnership firms

A partnership may be one of the following types:

1. ***Partnership at will :*** In this case any partner can, by giving the necessary notice, cease to be a partner. In other words, any partner can dissolve the partnership at any time he wishes by giving a notice of his intention.
2. ***Partnership for a definite period :*** Sometimes the partners may specify, at the time of entering into partnership, the period for which they wish to continue as partners. It is not open to any partner to withdraw for the specified period. If he does he will be liable in damages to the other partners.
3. ***Partnership for a single undertaking :*** Two or more partners may join in partnership to undertake a single venture, after the completion of which, the partnership is dissolved.
4. ***Limited partnership :*** In this type of partnership the liability of the partners is limited to their capital. The liability of at least one partner must be unlimited in such a firm. Partners with limited liability are known as limited partners and partners with unlimited liability are known as "general partners". Registration of such a firm is compulsory. The system of limited partnerships are not recognized by the Indian law. They are in existence in England.

5.3.3 Merits of Partnership Form

1. ***Ease of formation :*** A partnership can be easily formed. Unlike in the case of a joint stock company, no legal formalities are required for the formation of a partnership. Registration of firms is not compulsory although provision exists for it. The number of partners can be increased or decreased at the will of the partners without any legal formalities having to be gone through.
2. ***Larger resources :*** This form of organization enables the pooling or larger resources than sole proprietorship, because a number of persons (partners) contribributes to the capital of the business. Further, the partners can supplement their capital by borrowing from others on the basis of their private property. This enables the partnership to undertake business operations on a relatively larger scale and thereby reaping the economies of scale.
3. ***Unlimited liab1ility :*** The feature of unlimited liability is advantageous to the firm in two ways.
   (a) The partners are jointly and severally liable for all the losses of the firm. This ensures that the firm will be managed with a sense of responsibility by all the partners.
   (b) It becomes easier for the partners to raise loans on the basis of their private property.
4. ***Flexibility of organisation :*** The partnership form of organisation is extremely elastic and mobile. It can undertake new types or business without any legal formalities. It can decrease or increase capital at the will of the partners.
5. ***Promptness in taking decisions :*** The decisions in a partnership firm are quite prompt because partners often meet together to discuss various aspects of the business. Thus partner can take advantage of sudden business opportunities.
6. ***Balance Judgment :*** In addition to the pooling of capital resources, the partnership combines abilities and skills of two or more persons for handling the problems of the firm. The decisions are likely to be more balanced as compared to a sole proprietorship concern.
7. ***Reduced risk :*** The losses incurred by the firm will be shared by all the partners and hence the share of loss of each partner will be less than in the case of a sole trading concern.
8. Lastly, there is motivation for efficient management, as the profits of a partnership concern accrue to the partners themselves. This is not the case with joint stock companies, where directors do not personally gain except as shareholders.

5.3.4 Demerits of the Partnership

1. ***Lack of harmony :*** It is generally observed that there is friction and lack of harmony among the partners after the firm has worked for sometimes. The business may be paralysed and may come to an end because of difference of opinion between the partners.

2. ***Limited resources :*** The capital that can be pooled in a partnership is limited. The reason being that the number of partners in a firm is limited to ten in the case of firms doing banking business and to twenty in the case of other trading concerns. This makes the partnership form of organization highly unsuitable for business activities requiring large sums of capital.
3. ***Instability :*** The partnership firm has no independent legal existence separate from its partners. Therefore a partnership automatically ceases to exist when any one of the several partners goes out of the firm.
4. ***Limited risk-taking :*** The unlimited liability tends to restrict the enterprise of a partnership concern. The partners hesitate to explore new lines of business for fearing of placing their private property at risk.
5. ***Risk of implied authority :*** Every partner has an implied authority to bind the firm. A dishonest partners may land the firm and other partners in difficulties by his acts. The other partner may have to pay for the losses caused on account of the acts of the dishonest partner.
6. ***Lack of public confidence :*** A partnership may not enjoy public confidence because of the absence of the regulation and stricter legal control over its affairs.
7. ***Joint and several liability :*** From the point of view of liability, a partnership is even worse than sole proprietorship, because a partner is liable to the extent of his private property, not only for his own mistakes, but also for the mistakes, and dishonesty of the other partners. This is because partners are jointly and severally liable for the debts of the firm.

   Considering the merits and demerits of partnership firm, it is an ideal form of organization for small scale and medium size business having a limited market needs, limited capital and limited managerial skill. Most of the service enterprises such as transport and warehousing are also usually organized on partnership basis.

5.4 Joint Hindu Family Firm

The Joint Hindu Family firm is another form of business organization. It is not formed by an agreement or a contract but by the operation of Hindu law. Under this type of business organization, the business is owned by the co-owners or co-parceners of an estate belong to a joint Hindu family. The property of a joint Hindu family is inherited by a Hindu from his father grandfather and great grand father. This interest in inheritance is termed as coparcener intent and the members of Joint Hindu family are called co-parceners. The eldest member in the family known as "Karta" or the Karta has the right to control the affairs of the business. The Karta can barrow funds for conducting the business and his liability is limited. The liability of the co-parcener is limited to the their share in the business.

A joint Hindu family can enter into partnership with others. The death of a member does not dissolve its business. Dissolution can be possible only by mutual agreement between the members.

5.4.1 Features of Joint Hindu Family Firm

1. ***Member ship :*** The members in a Joint Hindu Family Firm arise by birth in the family. As such no outsider can acquire membership in such a business.
2. ***Male members :*** The Co-parcenery intent can be acquired only by male members of the family.
3. ***Karta :*** The right to manage the business vests in Karta alone. He has an implied authority to obtain loans for the purpose of business. Other members have neither any right to manage the business nor any right to take loans for the purpose of business.
4. ***Fluctuating share :*** The share of each member's interest fluctuates. The member's intent increases by death of any Co-parcener and decreased by birth of a new Co-parcener.
5. ***Liability :*** The liability of all the Co-parceners is limited to value of their share in the joint property. The liability of the Karta is unlimited and extends to all that he owns as his separate property.
6. ***Continued existence :*** The existence of a Joint Family business is not affected by the death or insolvency of the Co-parcener or the Karta.

5.4.2 Advantages of a Joint Hindu Family Firm

1. ***Continuity :*** Joint Hindu Family firm has relatively more continuous life as compared to a partnership firm, because it is not dissolved by the death or insanity of a coparcenor.
2. ***Centralised and efficient management :*** The management vests in the hands of the Karta who exercises full control over its activities. Secondly, Karta enjoys all the advantages of a sole proprietorship namely: (a) Prompt decisions and quick action, (b) Secrecy, (c) Flexibility in operation.
3. ***Share in profits :*** Every Co-parcener gets a share in the profits of the business irrespective of his contribution to the successful running of the business.
4. ***Insurance against contingencies :*** It serves as an insurance cover for maintaining the children, minors and the other members of the family.
5. ***Limited liability :*** The liability of the Co-parceners is limited to the extent of their shares except that of Kanrta.

5.4.3 Disadvantages

1. ***Lack of motivation :*** There is no encouragement to work hard and earn more because members who work hard do not get the direct benefits of their efforts. Further the right to share in incomes or profits irrespective of the efforts makes the members lazy and unenterprising.
2. ***Limited resources :*** Because of the limited capacity of the firm in having more members, in investing more capital and borrowing loans, the joint Hindu family firm has limited resources at its disposal.

3. The Karta exercises full control over the business activities and the other members have no right to interfere in the management of the business. This hampers the initiative and enterprise of the younger members of the family.

   The Joint Hindu Family Firm was a popular form of business organization in India. It is gradually losing grounds to the other firms of organization. This is because the Joint Hindu Family system as social institution is breaking down on account of the growth impact of industrialization and the consequential preference for individual family living.

5.5 Joint Stock Company

Another important form of business organization is the company form of organization or the Joint Stock Company. The company form of organization assumed importance after the industrial revolution, which resulted in the production and distribution of goods and services on a large-scale. This involved the investment of large sums of capital. The Sole Proprietorship and partnership forms of organization could not provide funds for large-scale production. In order to raise the necessary funds, even the small savings of scattered people had to be pooled. Thus the Joint Stock Company form of organisation arose. The capital of a Joint Stock Company is divided into shares of small value and these shares are subscribed by people with even small saving.

Definitions and features of a Joint Stock Company :

A company is a voluntary association of persons for the attainment of a common purpose with a capital divisible into units known as shares and with a limited liability. It is the creation of law and is known as an artificial person with a perpetual success in and a common seal. It exists only in contemplation of law. As per Lindley L.J., a company is "an association of many persons who contribute money or money's worth to a common stock, and employ it in some common trade or business and who share the profit or loss arising therefrom. The common stock so contributed is denoted in money and is the capital of the company. The proportion of capital to which each member is entitled is his share. Shares are always transferable although the right to transfer them is often more or less restricted". Chief Justice Marshall defined a company as "a persons artificial, invisible, intangible and existing only in the eyes of law".

5.5.1 Features of a Joint Stock Company

A joint stock company form of business organisaton has the following distinguishing features.

1. ***Separate legal existence :*** A company is different from its shareholders or members. It is treated by law as an entity separate from its members. In other words, it has an independent corporate existence. It can enter into contracts with its members or outside. Any of its members can enter into contracts with the company and the members are not liable for the acts of the company even if he holds the entire share capital. The company's property and money belong to the company and not to the shareholders.

2. ***Limited liability :*** The liability of the shareholders of a Joint Stock Company is limited by shares of guarantee. The individual shareholder need not contribute to the losses of the joint stock company beyond the face value of shares of the amount guaranteed by him.
3. ***Perpetual succession and a common seal :*** A company being an artificial person has a continuous existence. It is created by the process of law and it can be put to an end only by a process of law. It continues to exist even if all its members are dead.

   Since the company has no physical existence it can only act through agents and all such contracts entered into be its agents should be under its "common seal". It is the official signature of the company.
4. ***Transferability of shares :*** The capital of a company is divided into a number of units called "shares". These shares are transferable subject to certain conditions. A member may sell his share in the open market and realize his money. This provides liquidity to member and stability of the company since the company needs to refund the amount to the shareholder.
5. ***Separation of ownership and management :*** The members in a company are fairly scattered and hence all of them cannot participate in the day to day management of the company. The law therefore provides for the Board of Directors, which in turn is elected by the shareholders.
6. ***Number of members :*** The minimum number of members in case of private company is two, which in case of a public company the minimum is seven. The maximum number of members in case of a private company is 50, while there is no maximum limit for a public company.

5.5.2 Merits of a Company form of Organisation

1. ***Large financial resources :*** The joint stock company form of organization can raise larger resources for investments as compared to other forms of organizations by the issue of shares and debentures. This is because of two reasons (i) the capital of a company is divided into a number of shares of small denominations. This attracts investments by individual of even small incomes. (ii) The ease with which the investor can transfer his shareholdings is another attraction for the investors to invest in shares. This enable the company to raise vast funds and undertake business activities on a large scale.
2. ***Limited liability :*** The liability of shareholders of a joint stock company is limited to the face value of shares held by them or to the amount guaranteed by them. It means that their private properties are not attachable to recover the dues of the company. Thus, it makes the investments in a joint stock company less risky to the shareholder as compared to investment in other forms of organization.
3. ***Transferability of shares :*** The shareholders of a public limited company can transfer their shares or sell them and realize money. This feature imparts liquidity to the investments, and encourages investments in company form of organization. The existence of stock exchange has facilitated the purchase and sale of securities easily and quickly.

4. ***Benefits of large-scale operations :*** A company is in position to mobilise huge resources for investment and thereby undertake large scale operations. This results in economies in purchase, selling, advertising etc. This, in turn results in the reduction in the cost of production and thereby increasing the profit margin.
5. ***Perpetual succession :*** A company being an artificial person created by law has a continuous existence. Being a stable form of organization, it is suited for such business activities, which require a long period to establish.
6. ***Public confidence :*** A joint stock company is able to create and promote public confidence. This is because the activities of a company are regulated by the Companies Act. For example the companies are under legal obligation to get their accounts audited by a qualified chartered account and publish their audited accounts, director's report etc.
7. ***Tax benefit :*** Joint stock companies are liable to pay income tax at a flat rate fixed by the Finance Act from year to year. For higher incomes this rate is lower than that chargeable in the case of sole traders or partners in partnership firm.
8. ***Separation of ownership and management :*** In the case of a sole proprietorship concern and partnership firm the ownership control and management is united and the owners are the managers of the concern. In case of a company, there is complete separation of ownership from management.

   Individuals with an aptitude for business management get an opportunity to make use of their talent although they themselves might not have capital to start concerns of their own. This delinking of capital and business ability for the benefit of the individual and the community as a whole constitutes one of the greatest advantages of joint stock companies.

5.5.3 Demerits of a Company form of Organisation

1. ***Difficult and costly formation :*** The formation of a company involves fulfillment of number of legal formalities. For this purpose the provisions of the Companies Act are to be complied with and large amounts have to be spent in order to fulfill the preliminaries. In addition it is time consuming as well for, a number of sanctions and approvals are to be obtained from different authorities.
2. ***Oligarchic management :*** The management of a company is supposed to be conducted as per the decisions of the shareholders. In theory every shareholder has a right to participate in the annual general meetings and other meetings and exercise his right to elect directors, to appoint auditors and participate in other matters. But in practice companies are managed by a small group of shareholders who dominate and reign over the company. This is because of a number of factors such as lack of interest on the part of shareholders, lack of sufficient information about the working of the company etc.
3. ***Delay in administration :*** The administration of the affairs of a company is in the hands of officials who have no proprietary interest in the company. Therefore they lack initiative; quick decisions and prompt actions are absent. This leads to inefficiency and waste.

4. ***Fraudulent management :*** Sometimes a company may be floated by promoters just to collect capital and use it for personal gain. Misuse of property, goods and money by such managerial personnel harms the interest of the shareholders and may discourage the investing public.
5. ***Concentration of economic power :*** The Company form of organisation leads to the concentration of economic power. Large joint stock companies tend to from these levels into association or combinations. They acquire control over a number of business units by acquiring the shares of these units. This results in the concentration of economic power i.e. control over the assets of a number of companies by a few individuals. Concentration of econiomic power thus has bad consequences on the consumers, other forms of organization and the society. It may lead to monopoly power, destruction of small units and uneven distribution of income and wealth.
6. ***Delay in taking decisions :*** The working of a company is subject to number of regulations by the Companies Act and the various guidelines by the Company Law Board. Consequently it has to fulfill certain procedural formalities before it can take a policy decision. This results in unnecessary delay in taking decisions.

   From the merits and demerits discussed above, it may be concluded that the advantages of this form of organization outnumber its weaknesses. Most of the demerits arise out of mismanagement of the affairs. Despite its weakness the company form of organization is best suited to the business activities when :

   1. The required capital investment is heavy.
   2. The law does not permit the running of business in other forms of ownership. For example banking business cannot be run by sole proprietorship and partnership concerns.
   3. The scale of the business operations is very large.
   4. The owner of the business would like to take advantage of limited liability.

Superiority of a joint stock company as a form of business organization as compared to a sole proprietorship concern and partnership firm :

The sole proprietorship concerns and partnership firms could not supply the capital and managerial ability required by big business units. The joint stock company form of organization is a device, which enables the pooling of the small savings of the community. It enables the investor to have proprietary interest in huge commercial concern without any liability beyond the face value of his shares in the company. Further, a joint stock company is superior to the other forms of organisation in following respects.

1. A joint stock company can collect huge sums of money by way of share capital far beyond the reach of a single individual or of a partnership. This is because even individuals with comparatively small means can acquire some shares in a joint stock company and this contributes to its share capital.

   Besides, on account of its large size a joint stock company can undertake production on a large scale and realize the advantages of large-scale production.

2. A joint stock company is constituted on the basis of limited liability. This feature makes investment in a joint stock company less risky to the investor, than in a partnership or sole proprietorship concern. A shareholder of a joint stock company can never lose anything more then the face value of the shares taken by him. Further an investor need not invest all his money in one concern alone. He can distribute his risks between several companies by becoming a shareholder in several companies. Unlimited liability is a serious defect of sole proprietorship trading and partnership firms.
3. A shareholder in a joint stock company can transfer his shares to others without the necessity of having to obtain permission from anybody, at the same time, the company need not refund the money to the shareholder. Thus the investment which is fixed from the standpoint of the company is liquid from the standpoint of the investor. This is possible because of the existence of stock exchanges. On the other hand, a partner cannot sell his share without the consent of the other partners and many a time the firm is dissolved when a partner goes out.
4. A joint stock company has perpetual existence and its life is not affected by the death, bankruptcy or insanity of any shareholder. But a sole proprietorship concern or a partnership firm is dissolved on the death or insanity of its members.
5. The joint stock company form of organization can secure the services of the best managerial talent as compared to a sole proprietorship or partnership firm. This is because a joint stock company has more funds at its disposal as compared to the other forms of organization.

   Incorporated companies are those companies which are formed for the purpose of carrying on a business and registered under the Companies Act, 1956 or any other Act. Unincorporated companies are large partnership firms, which are not registered under the Companies Act or any other Act.

5.6 Co-operative Form of Organisation

The forms of organisation discussed so far run basically with a view to making profits. The co-operative form of organisation is different from the other forms of organisation in so far as set it is up with the main purpose of rendering service to its members in particular and to the society in general co-operative organizations have emerged primarily to protect and safeguard the economic interests of the relatively weaker sections in the face of exploitation by business men whose main objective is profit maximization. The idea of co-operative was evolved by Rober Own whose aim was the abolition of profits through the system of co-operatives. The essential features of a co-operative organization are service in place of profit and self-help in the place of dependence. Thus co-operative organization rests on the voluntary association of persons for the fulfillment of their economic interests. A co-operative organisation is defined as "an association of persons, usually to achieve a common economic end, through the formation of a democratically controlled business organisation, making equitable contributions to the capital required and accepting a fair share or risk and benefits of the undertaking".

5.6.1 Features of a Co-operative Organisation

The co-operative organisation, being different in its rationale and philosophy possesses certain features which are as follows:

1. ***Voluntary association :*** A co-operative society is a voluntary association of persons. Any person can join a co-operative society of his free will and can leave it at any time after giving due notice to the society. He cannot, however, transfer his shares to another person. The voluntary character has two major implications (a) None will be denied the right and opportunity to become its member and (b) the co-operative society will not compel anybody to become a member.
2. ***Capital :*** The capital of a co-operative society is procured by way of share capital from its members. Since co-operatives are generally formed by relatively weaker sections then share capital is generally limited. It procures the necessary funds from the government by way of loans or by way of grants and assistance from the government.
3. ***Democratic set-up :*** The management of co-operative organisation vests in the managing committee elected by members on the basis of "one-man, one-vote" irrespective of the number of shares held by them. It is the general body of the members which lay down the brand framework of policy within which the managing committee has to function.
4. ***Ideal of service :*** The main objective of a co-operative society is "service" unlike other forms of organisatins whose objective is profit motives. Besides, there is usually a limitation on the dividend that can be declared; only a moderate dividend is declared and a part of its is taken to the reserve fund; a part distributed as bonus to members, a part may be utilised for educational, charitable or other purposes.
5. ***Member's liability :*** The liability of members is limited in case of a co-operative society only when the society chooses to be a limited liability concern. It may even opt in form of unlimited liability.
6. ***Privileges :*** The co-operatives received special incentives from the government such as the exemption from income tax up to a certain limit and also from stamp duties and registration fees.
7. ***Separate legal existence :*** On incorporation, a co-operative society enjoys a separate and independent entity distinct from that of its members. As such, it has a perpetual life and is not altered by the entry and retirement of its members. It can sue and be sued in its own name, can own property and can enter into business contracts in its own name.

5.6.2 Merits of a Co-operative Society

As a form of organization, the co-operative society offers the following advantages.

1. ***Ease of formation :*** Being a voluntary association it is easy to form, as it does not entail any complicated legal formalities. Any adult persons can voluntarily form themselves into an association and get it registered with the registrar of co-operatives.

2. ***Democratic on management :*** The management of a co-operative is based on the basic democracy principle "One-man one-vote". A small group of shareholders cannot, therefore dominate its affairs even if its happens to command more capital than the other members.
3. ***Limited liability :*** The liability of the members is limited to a certain proportion of their capital contribution mentioned in the bye-laws of the society.
4. ***Scope for internal financing :*** Since the law lays down that the dividend on a share in any co-operative can not exceed 6 ½ per cent the balance of the surplus earned in any year, the funds can well be utlised for its growth, development and expansion.
5. ***Tax concession :*** The law gives a preferential treatment to co-operatives by exempting them from income tax up to a certain amount and exemption from certain registration fees and stamp duties.
6. ***Perpetual existence :*** As a co-operative society has a separate legal existence distinct from the of its members, it has a perpetual succession. Its life is not affected by the death insanity or retirement of its members.
7. ***Social service :*** Co-operatives foster fellow feeling among members and impart moral and educative values in their everyday life, which are essential for better living.
8. ***Reducing inequalities :*** Since the profits of a co-operative society are enjoyed by those people who are relatively of moderate means, this helps in raising the economic status of these people, thereby reducing the inequalities of income and wealth between the rich and the poor.

5.6.3 Demerits of co-operative society

1. ***Limited capital :*** The amount of capital that a co-operative society can raise is limited because of the membership remaining confined to a particular locality or region and also because of the principles of "one man one vote" and dividend restriction.
2. ***Excessive state regulation :*** Co-operatives are exposed to a considerable degree of regulation by the government. This interferes with the flexibility of its operation and efficiency of its management.
3. ***Inefficiency management :*** The management of co-operative societies is entrusted to a managing committee, which generally lacks of technical knowledge and experienced people. This is because it cannot attract proper managerial personnel on account of its limited capacity to pay attractive rates of remuneration.

   Lack of motivation : Since the co-operatives cannot offer dividends beyond a fixed rates, the members of the managing committee with whom rest the responsibility of managing the cooperatives, do not feel sufficiently motivated to do their best.

5.7 Public Enterprises and Their Types

1. ***On the basis of incorporation***

   (a) ***Chartered companies :*** Companies, which are incorporated under special character granted by a king or queen, are known as chartered companies. Such companies are governed by the character, which defines the nature of the company and at the same time incorporates them. An example of such a company was the East India Company. These companies find no place in India after independence.

   (b) ***Statutory companies :*** Companies, which are created by a special Act of the legislature, are known as statutory companies. Examples of such companies are the Reserve Bank of India, Unit Trust of India and have Industrial Finance Corporation of India. The provisions of the Companies Act, 1956 apply to them, if they are not consistent with the provisions of their special acts.

   (c) ***Registered companies :*** Companies, which are formed and registered under the Companies Act 1956 or were registered under any of the earlier Companies Act are known as registered companies.

2. ***On the basis of liability***

   On the basis of liability, companies may be classified into:

   1. ***Companies with limited liability***

      (a) Company limited by shares.

      (b) Company limited by guarantee.

      (a) ***Company limited by shares :*** In case of such a company the liability of the shareholder is limited to the amount unpaid on the shares held by him. The liability can be enforced by the company during its existence or during the winding up of the company. A company limited by shares may be a private company or a public company.

      (b) ***Company limited by guarantee :*** A company limited by guarantee is a company in which the liability of the members is limited to the amount which they under take to contribute to the assets of the company. In other words, the liability of the members is limited to the amount guaranteed by them. Such companies are not formed for the purpose of profit, but for the promotion of art, science, and culture. They may or may not have a share capital. Such a company may be either a public company or a private company.

   2. ***Companies with unlimited liability***

      Unlimited companies : These are companies in which the numbers have an unlimited liability. Every member of such a company is liable for the debts of the company, as in an ordinary partnership firm.

3. ***On the basis of control***

On the basis of control, companies may be classified into:

(a) Holding company

(b) Subsidiary company

(a) ***Holding companies :*** A holding company is a company, which has control over other company. A company is a holding company of another company if the holding company (a) controls the composition of the Board of Directors of another company or (b) exercises or controls more than half the total voting power of such company or (c) it holds more than half in nominal value of its equity share capital.

(b) ***Subsidiary company :*** A subsidiary company is a company, which is controlled by another company known as a holding company. It becomes the subsidiary of another company (holding company) if :

1. The composition of the Board of directors of the subsidiary company is controlled by the holding company, or
2. If more than ½ of the voting power in the subsidiary company is exercises by the holding company, or
3. If more than half of the nominal value of equity share capital of the subsidiary company is held by the holding company.

4. ***On the basis of ownership***

On the basis of ownership, a company may be a :

1. Government company
2. Non-Government company

1. ***Government company :*** A Government company is a company in which not less than 51 percent of the paid-up share capital is held by the Central government and/or by the State Government or partly by Central Government and partly by one or more State governments. The subsidiary of a government company is also a government Company. They are governed by the provision of the companies Act 1956, but the applications of these provisions may be restricted or modified by the Central Government. An annual report on the working and affairs of these companies must be placed and prepared before the legislature concerned.

2. ***Non-Government company :*** Such a company is controlled and operated by private capital :

5. ***On the basis of number of members***

(a) Private company

(b) Public company

(a) ***Private company :*** A private company is also known as a "Close corporation". A private company is a company, which by its articles has the following features:

1. restricts the right to transfer its shares
2. limits the number of members to fifty.
3. prohibit any invitation to the public subscribe for any shares in or debentures of the company. When two or more persons hold one or more shares jointly, they are treated as a single member.

A private company is in the nature of a partnership firm. It can be formed with a minimum of two members.

(b) ***Public company :*** A public company as per the Companies Act, 1956 is company, which is not a private company. In other words, a public company does not restrict the membership to fifty, is not prohibited from inviting the general public to subscribe its shares and debentures, and does not restrict the right of its members to transfer their shares.

A public company can be formed by a minimum of seven members although there is not maximum limit to its membership. It offers its shares to the public at large and is able to collect large sums of money. The shares of a public company can be transferred without any restriction. It must have the "word" "limited" in its name.

5.7.1 Conversion of a private company into a public company

1. ***Conversion by default :*** A private company becomes a pubic if it fails to comply with the essential requirements of a private company with regard to invitation of public for subscription to shares and debentures, number of members and transfer of shares. It ceases to be a private company, if it violates any of the three restrictions.
2. ***Conversion by operation of law :*** In such a case, the private company is termed as "Deemed public company". A private company becomes a public company.
   1. Where not less than 25% of its paid-up shares capital is held by one or more bodies corporate.
   2. Where its average annual turnover (sales) is not less than Rs. One crore for three consecutive financial year.
   3. Where it holds not less than 25 percent of the paid-up share capital of a public company.
3. ***Conversion by choice :*** A private company may become a public company by altering its articles of association that they do not contain the provisions, which make it a private company. One the date of alteration. It ceases to become a private company.

5.8 Public Enterprises and their Types

Public enterprise is one of the government participatio in business. There are certain areas such as defence, infrastructure, heavy industries and so on where private participation was not possible and hence government had to enter the business. The need for public enterprise was manifold: to accelerate the rate of economic growth by planned development, to speed up industrialisation, to increase infrastructural facilities, to promote balanced regional development, to increase employment opportunities, to promote employee welfare, and to reduce the disparities in income and wealth.

Public enterprises have many acheivements to their credit. Many basic and key industries have been set up, employment opportunities at different levels have been generated, generated funds for the government, many backward regions were developed because of setting up of public enterprises, import substitutes have been developed leading to conservation of foreign exchange, restricting the growth of monopolies, stimulating growth in private sector, taking over a number of sick units and putting them in order, creating a powerful network of financial system through development of financial institutions by nationalisation and so on.

5.8.1 Forms of Public Enterprises

There are three forms of public enterprises. They are (a) Departmental undertaking (b) Public Corporation (c) Government Company.

(a) Departmental undertaking is an extension to a government department. For instance, the Railway Board. It operates as per the guidelines of the ministry of railways. It has a good deal of financial freedom. It is organised and controlled by the civil servants. It has to follow the guidelines underlying the budget, accounting and audit controls.

In a departmental undertaking, the decisions are delayed, there is no incentive to put forth the best of the efforts for the employees and there is high degree of redtapism and bureaucracy.

(b) Public corporation is relatively a flexible organisation as it is created by a Statue by Parliament or the State Legislature. It need not go to any government department. It is governed by the contents of the Statute, that is, purpose, procedures to conduct and control its affairs. It has relatively larged degree of autonomy to take its own decisions, formulate its own budget, recruit its own staff and formulate its own procedures. The initial capital is provided by the government and the public corporation is created to make it more responsive to market changes, more dynamic and flexible. It is a body corporate with a separate existence by itself, it can but, sell or pledge the property, cansue and be sued by name. It has long life, common seal. For example, Life Insurance Coporation of India and so on. A public corporation has been viewed as a 'right combination of public ownership, public accountability and business management for public ends'.

It is true that the public corporation has made its mark on the Indian economy in terms of achieving the objectives of five-year plan to a significant extent. But a careful analysis of its performance reveals that there are certain lacunae in its functioning. The independence, initiative, flexibility were not really hundred percent. They were diluted by the political interference and pressures from time to time. The government machinery keeps playing with the policies of the corporation to its own disadvantage. There are a large number of cases of misuse of power also. With the result, the number of public corporations making profits or with strong financial background can be counted on fingers.

(c) Government company is created like any other joint stock company. 51 percent or more of the shares are held by the government, state or central or a combination of both. It is a body corporate with perpetual succession and a common seal. It is a right combination of operating flexibility of privately organised companies with the advantages of state regulation and control in public interest, for example, Hindustan Machine Tools.

Government company form offers six high degrees of flexibility. It can take over existing sick companies, it can be an industrial undertaking, a promotional agency, it can promote trade and commerce, it can safeguard national interests or it can invite private participation to obtain technical know-how and guidance for the magangement of the enterprise.

A Government company is just like a public compnay, with the blessings of the government. Formation of a government company is easy as per the procedure in the Companies Act. It doesn't require any statute for this purpose. It is free from the government interference, at least on paper. It has a high degree of operational flexibility. It can take advantage of the expertise of the private sector.

All this looks very bright on paper but in reality the position is altogether different. The government company has been the tool for the government to achieve their political objectives such as appointment of political leaders in the position of the directors. With the result, the agenda for the Government Company is more to satisfy the personal interests. The poor performance of the majority of government companies reveals that they lack necessary dynamism, initative, foresight and commitment to survive in a competitive environment. A government company is characterised by frequently changing directors, lack of necessary dynamism, initiative, foresight and commitment to survive in a competitive environment. A government company is characterised by frequently changing directors, lack of continuity in its policies and inability to respond to the market changes and initiatives in a competitive environment.

5.8.2 Problems faced by Public Enterprises

(a) Autonomy in many cases, is misued. The public enterprise is given autonomy to leave it independent in conducting its affairs. But this seldom happens. The political and ministerial interference, loyalty of the employees at different levels in the public enterprise to the political bosses manifests the misuse of autonomy.

(b) Public accountability refers to 'giving answers to the questions raised about the one's performance'. Public accountability is an administrative method of assuring responsible performance. Accountability takes three forms of control; (i) ministerial control (ii) parliamentary control and (iii) financial control. Despite the varied types of control, the targeted results could not be ensured to be achieved.

(c) Materials management is another weak area which is characterised by holding excessive stocks and poor control over material handling costs.
(d) Pricing policy is a sensitive area. It is because it has to be linked to the welfare objectives of the government and yet the same time, it should consider the requirements of the individual public enterprise in terms of growth and expansion in due course.
(e) Delay in project execution.
(f) Unrealistic production schedules.
(g) Over capitalisation.
(h) Disproportionate over heads.
(i) Over-staffing.
(j) Lack of progressive personnel policies.
(k) Inadequate return on capital.
(l) Organisation structure.
(m) More parliamentary interference than control.

5.9 Disinvestment in Post-Liberalisation, Privatisation and Globalisation Period

To keep pace with the globalisation, the Government of India by its Industrial Policy, 1991 opened up the Indian economy. Foreign companies started pumping their products and services into Indian markets. As a strategy to channelise the limited resources to productive sources, the Government of India has recently decided to disinvest good number of public enterprises by withdrawing its investments to a significant level. Sick units are straight away auctioned.

The Indian economy has been reeling under heavy tension from trade unions which protest against disinvestment. The government is not in a position to pump additional investments, unless it borrows from the World Bank, to keep most of the public enterprises going on. Government has not touched those public enterprises that have been making profits. It has been decided at the policy level that only those loss making public enterprises will be disinvested to a significant extent. Government of India proposes to raise Rs. 10,000 crore by disinvestment and the proceeds of such disinvestment are to be utilised (a) to meet fiscal deficity and (b) invest in the core sector for better productive use.

The Government of India wants to disinvest in profit making public enterprises (such as Bharat Sanchar Nigam Ltd, Mahanagar Telecom Nigam Ltd., Maruti Suzuki, BHPV. BHEL and so on) also.

5.10 Changing Business Environment in Post-Liberalisation Scenario

Economic reforms, as envisaged in New Industrial Policy of 1991, are now 15 years old and there is now ample evidence to assess their impact on Indian economy. The Indian industry for over 40 years since Independence was predominantly operating in a regulated and protected economy and hence remained an underperformer. During the implementation of Liberalisation

Privatisation and Globalisation policies, it could sustain extremely well the pressures in the new competitive environment.

In 1980s, the average industrial growth rate was around 8 percent. Later, in a few years, it was still less. But subsequently, you find the beginning of the possibility of new sustained growth of over 10 percent in the Indian economy. Indian industry has been doing very strong in every sector, to name a few promising ones such as automobile, infrastructure, banking and insurance, manufacturing, aviation, telecom, services. IT and IT-Enables services, retailing and Fast Moving Consumer Goods (FMCG). With fresh winds of competition blowing in all sectors have been performing extremely well. Every sector is stretching to attain world class standards in terms of quality and cost.

Mergers and acquisitions, setting up manufacturing bases at different geographical locations taking advantage of wage differentials, a great deal of re-engineering are some of the strategies we find across different sectors in Indian the economy. Access to new technologies worldwide was provided, legal hassles in importing them at rapid speed were minimized – hence there has been upgradation of quality in every sector. The firms welcomed the removal of licensing and moved forward to stengthen themselves through joint ventures, mergers and acquisitions, etc., and made themselves fit and strong to face competition worldwide.

Exporters welcomed all these strategic measures, such as the removal of import licesing and lowering of the tariffs as these facilitated them to compete internationally and increase value-added exports. All these measures culminated into considerable increase in the investment levels, foreign investment, and reduction in the formalities to be fulfilled after the onset of economic reforms in India.

This has resulted in every sector in Indian economy humming with vibrant business activity with many of the Indian companies going all out for acquiring foreign companies. It has also led to exports, high salary and compensation levels, technology upgradation and adoption of appropriate technologies, extensive increase in manufacturing capacities, large number of Special Export Zones and shopping malls all over the country, increase in computer literacy rate, overall improvement in the quality of life of the employees in particular and citizens in general.

5.10.1 The impact of economic reforms on Liberalisation, Privitisation and Globalisation

(a) *Attention to world market:* Many companies are setting their eyes on global markets. With their prudent financial polities, they have emerged cash rich and with liberal flow of foreign direct investments, they are poised to improve in world class ratings. For instance, Tata Steel emerged as the world's fifth largest steel company with its recent acquisition of Corus Group, UK. Thus many companies are now directing their efforts towards the world market.

(b) *Improvement in Work Culture* : Everywhere, including in government organisations, there is noticeable change in the work culture. The employees have realised the need for observing speed in response, customer focus and organisations have been focusing on 'high performing work culture'. The workers/employees have become more quality and cost conscious.

(c) *Focus on Capital Intensive Technologies/Processes:* For long time, the focus was on labour intensive policies and processes. Not considering the philosophy that 'capital intensive technologies will increase unemployment', most industries have been focussing on capital intensive technologies. So many ATMs set up by banks across every urban area are an example for this. Providing customer service of good quality have been prime considerations in considering capital intensive technologies to graduate from being labour intensive to capital intensive.

(d) *Downsizing and Rightsizing :* With a view to reducing the salary bill and enhancing the productivity per employee, every organization, without exception, has reduced the number of employees (head count) significantly through voluntary retirement schemes (popularly called the 'golden hand-shake). Thus organisations have successfully rightsized their employee count and today they are in a position to benchmark themselves in terms of productivity per employee. Trade unions and workers have also received such initiatives happily. Indian economy, which was otherwise considered the hotbed for trade union activity could sail through the economic reforms comfortably as the trade unions did not respond in a hostile manner.

(e) *Awareness and Stress on Quality and R & D :* The customer earlier used to trade off between price and quality. In other words, the trader used to successfully clear off his stocks of lower quality by marginally reducing the selling price. This trend has changed now. The quality awareness levels have considerable improved. The customer is seldom seen compromising on quality and with this trend, organisations have started earmarking huge budgets for R&D to attain world class quality in producing goods and rendering the services.

(f) *Scale Economies :* It is common to find leading companies in every sector to double/triple their volume of production to attain scale economies through rapid technological growth and increased productivity. In view of the encouragement for exports consequent to globalisation policies, Indian manufacturers such as Bajaj Auto, Bajaj Scooters, Maruti Udyog, etc., could export their products all over the world. Thus Indian leading business houses, which could successfully attain scale economies and identify the less contested business space in the world market, could transform themselves into Indian multinational in very less span of time.

(g) *Aggressive Brand Building* : The marketplace became increasingly competitive in view of domestic companies becoming more aggressive in promoting their brands and foreign companies invading Indian markets through their cost-effective quality products/service. Companies such as Reliance, Marks & Spencer, Pepsi, Coca-Cola, State Bank of India, ICICI Bank, Tanishk, Titan, Lee, Citizen, McDonald,

Intel, Ebay, Toyota, Business Today, etc., have successfully built their brand which are well-known and this adds tremendous economic value despite the fact that they cannot be quantified. Every product/service from these companies is synonymous with quality. Some of these are so smart that they built their company names into brands that give them an incredible edge over their competition. With their phenomenal access to media and huge advertisement budgets, they can make even a new product launch a smooth affair with little effort and time when compared to their competitors.

Like these, there have been many positive developments now encouraging the country to think in terms of strengthening these reforms further and moving to second generation reforms.

Summary

1. Buying and selling of goods with an aim of profit in a regular manner is known as *business*.
2. A person purchased scooter at 25,000 and sold it at market for 30,000. Is it a business? (True / False)
3. According to size, business is of three types namely:
   (a) Small scale
   (b) Medium scale
   (c) Large scale.
4. According to nature of activity, there are *three* types of business.
5. Buying and selling of goods is called *trading*.
6. Aids to trade are *transportation, banking, ware housing*.
7. Forms of business organisation are

   1. Public sector. 2. Joint sector. 3. Private sector.
8. Public sector is divided into *three* types namely:
   1. Departmental organizations.
   2. Public corporation.
   3. Government companies.
9. Private sector enterprises are owned and managed by *private individuals*.

10 Government owes a particular enterprise. Then it is called *public sector* enterprise.

11. In joint sector management is undertaken mainly by *private entrepreneurs*.
12. Private sector enterprises may be divided into *five* types.
13. Sole proprietorship is also called as *sole trading organisation*.
14. List out any two limitations of sole proprietorship:
    (a) Limited capital.
    (b) Risk bearing
15. Joint Hindu Family business is also called as *Hindu Undivided Family* business.
16. *Hindu* law governs Joint Hindu Family business.

17. Male members entitled for running a Joint Hindu Family business are called *Co-parceners.*

18. Types of partnerships.
    (i) Partnership at –will
    (ii) Particular partnership
    (iii) Partnership for a fixed duration.

19. Partners who do not take active part in management are called sleeping or dormant partners.

20. *Nominal* partners do not have interest in the business but lend their name to the firm.

21. Any two demerits of partnership
    1. Uncertainty of existence
    2. Difficulties of expansion.

22. Maximum number of partners in partnership is *20* and is *10* in case of bank.

23. A voluntary association of persons for mutual benefit through self-help and collective effort is called *co-operative* organisation.

24. Main types of co-operative societies are 6 numbers of types.

25. A voluntary association of persons having separate legal existence, perpetual succession and a common seal is called a *company.*

26. Members of a company have *limited* liability.

27. Companies are classified into 3 types namely

    (i) Public company (ii) Private company (iii) Government company

28. Minimum number of members in a public company is *7* and maximum is unlimited.

29. Give two examples for genetic industry (a) prawn culture (b) fish culture.

30. Documents that are to be filed while registration of a company.
    (a) Memorandum of association
    (b) Articles of association
    (c) Prospectus.

31. *The memorandum of association* is the principal document of the company.

32. List out any three features of public enterprises.
    (a) State control
    (b) State ownership
    (c) State financing.

33. Types of public enterprises are
    (a) Departmental Undertaking
    (b) Public corporation
    (c) Government Company.
34. In Joint Hindu Family business, the oldest member is known as Karta.
35. Sony and coco-cola are examples of multinational companies.
36. Shares are transferable in public limited company.
37. Trade is of 2 types namely

    (i) Internal trade (ii) External trade
38. External trade is of 2 types namely

    (i) Import trade (ii) Export trade.
39. Types of business based on nature of activity are
    (a) Industrial business
    (b) Trade business
    (c) Service business.
40. Wholesale trade and retail trade are the two types of internal trade.

Eassy Questions

1. Discuss the factors that help in choosing a suitable form of business or organization.
2. "Small is beautiful". Do you think ,this is the reason for the survival of the sole trader form of bussiness organisation?

   Support your answer with suitable examples.
3. Explain the features of sole trader form of organization. Discuss the advantages and limitations of sole trader form of organization.
4. Explain the features of partnership form of organization. Discuss te advantages and limitations of partnership form of organization.
5. What are the reasons for joint stock company being popular as a form of business organization? Explain.
6. Give the reasons for the failure of cooperative society form of business organization to some extent.
7. Explain the need for public enterprise in India? Do you think public enterprise as a whole have fulfilled that need?

8. What are the objectives of sole proprietorship?
9. What are the types of partners in partnership business organizations?
10. What are the advantages and limitations of cooperative society form of business organization?
11. What are the advantages and limitations of joint stock company.
12. Profit maximization is the prime motive of business organization. Discuss.
13. Differentiate sole properties ship and partnership firm.
14. Differentiate joint stock company and cooperative society form business.

Short Questions

1. Write short note on (a) Sole proprietorship
2. Write short note on (b) Partnership firm
3. Write short note on (c) Joint Hindu Family Business
4. Write short note on (d) Cooperative Society Business
5. Write short note on (e) Joint Stock Company
6. Write short note on (f) Multi National Company
7. Write short note on (g) Public Enterprise
8. Write short note on (h) Ziberalisation
9. Write short note on (i) Privatisation
10. Write short note on (j) Globalization
11. Write short note on (k) Holding company
12. Write short note on (l) Subsidiary company
13. Write short note on (m) Government company
14. Write short note on (h) Non-Government company

CHAPTER 6

Capital and Capital Budgeting

6.1 Introduction

Every business needs funds for two purposes – for its establishment and to carry out its day-to-day operations. Funds needed for long- term purposes to create production facilities, through purchase of fixed assets etc., is called fixed capital. Funds needed for short-term purposes for the purchase of raw materials, payment of wages and other day-to-day expenses etc., is known as working capital. In other words, working capital refers to that part of the firms capital which is required for financing short-term or current assets such as cash, marketable securities, debtors and inventories.

Gerstenberg has suggested the term 'Circulating capital' for application to all the assets of a company that one changed in the ordinary course of business from one form to another, for instance from cash to inventories, from inventories to receivable and book debts, from receivables and book debts back into cash. In simple words, circulating capital is the sum of working capital and current liabilities. Hence working capital is also known as revolving or circulating capital or short-term capital.

Working Capital : For every busines what ever amount of money utilising for the purpose of starting of the business or establing of business is known as 'working capital'.

6.2 Concepts of Working Capital

Working capital, also known as short-term capital largely deals with the management and control of current assets and current liabilities. Two distinct views may be noted as regards the definition of working capital.

1. Net working capital
2. Gross working capital

Net working Capital : According to this concept working capital means total current assets less the total current liabilities. This concept is supported by authorities like Lincoln, Saliers and Stevens.

Arguments in favour of this view are :

(i) Long usage sanctions support this definition of working capital.

(ii) This concept of working capital helps the investors and the creditors of a firm to judge its financial soundness and margin of the protection.

(iii) The surplus of current assets over current liabilities can always be relied upon to meet contingencies since the enterprise is under no obligation to return this amount.

(iv) This definition is of great use in discovering the true financial position of the companies possessing the same amount of current assets.

Net working capital may be positive or negative. Net working capital is positive when the current asset exceed the current liabilities and negative when current liabilities are more than the current assets. Liabilities which are intended to be paid in the ordinary course of a business within a short period out of the current assets or the income the business are the current liabilities.

Examples of Current Liabilities :

1. Sundry creditors (Bill payable and Accounts payable)
2. Trade advances (given to the company for supply of goods)
3. Short-term borrowings from banks and others.
4. Short-term loans from others
5. Provisions (for taxes, bad debts, etc).

6.2.1 Gross working capital : In its broad sense, the term working capital refers to the gross working capital and represents the amount of funds invested in current assets. This view is supported by Field, Baker, Malott and Mead.

Arguments in favour of this view are

1. Profits are earned with the help of assets which are partly fixed and partly current.
2. This definition takes into account the fact that with every increase net concept of working capital there will be no change.
3. The management is more concerned with the total current assets as they constitute the total funds available for operating purposes than with the sources from where the funds come.

   The main items that comprise current assets are:

   (i) Cash (a) in hand (b) in bank and (iii) in transit.

   (ii) Investments (only short-term investments)

   (iii) Investories (Comprising (a) Raw materials, Consumable stores (b) Work in process and (c) Finished goods)

(iv) Sundry debtors (also known as Bills Receivable or Accounts Receivable)

(v) Loans and advances (Given by the company to others).

But in practice, the working capital management concerns the management of total current assets and the total current liabilities, too which in fact, varies, depending upon the level of current assets required. Thus, the term, 'Net working Capital' is an accounting concept, not having much of economic or financial significance. These two concepts of working capital are not exclusive, rather both have their own merits.

In fact, working capital management not only pertains to the management of current assets. But it also involves the management of current liabilities, because these arise due to the volume and value of the current assets required. The net concept of working capital may be suitable only for proprietory form of organisation such as sole-trader or partnership firms. But the gross concept is very suitable to the company form of organisation where there is a diverse ownership and separate management and control.

6.3 Need of Working Capital

The basic objective of financial management is maximisation of shareholder's wealth. This is possible only when the company earns sufficient profit. The magnitude of sales determines the amount of profit. However, there is an operating cycle involved in the sales and realisation of cash. Working capital is required during this period in order to sustain the sales activity (operating cycle is the time gap between the sales and their actual realisation in cash). Thus working capital is needed for the following purposes:

1. For the purchase of raw materials.
2. To pay wages, salaries and incur day-to-day expenses.
3. To provide credit facilities to the customers.
4. To meet the selling costs as packing, advertising etc.
5. To maintain the inventories of raw material, work-in-progress.

6.3.1 Classification of Working capital

Working capital can be studied under two heads:

(i) On the basis of concept.

(ii) On the basis of time.

Conceptual basis of working capital as gross working capital and net working capital has been studied earlier.

The classification of working capital

(a) fixed, regular or permanent, and

(b) variable, seasonal or special

Table 6.1 Classification of working capital

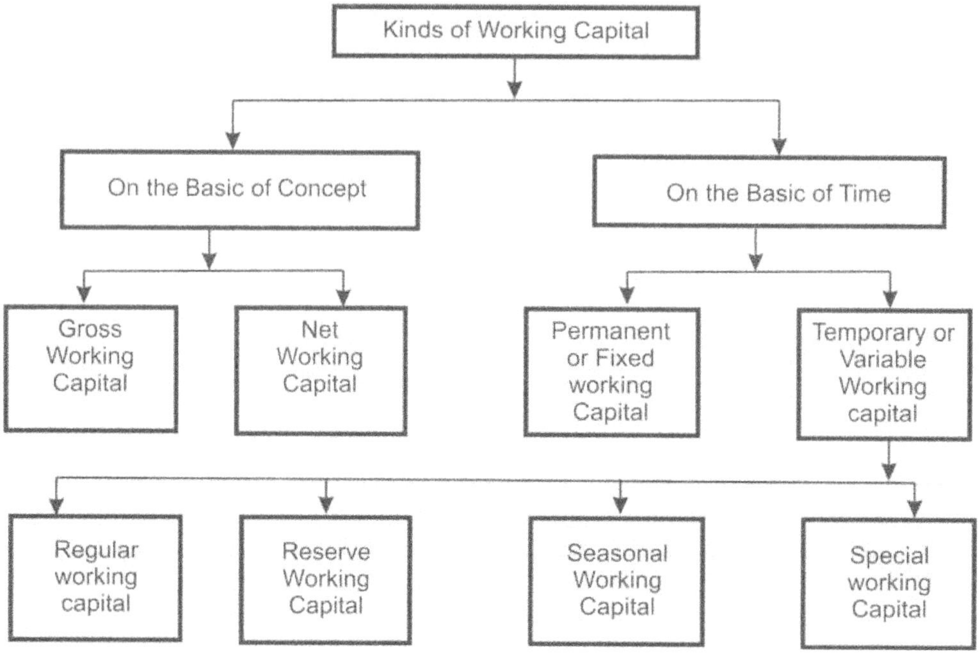

(i) ***Permanent or fixed working capital :***

A part of investment in current assets is as permanent as the investment in fixed assets. This refers to that minimum amount of investment in all current assets which is required to ensure effective utilisation of fixed facilities and for maintaining the circulation of current assets. This minimum level of current assets is called permanent or fixed working capital.

Characteristics of permanent working Capital :

The permanent working capital increases with the size of the business. In other words as the business grows, the requirements of permanent working capital also increases due to the increase in current assets.

(ii) ***Permanent working capital can further be classified into two types :***

Regular working capital and reserve working capital. Regular working capital is required to ensure circulation of current assets from cash to inventories, from inventories to receivables and from receivables to cash and so on.

Reserve working capital is the excess amount over the requirement for regular working capital which may be provided for contingencies that may arise at unstated periods such as strikes, depression etc.

Permanent working capital is permanently needed for the business and therefore it should be financed out of long term funds.

(iii) ***Temporary or variable working capital :*** The amount of such working capital is variable from time to time on the basis of business activities. Temporary working capital differs from permanent capital in the sense that it is required for short periods and cannot be permanently employed gainfully in the business.

Characteristics : It is the amount of working capital which is required to meet the seasonal demands and some special exigencies.

Variable working capital can be further classified into two types :

(a) Seasonal working capital and (b) Special working capital.

Seasonal working capital : This represents the capital required to meet the seasonal needs of the enterprise.

Special working capital : It is that part of working capital which is required to meet special exigencies such as launching marketing campaigns for conducting research etc.

(iv) Temporary working capital is generally financed from short-term sources on finance such as bank credit.

The permanent working capital is stable or fixed over time while temporary working capital fluctuates. We find permanent working capital increasing over a period of time due to expansion of business without any fluctuation but there is fluctuations in variable working capital which is sometimes increasing and sometime decreasing.

6.4 Importance of Working Capital

A manufacturing concern needs adequate supply of raw materials to process for uninterrupted flow of production without which it is sure to collapse. Working capital, this is the life-blood of a business. No business can run successfully without an adequate amount of working capital. It must be noted that working capital must be adequate, it should be neither excessive nor inadequate. Because both the situations are dangerous. Excessive working capital represents idle funds which earn no profits for the firm. Inadequate working capital on the other hand results in production interruptions due to insufficient funds for running the operations which further bring down the profitability.

(i) ***Good running of the Business :*** Adequate working capital helps in the smooth running of the business by providing uninterrupted flow of production.

(ii) ***Good Will :*** This firm also makes prompt payments due to the availability of sufficient working capital. This helps in creating and maintaining good will.

(iii) ***Increases credit worthiness :*** The high solvency and good credit standing of a firm enables the bank and other to arrange loans on easy and favourable terms.

(iv) ***Uninterrupted supply of raw materials :*** Sufficient working capital ensures regular supply of raw materials and continuous prodution.

(v) ***Regular day-to-day Commitment :*** Sufficient working capital of a firm enables it to pay salaries, wages and other day-to-day payments regularly. This raises the morale of its employees.

(vi) ***Cash discount :*** Adequate working capital enables a concern to make use of cash discounts on the purchases and hence it reduces costs.

(vii) ***Exploitation of favourable market conditions :*** When the firm has adequate working capital it can exploit favourable market conditions such as purchasing its requirements in the bulk when the prices are lower and by holding its inventories for higher prices.

(viii) ***Increase the confidence of investors :*** Sufficiency of working capital enables a concern to pay quick and regular dividends to its investors as there may not be much pressure to plough back profits. This gains the confidence of its investors and creates a favourable market to raise additional funds in the future.

(ix) ***Ability to face crisis :*** When a firm has to face business crisis in emergencies such as depression there is much pressure on working capital. Adequate working capital enables the concern to face the crisis much effectively without undergoing any sort of pressure.

(x) ***High morale :*** The ability to meet all reasonable demands for cash without inordinate delay is a great psychological factor to improve all – round efficiency in the business and to create self – confidence in the person at the helm of affairs of the company. This enhances financial position which in turn enhances the general morale of the management.

6.5 Excess or Inadequate Working Capital

The working capital of a firm should be adequate and it should be neither short nor excess. Both excess as well as short working capital positions are bad for any business. However, it is the inadequacy of working capital which is more dangerous from the point of view of the firm.

6.5.1 Disadvantages of Inadequate Working Capital

(i) ***Loss of reputation :*** A concern with inadequate working capital loses its reputation as it cannot pay its short – term liabilities in time.

(ii) ***Lowers creditworthiness :*** As it cannot pay the credits in time it loses its creditworthiness and will not be able to get good credit facilities.

(iii) ***Cash Discounts :*** As the firm cannot buy its requirements in bulk due to inadequate working capital it cannot avail of discounts etc.,

(iv) ***Difficulty in exploiting favourable market conditions :*** Due to lack of working capital it becomes difficult for the firm to exploit favourable market conditions and undertake profitable projects.

(v) ***Irregularity in payment of day-to- day expenses :*** The firm cannot pay day – to – day expenses of its operations and creates inefficiencies , increases costs and reduces the profits of the business.

(vi) ***Low Rate of Return :*** With the shortage of working capital, the rate of return on investment also falls.

(vii) ***Inefficient use of Fixed Assets :*** With the shortage of working capital, the rate of return on investment also falls.

(viii) ***Efficient use of Fixed Assets :*** It becomes impossible to utilise efficiently the fixed assets due to the non-availability of liquid funds.

6.5.2 Disadvantages of Excessive Working Capital

(i) ***Idle funds :*** Excess of working capital represent idle funds which earn no profits for the business and hence the business cannot earn a proper rate of return on its investments.

(ii) ***Low rate of Return :*** Due to low rate of return on investments, the value of shares may also fall.

(iii) ***Unnecessary purchase of Inventories :*** The excessive working capital lead to unnecessary purchasing and accumulation of inventories causing more chances of theft, waste and losses.

(iv) ***Defective Credit Policy :*** Excessive working capital implies excessive debtors and defective credit policy which may cause higher incidence of bad debts.

(v) ***Speculative Transaction :*** The working capital in excess give rise to speculative transactions.

6.5.3 Working Capital Cycle

The operating cycle refers to the average time that elapses between the acquisition of raw materials and the final cash realisation. This concept is new and is gaining more and more importance in recent years. This is also known as 'working capital cycle'.

Cash is used to buy raw materials and other stores, so cash is converted into raw materials and inventory. Then the raw material and stores are issued to the production department. Wages are paid and expenses are incurred in the process and work in process comes into existence. Work-in-process becomes finished goods. Finished goods are sold to customers on credit. In the course of time, these customers pay cash for the goods purchased by them. 'Cash' is retrieved and the cycle is completed. Thus, operating cycle consists of four stages:

1. The raw materials and stores inventory stage.
2. The work-in-progress stage.
3. The finished goods inventory stage
4. The receivable stage.

The operating Cycle can be represented as

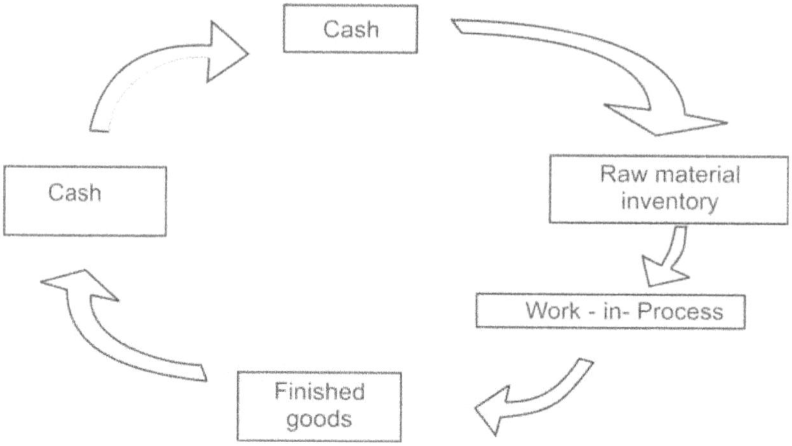

Fig. 6.1 Operating cycle

Production Management :

Manufacturing cycle is a part of operating cycle and influences it directly. The longer the manufacturing cycle, the longer will be the operating cycle and higher will be the firm's working capital requirements. The following measures may be taken to control the manufacturing cycle:

(i) Proper maintenance of plant, machinery and other infrastructural facilities.

(ii) Proper planning and co-ordination at all levels of activity.

(iii) Selection of the shortest manufacturing cycle out of various alternatives.

Marketing Management :

It is necessary to synchronise the sale and production policies as far as possible. Lack of proper matching increases the operating cycle period. Effective advertisement, sale of promotion activities etc., reduce the storage period of finished products.

Sound credit and collection policies :

The finance manager should adopt sound credit and collection policies to minimise the investment in working capital in the form of book debts. The firm should be selective and prudent in granting credit terms to its customers because slack collection policies will tie up funds for long period, increasing length of operating cycle.

Proper Monitoring of External Environment :

The factors of external environment like fluctuations in demand, competitors, production and sales policies, government fiscal and monetary policies etc., influence the length of the operating cycle. Therefore the management should evaluate the changes in these factors to minimise their adverse impact on the length of operating cycle.

Other suggestions :

Use of human resources development technique in the organisation enhances the morale and seal of employees thereby reduces the length of operating cycle.

Importance of Operating Cycle Concept :

The operating cycle concept is an important concept because it is useful to ascertain the requirement of cash and working capital to meet the operating expenses of a growing concern. Management must ensure that this cycle does not become too long because the longer the operating cycle, the more working capital funds the firm needs. This concept measures the working capital fund requirements more precisely, traces its changes and determines the optimum level of working capital requirements.

Reasons for Prolonged Operating Cycle :

The reasons for longer operating cycle period are as follow:

(i) Purchase of materials in excess / short of requirements.

(ii) Buying materials of inferior quality or defective materials.

(iii) Inability to purchase during seasons.

(iv) Defective inventory policy.

(v) Lack of proper planning in production, co-ordination and control.

(vi) Lack of proper monitoring of external environment etc.

(vii) Use of outdated machinery, technology.

(viii) Poor maintenance and upkeep of plant, equipment and infrastructural facilities.

Remedial measures of prolonged operating cycle :

Every management aims to reduce the length of operating cycle or the number of operating cycles in a year. The following are a few remedies that become handy in controlling the length of operating cycle period.

Purchase Management :

It is the responsibility of the purchase manager to ensure the availability of right type of materials in right quantity of right quality at right price on right time and at right place. These six R's contribute greatly in the improvement of length of operating cycle. If the measures are adopted properly, they will help in minimising not only the length of operating cycle period but also the working capital requirements.

6.6 Determinants of Working Capital

The working capital requirements of a concern are constantly affected by the criss – crossing economic currents flowing about the business. The nature of a firm's activities, the economic health of the country, the state of economic situation are all part of these shifting forces. It is difficult to rank them because all such factors are of different importance and the influence of individual factors change for a firm over time. However, the following are important factors.

(i) ***Nature of Business :*** A company's working capital requirements are basically related to the kinds of business it conducts. Public utilities basically related to the kinds of business it conducts. Public utilities need very limited working capital because they offer cash sales only and supply services, not products, trading concerns have to invest proportionately high amounts in current assets as they have to carry stock in trade, accounts receivable and liquid cash. The industrial units also require a large amount of working capital though it varies from industry to industry, because of the lack of uniformity in the asset structure of various industries. Generally speaking, trading and financial firms require relatively very large amount, public utilities comparatively small amounts, whereas manufacturing concerns stand between these two extremes, their needs depending upon the character of which they are a part.

(ii) ***Production Policy :*** Strong seasonal variations result in special working capital problems in controlling the internal financial swings that may take place. In such cases, the requirement of working capital depends upon the production policy. The choice rests between keeping the production steady by accumulating inventories and curtailing the production during the slack season and increasing it during the peak season. In the former instance, the uniform manufacturing rate minimises fluctuations of production schedules but enlarged inventory creates special risks and costs. In the latter cse, inventories are kept at minimum levels but the production manager has to shoulder the responsibility of constantly adjusting his working staff. Thus, it is obvious that a firm will require higher working capital if the policy is to keep production steady by accumulating inventories.

(iii) ***Manufacturing Process :*** In the manufacturing business, the working capital requirement is directly proportionate to the length of the manufacturing process. The longer it takes to make product and the greater its cost, the larger the inventory tied up in its manufacture with progressive increment of labour and service costs before the finished product is fully obtained. Therefore, if there are alternative processes of production in the manufacturing process, the process with the shortest production period should be chosen.

(iv) ***Growth and expansion of business :*** As the composition of working capital in growing company also shifts with economic circumstances and corporate practices, growing industries require more working capital than those that are static, other things being equal. However, it is difficult to determine the relationship between the growth in the volume of business and the growth in the working capital of a business.

(v) ***Seasonal variations :*** The raw materials of certain industries are not available throughout the year. In such cases, the firms have to purchase the raw materials in bulk during the season to ensure uninterrupted flow and process them during the entire year. Due to this, a huge amount gets blocked in the form of material inventories during such season, giving rise to more working capital requirements. Thus, it can be concluded that a firm requires larger working capital during the busy season than in the slack season.

(vi) ***Turn of circulating capital :*** The speed with which the working capital completes its operating cycle (i.e., conversion of cash into inventory of raw material and stores, inventory of raw material into inventory of finished goods, inventory of finished goods into book debts or accounts), reveivable and book debt into cash account, play an important and decisive role in judging the adequacy of working capital.

(vii) ***Terms of purchase and sales :*** The place given to credit policy by a company in its dealings with creditors and debtors affects considerably the requirements of working capital. A company purchasing its requirements on credit business and selling its finished products on cash basis, will require lesser amount of working capital. On the other hand, a concern buying its requirements for cash and allowing credit to its customers, may find itself in a tight position. This is because it will need large amount of working capital as very huge amount of funds are bound to be tied up in debtors and bills receivables.

(viii) ***Business cycle :*** Business cycle refers to alternate conditions of inflation and depression. The expansion of business units caused by the inflationary conditions creates demand for more and more capital. Usually the need for working capital under such conditions increases. On the other hand, if there is contraction in the volume of business done by an enterprise, it may result in increasing the cash position because of reduction in inventory and receivable that usually accompanies a decline in sales and the curtailment of capital expenditures. Thus, a business during depression may give a misleading appearance of financial strength, except where substantial operating losses are incurred.

(ix) ***Scale of operations :*** The size of a business concern which may be measured in terms of scale of operations directly influences the working capital requirements of that concern. Greater the size of a business units, larger the amount of working capital required. However, due to high overhead charges, inefficient use of available resources, even a smaller concern may need more working capital.

(x) ***Rate of stock turnover :*** The quantum of working capital required is inversely proportional to the velocity with which the sales are effected. A firm with a high rate of stock turn over will need lower amount of working capital. ON the contrary, a firm with low rate of stock turn over need larger amount of working capital. For eg., The working capital requirements of a provision store is lower than that of a precious stone dealer.

(xi) ***Dividend Policy :*** The dividend policy of a concern also influences the requirements of its working capital. A firm that maintains a steady high rate of cash dividend irrespective of its generation of profits requires more working capital than the firm that retains larger part of its profits and does not pay so high rate of cash dividend.

(xii) ***Other factors :*** Lack of co-ordination between the production and distribution policies in a company results in a high demand for working capital. Hence specialisation in the distribution of production facilities and lack of transport facilities also cause requirement of high amount of working capital.

6.7 Financing of Working Capital

The working capital requirements of a concern can be classified as:

(i) Permanent or fixed working capital requirements.

(ii) Temporary or variable working capital requirements.

Permanent working capital is financed from long – term sources of funds for meeting the margin money for working capital loans as also a portion of the working capital requirements. Temporarily variable working capital requirement of a firm may be met with short – term sources of funds.

6.7.1 Sources of Working Capital

FIXED	VARIABLE
1. Shares	1. Commercial banks
2. Debentures	2. Indigenous bankers
3. Public Deposits	3. Accruals
4. Ploughing back of profits	4. Trade credits
5. Loans from financial institutions	5. Advances.
	6. Accounts Receivable
	7. Instalment Credit
	8. Commercial paper.

Table 6.2 Sources of working capital

Sources of working capital

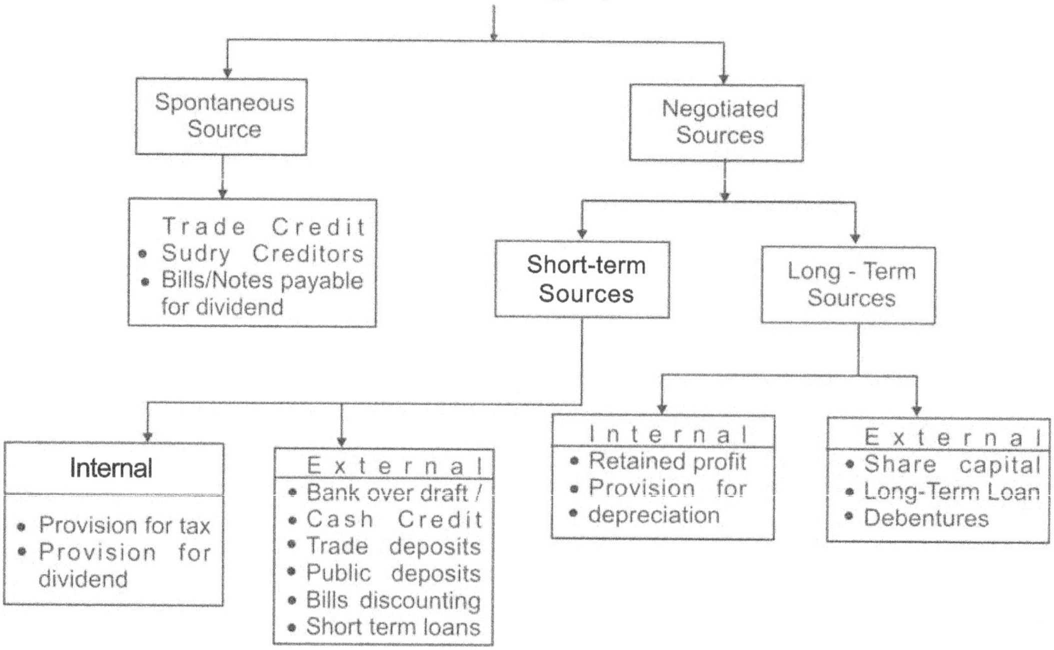

The working capital finance may also be classified into the following :

(i) ***Spontaneous source of Finance :*** Finance which naturally arise in the course of business is called as spontaneous financing. Eg. trade credit, credit from employees etc.

(ii) ***Negotiated Financing :*** Financing which has to be negotiated with lenders, say commercial banks, general public, financial institutions is called negotiated financing. This is more expensive and inconvenient method of raising funds and may be short-term or long – term in nature.

6.7.2 Finance Mix of Working Capital

Now, let us study the various sources of funds according to the first classification.

Fixed / Long-Term working capital : The permanent working capital helps the enterprise to have an uninterrupted use for a sufficiently long period. The following are the sources of long-term funds

(i) Retained earnings

(ii) Share capital

(iii) Debentures

(iv) Public Deposits

(v) Term loans.

(i) ***Retained earnings :*** It represents the retention of a major portion of the net profit to be ploughed back in the business so as to result in the over all growth of the shareholders wealth. As it is internal sources of finance, the company does not have to depend or negotiate with outsiders like creditors or even the share holders. By this source of financing the company's capacity and possibility to expand and modernize goes up and its prospects, too, therewith. Retained earnings mitigates the risks of dilution of control and avoids the issuance of fresh equity shares thus eliminating the possibility of downward trend in the price of its shares in the stock market. But excessive resort to retained earnings may lead monopolies, misuse of funds, overcapitalisation etc.

(ii) ***Share Capital:*** Another important source for raising the permanent capital is the issue of shares. There are two types of shares (a) Equity shares and (b) Preference share. Equity shares may by well considered as the most significant long-term source of finance, in as much as it represents the perpetual and permanent capital of the company and thus, there is no liability on the part of the company, to repay it at any point in time, during its entire life span. Preference shares are those which carry the preferential rights in respect of dividend at a fixed rate and in regard to the repayment of the capital at the time of winding up of the company. On account of there advantages the company should issue shares to raise maximum amount of permanent capital.

(iii) ***Debentures :*** As against the equity shareholders, who are considered as the owners the company, the debenture holders are considered to be the company's creditors. As already said debentures are issued for raising long – term debts. The debenture capital is like the funds lent to company at an agreed rate of interest and repayable after the stated and agreed period from the date of allotment. Besides the company has the legal obligation to pay the amount of interest at specified rate and specified time, and redeem the debentures on due date. The interest on debentures is a charge against profit and loss amount. They are generally given floating charge on the assets of the company. When the debentures are secured they are paid on priority to other creditors. The issue of debentures does not entail any risk of dilution of control. Also as the company is legally bound to pay the principal and interst, the investment in debentures is relatively a secured channel of investment for investors.

(iv) ***Public Deposits :*** Public Deposits are the fixed deposits accepted by a business enterprise directly from the public. This was a very popular source of raising short-term and medium-term finance in the absence of banking facilities. The public deposits as a source of finance have a large number of advantages such as very simple and convenient source of finance. But the major disadvantages of this source of financing are it is uncertain, unreliable, unsound and inelastic source of finance. The issue of public deposits is governed by certain limits laid down by RBI. Non-Banking concerns cannot borrow by way of public deposits more than 25% of its paid-up capital and free-reserves.

(v) ***Loans from Financial Institutions :*** There are some financial institutions like commercial Banks, LIC, IFCI, SFC etc., which provide short- term, medium-term and long-term loans. However, this source of finance is more suitable to meet the medium- term demands of working capital. These loans are charged with fixed rate of interest and the amount of the loan is to repaid by way of easy instalments in a number of years.

Variable or Short-term Sources

1. ***Trade Credits :*** As per the trade practices, all the manufacturers and traders have to supply a larger portion of their goods, on credit basis, on some credit term or the other, depending upon the trend in the specific line of business and or the market reputations and position of the seller companies. The credit-worthiness of a firm and the confidence of the suppliers are the main basis of securing trade credit. Prompt payments facilitate further liberalization of the credit terms, unduly delayed payment may adversely affect the quality of supplies and services, as also the competitive pricing thereof. Trade credits are almost an automatic and spontaneous source of finance which is generally available without much of negotiations. And these constitute a very important source of finance generally as much as 25% to 50% of the total short – term source for financing working capital requirements.

2 **Indigenous Bankers:** Prior to the establishment of commercial banks, private money- lenders and other county bankers used to be the only source of finance. But now-a-days with the development of commercial banks they have lost their monopoly. However, there are some business houses that depend upon indigenous bankers for obtaining loans to meet their working capital requirements even today.

3. ***Instalment Credit :*** By this method the assets are purchased and the possession of goods is taken immediately but the payment is made in instalments over a pre-determined period of time. The general practice is that interest is charged on the unpaid price or it is adjusted in the rice. This method provides funds for sometime and therefore many businesss houses which have difficult fund position use this as a source of short- term working capital.

4. ***Accruals :*** These simply represent a liability that a firm has to pay for the services already received by it. The most important items of accruals are wages and salaries, interest and taxes. The amount of accruals varies with the change in the level of activity of a firm. When the activity level expends, accruals also increase and hence provide a spontaneous source of finance. They also represent a free source of finance as there is no need to pay interest on accrued expenses. However, it must be noted that it may not be desirable or even possible to postpone these expenses for a long period as any delay or default in payment may attract penalties. Even then, they serve as a spontaneous, interest free, limited source of short – term financing.

5. ***Advances :*** It is a cheap source of finance and is preferred by some firms having long production cycle in order to minimise their investment in working capital.

6. ***Deferred incomes :*** Deferred incomes represent the funds received by a firm for which it has to supply goods or services in future. These funds increase the liquidity of the firm and serve as an important source of short – term finance.

7. ***Commercial Paper (CP) :*** The commercial paper has become a popular debt instrument of the corporate world. CP is a debt instrument for short- term borrowing, that enables a highly- rated corporate borrowers to diversify their sources of short-term borrowings and provides an additional financial instrument to investors with a freely negotiable interest rate. The maturity period ranges from three months to less than 1 year. Commercial paper is short-term unsecured promissory note issued by corporations with high credit ratings.

   An important feature of commercial paper is that the firm may raise large amount of funds which is not possible from a single bank. It is a form of promissory note, negotiable by endorsement and delivery. High credit ratings fetching a lower cost of capital and wide range of maturities are the advantages of issue of commercial paper. The limitation of the usage of commercial paper to blue chip companies only is the main drawback of the commercial paper.

8. ***Working Capital Finance from Banks :*** Today, banks constitute the major supplies of working capital credit to any business activity. The various schemes of working capital financing followed by the banks are as follows.

(i) ***Drawer Bills Scheme :***

Generally the seller is provided with bill limit to finance his receivables arising out of sale of finished goods. In the case of drawer bills, banker primarily sees the creditworthiness of the drawer of the bills. In case of drawer bills, the bill limit is provided to the purchaser of goods to acquire raw materials. Two systems of drawer bills are given below.

(a) ***Acceptance System :*** Under this arrangement of company draws a bill of exchange on a bank. The bank accepts the bill thereby promising to pay out the amount of the bill at some specified future date. The bill itself is then worth and can be sold either at once or when the funds are needed. Generally the bills are sold in the money market i.e. discount houses.

(b) ***Bills Discounting System :*** Bills discounting is the oldest and simplest form of securitisation. Under this system, the drawer sends a bill to the buyer or his bank. The buyer in turn discounts the bill and sells the proceeds to seller. In the books of the buyers bank, the bill will remains as 'bill discounted'. The bank earmarks suitably the drawing power available against stocks after providing the prescribed margin.

(ii) ***Bank Overdrafts :***

Overdraft means an agreement with a bank by which current account holder is allowed to withdraw more than the balance to his credit upto a certain limit. This kind of short-term borrowing is very flexible and can be easily and quickly repaid. There are no restrictions for operation of overdraft limits. The bank charges the interest on daily overdrawn balances.

(iii) ***Line of credit :***

Line of credit is a commitment by a bank to lend a certain amount of funds on demand specifying the maximum amount of unsecured credit the bank will permit the customer to lend at any point of time. An extra cost over the normal rate of interest is charged by the bank as it keeps the funds readily available to make useful for the customer at all times.

(iv) ***Revolving Credit :***

By this facility the bank gives the customer certain amount of credit facility on continuous basis. The borrower is not allowed to exceed the limits sanctioned by the bank. Such credit facilities will be given by the banks to their customers in the form of overdraft facility. In consumer financing credit cards are familiar ones for this kind of financing.

(v) *Bridge loans :*

The bridge loans are made available by the banks and financial institutions, when the source and timing of the funds to be raised is known with certainty. The cost of bridge loans is normally higher and they are provided to speed up implementation of the projects when there is a time gap for access of funds.

(vi) *Transaction loans :*

These are loans provided by the banker for a short period for a specific activity. When the customer receives payment, the loan will be repaid by the customer. The lender will evaluate the ability of the borrower and the cash flow of the borrower before sanctioning this type of loan.

6.7.3 Determing the Working Capital Financing Mix

Long- term and short- term sources of finance are the two main sources of financing working capital requirements. The finance manager has to make use of both long-term and short- term sources of funds in a way that the overall cost of working capital is the lowest and the funds are available on time and for the priod they are really needed.

There are three basic approaches for determining an appropriate working capital financing mix.

Table 6.3 Working capital financing mix

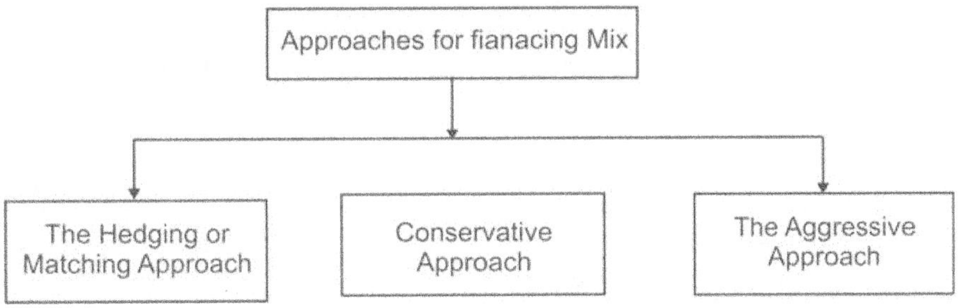

1. ***Heading or Matching Approach :*** The term hedging with reference to financing mix, refers to 'a process of matching maturities of debt with the maturities of financial needs'. According to this approach, the maturity of sources of funds match the nature of assets to be financed. This approach is, therefore, also known as " matching approach. This approach divides the requirements of total working capital funds into two categories. (a) Permanent or fixed working capital: It is the minimum amount required to carry out normal business operation. It does not vary over time. (b) Temporary or seasonal working capital: Funds which fluctuate over time and are required to meet special exigencies.

   The hedging approach suggests that the permanent working capital requirements should be financed with funds from long-term sources while the seasonal working capital requirements should be financed with funds from short-term sources.

2. ***The conservative Approach :*** A firm is said to be following the conservative policy when it depends more on long – term funds for its financing needs. This approach suggests that the entire estimated investments in current assets should be financed from long-term sources and the short-term sources should be used only for emergency requirements. As the firm relies more on long – term financing the risk is minimised.

   Trade-off Between Hedging and conservative Approaches :

   Both the hedging and conservative approaches represent two extreme situation and neither of them can serve the purpose of efficient working capital management. A trade off between these two can give satisfactory results. The level of trade off will differ from case to case depending upon the perception of the risk by the persons involved in financial decision making. However, one way of determining the trade off is by finding the average of maximum and minimum requirements of current assets. The average capital so obtained may be financed by long – term funds and the balance by short- term funds.

   For example, if during the quarter ending 30,March 1998, the minimum working capital required is estimated at Rs.10,000 while the maximum at Rs.30,000 the average level comes to Rs.20,000 (i.e, (10,000 + 30,000) divided by 2). The firm should therefore finance Rs.20,000 form long-term sources while any extra capital required any time during the period from short-term sources.

3. ***The Aggressive Approach :*** According to this approach, the entire estimated requirements of current assets or working capital should be financed from short – term sources or even a part of fixed assets investments be financed from short – term sources. The finance mix becomes more risky, less costly and more profitable by following this approach.

6.8 Management of Different Components of Working Capital

Cash is the most important liquid assets that a business owns. It may be compared to the blood of the human body. As blood gives life and strength to the human body, the cash imparts profits and solvency to the business organisation. The main pre-occupation of a business should cash, which is the starting point and the finishing point. Thus, it is the sole asset at the commencement and the termination of a business.

Cash is one of the current assets of a business. However, it is the most unproductive of all the assets. While fixed assets like machinery, plant etc., and current assets such as inventory will help the business in increasing its capacity, csh in hand is devoid not only of earnings power, but is, on the contrary, expensive to retain. It is in this context that planning for cash requirements has become an essential management function of any business.

Nature of Cash :

The term “cash” in a narrower sense includes coins, currency notes, cheques, bank drafts held by a firm with it and the demand deposits held by it in banks. In its broad sense, it also includes “ near cash assets” such as marketable securities and deposits with banks.

Cash itself does not produce goods or services. It is used medium to acquire other assets. A business has to keep required cash for meeting various needs. The assets acquired by cash again help the business in producing cash. There remains a gap between cash inflows and cash outflows. The objective of cash management is to make the most effective use of funds on one the hand and to accelerate the inflow and decelerate the outflow of cash on the other. However, a perfect synchronisation of cash inflows and cash outflows is only an ideal situation.

6.8.1 Motives for Holding Cash

A company may hold the cash with the various motives as stated below:

1. ***Transaction Motive :*** The company needs cash for making transactions in the day – to – day operations like purchases, wages or salaries, various expenses etc., similarly, the company a may receive the cash basically from its sales operations. However, there is no complete synchronisation between cash receipts and payments. In such situations, the company will like to hold the cash to honour the commitments whenever they become due. This requirement of cash balances to meet routine needs is known as transaction motive.
2. ***Precautionary motive :*** In addition to the requirement of cash for routine transactions, the company may also require the cash to meet various contingencies Eg: A sudden decline in the collection from the customers, increase in the price of the raw materials etc., Such contingencies arise often in a business. The company must hold the cash to meet such contingencies, or it should be in " Position to rise finances at a short period. The more is the possibility of such contingencies, the more is the amount of cash kept by the firm for meeting them. This need of cash is known as precautionary motive.
3. ***Speculative motive :*** The company may like to hold cash for investing in profitable opportunities as and when they arise. Such opportunities do not come in a regular manner. Eg: purchase of land, stocks, shares etc., such opportunities can be availed of if a firm has cash balance with it. These transactions are speculative because prices may not move in a direction in which we suppose them to move. This need to hold the cash for such purposes is known as speculative motive.

6.8.2 Objectives of Cash Management

There are two basic objectives of cash mangement.

(i) To meet the cash disbursements needs as per the payment schedule.

(ii) To minimise the amount locked up as cash balances. These two objectives are mutually contradictory and therefore, it is a challenging task for the finance manager to reconcile them and to have the best in this process.

1. ***Meeting cash disbursement :*** The basic objective of cash management is to meet the payments schedule. The business has to make payment for the purchase of raw materials, salaries and to meet the various requirements of the firm at different periods of times. The business activity may come to a grinding halt if the payment schedule is not maintained.

6.8.3 Minimising funds locked up as cash balances

This process of minimising the cash balances involves two conflicting aspects. A higher balance ensures proper payment with all its advantages. But this will result in a large balance of cash remaining idle. On the other hand low level of cash balance may result in failure of the firm to meet the payment schedule. Therefore, the finance manager should try to have an optimum amount of cash as balance keeping the above facts in view.

6.9 Capital Budgeting

A capital expenditure may be defined as an expenditure incurred for acquiring or improving the fixed assets, the benefits of which are expected to be received over a number of years in future. The capital expenditure decisions of a firm therefore, usually involve large sums of money, have long – time spans and carry some degree of risk and uncertainty. The planning and control of capital expenditure is termed as 'capital budgeting'. In otherwords capital budgeting is the art of finding assets that are worth more than they cost, to achieve a predetermined goal, i.e., optimising the wealth of a business enterprise. Thus, the capital budgeting decisions are decisions as to whether or not money should be invested in long – term projects. It includes analysis of various proposals regarding capital expenditure to evaluate their impact on the financial situation of the company and to choose the best out of various alternatives. The function of finance in this area is to enable the management to take a proper capital budgeting decision.

According to G.C.Philippatos, "Capital budgeting is concerned with the allocation of the firm's scarce financial resources among the available market opportunities. The consideration of investment opportunities involve the comparison of the expected future streams of earnings from a project with the immediate and subsequent streams of expenditure for it".

Charles T. Horngreen has defined capital budgeting as, "Capital budgeting is long-term planning for making and financing proposed capital outlays".

Thus, capital budgeting decision may be defined as "The firm's decision to invest its current funds most efficiently in long-term projects, in anticipation of an expected flow of future funds over a series of years".

It therefore involves the process of generation of investment proposals, estimation of cash flows for the proposals, evaluation of cash flows, selection of projects based upon an acceptance criterion and finally continuous revaluation of investment projects after their acceptance.

6.10 Importance of Capital Budgeting

Capital budgeting means planning for capital assets. They are the most crucial and critical decisions for a business to take. The importance capital budgeting arises mainly due to the following reasons:

(i) ***Long-Term effect on business operations :*** Capital budgeting decisions have a long-term and significant implications on the operations of a business. An unwise decision may affect the long-term survival of the company. The investment decision taken today not only affects the present earnings of the shares but also the growth and profitability of the firm in the future.

(ii) ***Large amount as investments :*** Capital budgeting decisions involve large amount of funds. But the funds available with the firm are always limited and the demand for funds exceeds the resources. Therefore it is necessary to take the decisions very carefully and control its capital expenditure.

(iii) ***Irreversible :*** The capital budgeting decisions are of irreversible nature of due to the fact that it is difficult to find the market for such capital goods. Once the decision for acquiring a permanent asset is taken, it becomes very difficult to dispose off these assets and the only alternative is to scrap these assets which involve huge losses.

(iv) ***Difficulties of investment decisions :*** The long – term investment decisions are difficult to make because it involves the assessment of future events which are difficult to ascertain. The investments are required to be made immediately but the returns are expected over a number of years.

(v) ***Ability to compete :*** It has been observed that many firms fail not because they have too much capital equipment but because they have too little ability to compete. At times the conservative approach of having small amount of capital equipment may also be fatal if other competitors install modern and automated equipment that permit them to produce a better product and sell at a lower price. Hence the investment decisions must consider the investment in capital assets so that the company can face and meet the competition from other companies in the same industry.

(vi) ***National importance :*** Investment decision is of national importance because it determines the employment, economic activities and economic growth of a county.

6.11 Capital Budgeting Process

Capital budgeting process is very complex as it involves decisions relating to the investment of current funds for the benefit to be achieved in capital budgeting process are as follows:

(i) Project generation
(ii) Project evaluation
(iii) Project selection
(iv) Project execution
(v) Performance review.

(i) ***Project generation :*** The capital budgeting process starts with the identification of investment proposals to be undertaken depending upon its future plans of activity. The proposal about potential investment opportunities may originate form the top management or may come from any officer of the organisation. The departmental head then analyses the various proposals and groups them according to the following categories.

(a) ***Replacement of equipment :*** The existing out – dated equipment and machinary can be replaced by purchasing new and modern equipment.

(b) ***Expansion :*** By purchasing additional equipment the company can increase its product lines.

(c) ***Diversification :*** The company can produce various products and diversity its product lines.

(d) ***Research and Development :*** By this the company can incur heavy expenditure with a view to innovate new methods of production, products etc.

(ii) ***Project Evaluation :*** The next step in the capital budgeting process is to evaluate the profitability of various proposals. The process of project evaluation comprises two steps.

(a) ***Estimation of benefits and costs :*** These must be measured in terms of cash flows. Benefits to be received are measured in terms of cash inflows and costs to be incurred are measured in terms of cash outflows.

(b) ***Selection of appropriate criterion :*** There are many methods to evaluate the profitability of various proposals. The selection of an appropriate method to judge desirability of the project is also a step in project evaluation. However, it should be noted that the various proposals to be evaluated may be classified as

(i) Independent proposals

(ii) Contingent proposals

(iii) Mutually exclusive proposals.

Independent proposals are those which do not compete with one another and the same may be either accepted or rejected on the basis of a minimum return on investment required. The proposals whose acceptance depends upon the acceptance of one or more proposals are the contingent proposals. Mutually exclusive proposals are those which compete with each other and one of those may have to be selected at the cost of the other.

(iii) ***Project selection :*** After evaluating various proposals, the unprofitable or uneconomic proposals may be rejected straight away. But there is no standard administrative procedure for approving the investment decisions. Hence, it is very essential to rank the various proposals and to establish priorities after considering urgency, risk and profitability involved there in.However, the proposals are scrutinised at multiple levels and the final approval of the project generally rests with the top management of the company. Sometimes the top management may delegate authority to approve certain types of investment proposal. The top management may delegate authority by limiting the amount of cash outlay, prescribing the selection criteria and holding the lower management levels accountable for results.

(iv) ***Project Execution :*** It is not possible to implement the project just by preparing a capital expenditure budget and incorporating a particular proposal in the budget. A request for authority to spend the amount should further be made to the Capital Expenditure Committee which may like to review the profitability of the project in the changed circumstances. The funds for the purpose of the project execution must be spent only after obtaining the approval the finance controller. Further, to have an effective control, it is necessary to prepare monthly budget reports to show clearly the total amount allocated amount spent and the amount in hand.

While implementing the project, it is better to assign responsibility for completing the project within the given time frame and cost limit so as to avoid unnecessary delays and cost over runs. Network techniques such as PERT and CPM can also be applied to control and monitor the execution of the project.

(v) ***Performance Review :*** This is the last stage in the process of capital budgeting and involves the evaluation of the performance of the project. The evaluation is made by comparing the actual expenditure on the project with the budgeted one and also by comparing the actual return from the investment with the anticipated return.

6.12 Capital Budgeting Appraisal Techniques

A business firm has a number of proposals regarding various projects in which it can invest funds. But the funds available with the firm are always limited and it is not possible to invest funds in all the proposals at a time. The capital budgeting appraisal methods of evaluation of investment proposals will help company to decide upon the desirability of an investment proposal depending upon their relative income generating capacity and rank them in order of their desirability. These methods provide the company a set of norms on the basis of which, either it has to accept reject the investment proposal. The crucial factor that influences the capital budgeting decision is the profitability of the prospective investment. There are many methods of evaluating profitability of capital investment proposals. The criterea for the appraised of investment proposals are grouped into two types, viz.,

1. *Traditional Methods :*
   (a) Pay back period method
   (b) Improvement of Traditional Approach to Pay Back Period Method.
   (c) Accounting Rate of Raturn.
2. *Time-Adjusted method / Discounted cash Flow Mehtod :*
   (a) Net Present Value (NPV)
   (b) Internal Rate of Return (IRR)
   (c) Profitability Index (PI)

6.12.1 Traditional Methods

These methods determine the desirability of an investment project on the basis of its useful life and expected returns. These methods will not take into consideration the concept of 'time value of money' and depend upon the accounting information available from the books of accounts of the company.

6.12.2 Pay-back Period Method

This is the most popular and widely recognised traditional method of evaluating the investment proposals. It is based on the principle that every capital expenditure pays itself back within a certain period out of the additional earning generated from the capital assets. The pay-back period may be defined as "as the number of years required to recover the original cash outlay invested in a project". It can be calculated with the help of the following formual:

$$\text{Pay back period} = \frac{\text{Cash outlay}}{\text{Annual cash inflows}}$$

6.12.3 Acceptance rule

Under this method, various investments are ranked asccording to the length of their pay back period in such a manner that the investment with a shorter pay back period is preferred to the one which has longer pay back period. The pay back period can also be used as an accept or reject criterion. In case of evaluation of a single project, it is adopted if it pays back for itself within a period specified by the management and if the project does not pay back itself within the period specified by the management then it is rejected.

6.12.4 Merits

The following are the merits of the pay back period method.

1. It is one of the easiest methods of evaluating the investment projects.
2. The main advantage of this method is that it is simple to understand and easy to calculate.
3. It does not involve any cost for the computation and requires lesser time and labour as compared to other methods of capital budgeting.
4. This method is most suitable when the future is uncertain. The shorter the pay back period, the less risky is the project. Therefore, it can be considered indicator of risk.
5. It may be a suitable techniquie where risk of obsolescence is high. In such cases, projects with shorter pay back period may be preferred as the changes in technology may make other projects obsolate before the costs are recovered.
6. Due to its short-term approach, this method is particularly suitable to a firm which has shortage of cash or whose liquidity position is not particularly good.

6.12.5 Demerits

1. It ignores the returns from a project after the completion of pay back period for example, there are two projects. A having a pay back period of 5years while another project B with a pay back period of 3years. Thus B is preferred. But it is quite possible that project may generate good cash inflows after 5years till he end of 10years, while a project B may stop generating cash inflows after 3years only. In such cases, project A may prove to be more advantageous. Thus, it may not be appropriate to ignore earnings after the pay back period especially when these are substantial.
2. It ignores the time value of money and does not consider the magnitude and timing of cash inflows. It treats all cash flows equally though they occur in different periods. The fact that cash received today is more important than the same amount of cash received after some period is ignored by this method.

3. It does not take into account the cost of capital which is a very important factor in making sound investment decisions.
4. It ignores the cash generation beyond the pay back period and this can be seen more a measure of liquidity man of profitability.
5. It does not take into account the interest factor involved in an investment outlay.
6. It treats each asset individually in isolation with other assets. White assets cannot be treated in isolation in real practice.
7. The method is delicate and rigid because even a slight change in the division of labour and cost of maintenance will effect the earnings and such instances may also affect the pay back period.

   Though this method violates the first principle of rational investor behaviour namely that large returns are preferred to smaller ones, this method can be applied in assessing the profitability of short and medium term capital expenditure projects.

6.12.6 Improvements in Traditional Approach to Pay Back Period Method

(a) ***Post-pay back profitability method :*** The major disadvantage of pay back period method is that it does not take into account the cash oflows earned after pay back period and hence the true profitability of the project cannot be assessed. Hence, the pay back period method is improved by taking into account the returns receivable beyond the pay-back period. This returns are called post pay back profils.

$$\text{Post-pay back profitability Index} = \frac{\text{Post-pay back profits} \times 100}{\text{Investment}}$$

(b) ***Pay back reciprocal method :*** An alternative way of expresing the pay back period as the pay back period reciprocal which is expressed is

$$\text{Pay back reciprocal} = \frac{\text{Annual cash inflow}}{\text{Total Investment}}$$

However, this method is applicable only when (i) Equal cash inflows are generated every year (ii) The project under consideration has a long-life which must be atleast twice the pay back period.

The pay – back reciprocal can be calculated in percentage by multiplying the above by 100. The higher the pay – back period reciprocal the more worth while the project becomes. The only relevance of this calculation is that laymen may be happier in discussing the percentage measure.

(c) ***Post-pay back period method :*** Another limitation of the pay – back period method is that it ignores the life of the project beyond the pay- back period. The post pay-back period method takes into account the period beyond the pay-back period. According to this method, a project can be accepted if it gives the greatest post pay-back period. This method is also known as surplus life over pay-back method and can be employed successfully where the various projects under consideration do not differ significantly as to their size and the expected cash inflows are even throughout the life of the project.

(d) ***Discounted pay-back method :*** This method takes into consideration the time value of money which is ignored by pay- back period method. Under this method the present values of all cash outflows and inflows are computed at an appropriate discount rate. The present values of all inflows are cumulated in order of time period at which the cumulated present value of cash inflows equals the present value of cash outflows is known as discounted pay-back period. The project with a shorter discounted pay-back period is accepted.

6.13 Accounting Rate of Return (ARR) Method

This is known as Rate of Return method for the reason that under this method, the account concept of profit is used rather than cash inflows. According to this method, capital projects are ranked in order of earnings. This method employs the normal accounting technique to measure the profitability of the investment proposal. It can be determined by dividing average income less taxes by the average investment i.e., average book value after depreciation.

$$\text{Average Rate of Return} = \frac{\text{Average net income}}{\text{Average investment}}$$

6.13.1 Acceptance Value

On the basis of this method projects which yield the highest earnings are selected and others are ruled out. The return on investment method can be expressed in several ways as follows:

(a) ***Average rate or return method :*** Under this method average annual profit is calculated and then it is divided by the total capital outlay of the project other words, it establishes the ratio between the average annual profits and total investment of the project.

$$\text{Thus average rate of Return} = \frac{\text{Total profits (After depreciation and taxes)}}{\text{Net investment in the project} \times \text{No. of years of profits}}$$

$$\text{or} \quad \frac{\text{Average Annual profits}}{\text{Net investment in the project}} \times 100$$

(b) ***Earnings per unit of investment method :*** As per this method the total profit after tax and depreciation is divided by total investment.

$$\text{Earnings per unit of investment} = \frac{\text{Total profit}}{\text{Net investment}} \times 100$$

The higher the earnings per unit, the project deserves to be selected.

(c) ***Return on average amount of investment method :*** In this method the percentage return on average amount of investment is calculated. The average investment is calculated by dividing the outlay of the projects by two. As formula,

Average investment = Unrecovered capital at the beginning + Unrecovered

$$\frac{\text{Capital at the end}}{2}$$

or $$\frac{\text{Initial investment + scrap due}}{2}$$

or $$\frac{\text{Investment}}{2}$$

(d) ***Average Return on Average Investment method :*** Under this method, average profit after depreciation and taxes is divided by the average amount of investment. This can be expressed as Average on Average investment.

$$= \frac{\text{Average Annual profit after depreciation and taxes}}{\text{Average investment}}$$

$$= \frac{\text{Average annual profit}}{\frac{\text{Net investment}}{2}}$$

6.13.2 Merits

1. It is very simple to understand and calculate.
2. Unlike pay-back period method, this method takes into consideration the entire earnings of a project in calculating the rate of return and earnings upto pay- back period and hence gives a better view of profitability.
3. This approach gives due weight to the profitability of the project.
4. Where a number of capital investment proposals are being considered, a quit decision can be taken by use of ranking the investment proposals.
5. This method is based upon accounting concept of profits, and therefore can be readily calculated from the financial data.

6.13.3 Demerits

1. This method also like pay – back period method ingnores the time factor which is very crucial in business decision.
2. It ignores the cash flows which are more important than the accounting profits.
3. This method uses straight line of method of depreciation. Therefore the method will not be easy to use and will not work practically once a change in method of depreciation takes place.
4. One of the important disadvantages of this method is that its results by different methods are inconsistent.
5. This method ignores the distinction in the size of investment required for individual projects. Competing investment proposals with the same accounting rate of return may require different amounts of investment.
6. It is biased against short-term projects.

6.14 Discounted Cash Flow Techniques or Modern Techniques

The method of computing expected rates of return is the present value method, popularly known s DCF Method. It involves the present value of the cash benefits at a rate equal to the firm's cost of capital. These methods consider the magnitude and timing of cash flows in each period of a projects life. To determine the desirability of the project the financial executive compares the peresent value with the cost of the proposal.

6.14.1 Acceptance rule

If the present value is greater than the net investment, the proposal should be accepted. On the other hand, if the present value is smaller than the net investment the return is less than the cost of financing. Making investment in this case will cause a financial loss to the firm.

The present value methods are:

(i) Net present value method (NPV).

(ii) Internal rate of return method (IRR).

(iii) Profitability Index method (PI).

6.15 Net Present Value Method

This is the modern method of evaluating investment proposals and takes into consideration the time value of money. We know, the objective of the firm is to create wealth by existing and future resources to produce goods and service. To create wealth, the cash inflows must exceed the present value of all anticipated cash outflows. The net present values of all inflows and outflows of cash occuring during the entire life of the project is determined separately for each year by discounting these flows by the firm's cost of capital or at a predetermined rate. The method discounts the net cash flows from the investment by the minimum required rate of return and deducts the initial investment to give the yield from the funds invested.

6.15.1 Acceptance Rule

If the yield is positive or zero, i.e., when present value of cash inflows exceeds or is equal to the present value of cash outflows, the project is acceptable. If it is negative the project is not acceptable. If there are two mutually exclusive projects to be selected the projects should be ranked in order of net present value i.e., the first preference should be given to the project having maximum positive net present value.

The present value can be found by the following mathematical formula.

PV = 1/(1 + r) power n

where PV = Present value

r = Rate of interest or discount rate

n = Number of years.

6.15.2 Merits

1. It recognises the time value of money.

2. It is based on the entire cash flows generated during the useful life of the asset and the true profitability of the investment proposal can be evaluated.
3. It is consistent with the objective of wealth maximisation of the owners.
4. It is based on the assumption that cash flows determine the wealth of shareholders.
5. Cash flows are subjective than profits.

6.15.3 Demerits

1. It is difficult to understand and compute.
2. The net present value is calculated by using the cost of capital as a discount rate. Calculation of cost of capital is itself complicated. Moreover, desired rates of return vary from year to year.
3. It is an absolute measure and does not give solutions when two projects are being considered involving different amounts of investment.
4. It may not give satisfactory results where two projects having different effective lives are compared.
5. It disregards the initial investment involved and emphasises the comparison of net present value.

6.16 Internal Rate of Return Method

This method is popularly known as time adjusted rate of return method discounted rate of return method. The internal rate of return is defined as the rate of return which equates the present value of anticipated net cash flows with the initial outflow. The Internal Rate of Return is also defined as the rate at which present value is zero. The internal rate of return is found by trial and error method.

Calculation of Internal Rate of Return :

(i) Compute the present value of cash flows from an investment, by using an arbitrarily selected interest rate.

(ii) Then compare the present value so obtained with the investment cost.

(iii) If the present value is higher than the cost, we take a high rate of interest go through the procedure again to determine the present value. Conversely, it the present value is lower than the cost, lower the interest and the process should be repeated.

(iv) The procedure is to be continued until the present value of the flows from the investment are approximately equal to its cost.

(v) The interest rate that brings about equality is the internal rate of return.

6.16.1 Acceptance Rule

If the internal rate of return exceeds the required rate of return, the project is acceptable. Conversely, if the projects internal rate of return is lower than the required internal rate of return, it is not acceptable. The internal rate of return technique is significantly used in case of ranking the proposal. The projects with the highest rate of return will be ranked first compared to the lowest rate of return.

6.16.2 Merits

(i) It considers the time value of money.

(ii) It takes into account the total cash inflows and each outflows.

(iii) It considers the profitability of the project for its entire economic life and hence enables evaluation of true profitability.

(iv) It provides for uniform ranking of various proposals due to the percentage rate of return.

(v) It is in conforming with the firm's objective of maximisation of profitability and is considered to be a more reliable technique of capital budgeting.

6.16.3 Demerits

(i) It is difficult to understand and evaluate.

(ii) It involves very complicated computational work based on trial and error method.

(iii) It produces multiple rates and may not give unique answer in all situations.

(iv) The results of internal rate of return method may differ when the projects under evaluation differ in their size, life and timings of cash flows.

6.17 Profitability Index Method

It is also time – adjusted method of evaluating the investment proposals and is sometimes called the Benefit – Cost ratio. The profitability Index is the present value of an anticipated net future cash flows divided by the initial out lay.

$$\text{Profitability Index} = \frac{\text{Present value of cash inflows}}{\text{Present value of initial cash outflows}}$$

$$\text{or} \quad = \frac{\text{Present value of cash inflows}}{\text{Initial cash outlay}}$$

The profitability Index may be found for net present values of inflows

$$\text{PI(Net)} = \frac{\text{Net present value}}{\text{Initial cash out lay}}$$

6.17.1 Acceptance rate

If the profitability index is more than one, the project is accepted and the project is rejected if the profitability index is less than one. In case of ranking various projects, projects with higher profitability index are ranked higher than the other with lower profitability index.

6.17.2 Merits

(i) It takes into account the time value of money.

(ii) If involves less computational work than internal rate of return method.

(iii) Selection of the projects on the basis of the value of index is easier.

(iv) Useful in ranking of projects on the basis of the value of index.

(v) It takes into account the entire stream of cash flows generated during the useful life of the asset.

6.17.3 Demerits

(i) It is difficult to understand.

(ii) It is very difficult to understand the analytical part of the decision on the basis of profitability index.

6.18 Final Choice of Evaluation Method

The choice of the evaluation technique depends upon the objective of the management in the investment decisions. However, those projects will be in the interest of shareholders which can earn more rate of return than other alternative investment opportunities.

PROBLEMS

1. Prepare an estimate of working capital requirement from the following information of a trading concern :

(a)	projected annual sales	1,00,000 units
(b)	selling price	6 per unit
(c)	% of net profit on sales	25%
(d)	average credit period allowed to customers	8 weeks
(e)	average credit period allowed by suppliers	4 weeks
(f)	average stock holding in item of sales requirement	12 weeks
(g)	allow 10% for contingencies.	

Solution :

Statement showing working capital requirement

Current assets :

$$\text{Debtor (8 weeks)} = \frac{1,00,000 \times 8}{52} = 92,308$$

stock (12 weeks) = $\frac{6,00,000 \times 12}{52}$ = 1,38,462

2,30,770

Less current liabilities :

Creditors (4 weeks) = $\frac{6,00,000}{52} \times 4$ = 46,154

net working capital 1,84,616

Add 10% for contingencies 18,462

Working capital required Rs. 2,03,078

2. A project requires an investment of Rs. 5,00,000 and has a scrap value of Rs. 20,000 after 5 years. It is exprcted to yield profit after depreciation and taxes during the five years amounting Rs. 40,000, Rs. 60,000, Rs. 70,000, Rs. 50,000, Rs. 20,000. Calculate the average rate of return on investment.

Solution:

Total profit = 40,000 + 60,000 + 70,000 + 50,000 + 20,000 = 2,40,000

Average profit = $\frac{2,40,000}{5}$ = 48,000

Net investment in the profit = 5,00,000 – 20,000 = 4,80,000

$$\text{Average rate of return} = \frac{\text{Average annual profit}}{\text{Net investment in the project}} \times 100$$

$$= \frac{48,000}{4,80,000} \times 100 = 10\%$$

3. Where cash inflows are uniform. An equipment requires an initial investment of Rs. 12,000. The annual cash inflow matched at 4000 for 5 years. Calculate IRR.

Solution:

$$F = \frac{1}{c}$$

Where F = Factor to be located

I = Original investment

C = Cash inflow per year

$$F = \frac{12000}{4000} = 3$$

This factor of 3 should be located in table in the line of 5 years. The discount % would be somewhere between 18% i.e. 3.127 and 20 % i.e. 2.991. It indicates IRR is more than 18% but less than 20%. A more exact interplation can be done. However, such an effort may not be very useful in this case since 2.991 is very nearer to 3 and hence IRR can be taken as 20%.

4. From the following information prepare a statement in columnar form showing the estimated working capital requirements :

   (a) in total

   (b) as regards each constituent part of working capital. Budgeted sales Rs.2,60,000 per annum. Analysis of cost of each unit :

raw material	3
labour	4
overheads	2
profit	$\frac{1}{10}$

   It is estimated that :

   (a) Pending use, raw materials are carried in stock for three weeks and finished goods for 2 weeks.

   (b) Factory processing will take three weeks.

   (c) Suppliers will give five weeks credit and consumers will require eight weeks credit.

It may be assumed that production and overheads accrue evenly throughout the year.

Solution :

Statement of working capital requirements :

Inventories :	**Rs**
Stock of raw materials (26,000 units $\times \frac{3}{52} \times 3$)	4,500
Work-in-progress	
Raw materials (26,000 $\times \frac{3}{52} \times 3$)	4,500
Labour(26,000 $\times \frac{3}{52} \times 4$)	6,000
Overheads (26,000 $\times \frac{3}{52} \times 2$)	3,000
	18,000

Stock of finished goods :

Raw materials (26,000 units $\times \frac{2}{52} \times 3$)	3,000
Labour(26,000 $\times \frac{2}{52} \times 4$)	4,000
Overhead	$\left(26000 \times \frac{2}{52} \times 2\right) = 2000$
Sundry debtor	$\left(9 \times \frac{26000}{52} \times 8\right) = 36,000$
less : Sundry creditors $\left(\frac{26,000 \times 10 \times 5}{52}\right)$	25,000
Net working capital required	**38,000**

5. A project requires Rs. 20,000 as initial investment and will give in general an annual cash inflows (CIF's) of Rs.5000 for 10 years. Calculate pay back period.

Solution :

Initial investment = Rs. 20,000

Annual CIF's = Rs. 5000

$$\text{PBP} = \frac{\text{Initial investment}}{\text{Avg. Annual cash flows}}$$

Avg Annual cash flows = Rs. 5000

$$\text{PBP} = \frac{20,000}{5,000} = 4 \text{ years.}$$

6. A project costs Rs. 50,000 and yields annual cash inflow of Rs. 20,000 for 6 years. Calculate its pay back period.

Solution :

$$\text{Pay back period} = \frac{\text{Investment}}{\text{Annual cash inflow}} = \frac{50,000}{20,000}$$

$$= 2.5 \text{ years}$$

7. Determine the pay back period for a project whose cash outlay is Rs. 12,000 and cash inflow is Rs. 3,000, Rs. 8,000 and Rs. 12,000 in first, second and third years respectively.

5	150000	600000

PBP = 4year + 50000/150000 = 4.33years

b. ARR = Avg. annual EATs/Avg. Investments

Avg. Annual EATs = 100000/5 =20000

Avg. investment = Net working capital +S.V +1/2(cost-S.V)

= 0 + 0 + 1/2 (500000-0)

Therefore ARR = 20000 × 100/250000

= 8%

c. NPV at 15 %

Year	CFATs	PVIF@15%	PVs
1	100000	0.8696	86960
2	100000	0.7561	75610
3	125000	0.6575	82188
4	125000	0.5718	71475
5	150000	0.4972	74580
		390813	
	(-) initial investment	500000	
	NPV	(109187)	

Therefore NPV = (109187)

d. IRR Calculation:

Step 1:

Calculation of Fake pay back period:

$$FPBP = \frac{\text{Initial Investment}}{\text{Avg. CFATs}}$$

Avg. CFATs = 600000/5 =120000

FPBP = 500000/120000 = 4.1667 Years.

Step 2:

PVAF table indicates that value closes to 4.1667 against 5years is 4.2124 at 6%

Step 3:

Calculation of NPV at 6%.

Year	CFATs	Pvif @ 15%	PVs
1	100000	0.9434	94340
2	100000	0.8900	89000
3	125000	0.8396	104950
4	125000	0.7921	99013
5	150000	0.7473	112095
			499398
		(-)initial investment	500000
		NPV	(602)

Calculation of NPV at 3%

Year	CFATs	PVIF @15%	PVs
1	100000	0.9709	97090
2	100000	0.9426	94260
3	125000	0.9151	140388
4	125000	0.8885	111063
5	150000	0.8626	129390
			546191
		(-)initial investment	500000
		NPV	(46191)

$$IRR = LR + \frac{\text{NPV at LR} \times \Delta R}{\Delta \text{PVCIFs}}$$

= 3 + 46191 x 3/46793

= 5.96%

e. BCR calculation:

Year	CFATs	PVIF @15%	PVs
1	100000	0.9091	97910
2	100000	0.8264	82640
3	125000	0.7513	93913
4	125000	0.6830	85375
5	150000	0.6209	93135
		445973	
	(-)initial investment	500000	
	NPV	(54027)	

Solution :

Year	Annual cash inflow Rs.	Accumulated annual cash inflow (AACI) Rs.
1	3,000	3,000
2	8,000	11,000
3	12,000	23,000

$$\text{Pay back period} = 2 + \frac{\text{Cash outlay - AACI of 2nd year}}{\text{AACI of 3rd year} - \text{AACI of 2nd year}}$$

$$= 2 + \frac{12{,}000 - 11{,}000}{23{,}000 - 1200} = 2 + \frac{1}{11000} = 2 + 0.09$$

$$= 2.09 \text{ years}$$

Problem 3

A project whose cost is 8,00,000 yields a profit of Rs. 80,000 after depreciation at 12% per annum but before tax of 40% calculate the pay back period.

Solution :

Profit before tax Rs. 80,000

(-) Tax at 40% = 80,000 × 40/100 = Rs. 32,000

Profit after tax = Rs. 48,000

Depreciation at 12% per annum

Depreciation = 8,00,000 × 12/100

= 96,000

Profit before depreciation but after tax = 48,000 + 96,000

= 1,44,000

$$\text{Pay back period} = \frac{\text{Cost of project}}{\text{Annual cash inflow}}$$

$$= \frac{8{,}00{,}000}{1{,}44{,}000}$$

$$= 5.56 \text{ years}$$

Problem 4

Calculate the average rate of return for a project from the following

Investment Rs. 20,000

Expected life 4 years

Net income of the project

Year	Cash inflow
1	5000
2	3000
3	1000
4	1000
Total =	**10,000**

Solution :

$$\text{Average investment} = \frac{20{,}000}{2}$$

$$= 10{,}000$$

$$\text{Average Earnings} = \frac{10{,}000}{4}$$

$$= 2{,}500$$

$$\text{Average rate of return} = \frac{\text{Average earnings}}{\text{Average investment}} \times 100$$

$$= \frac{2500}{10{,}000} \times 100$$

$$= 25\%$$

Problem 5

A project 'Y' requires an investment of Rs. 75,000 and has a scrap value of Rs. 2,000 after five years. It is expected to yield profits after depreciation and taxes during five years amounting to Rs. 2,000, Rs. 5,000, Rs. 3,000, Rs. 6,000, Rs. 1,500. Calculate (ARR).

Solution :

Total earnings for 5 year = Rs. 2000+5000+3000+6000+1500 = 17,500

$$\text{Average earnings} = \frac{17{,}500}{5}$$

$$= 3{,}500$$

Average investment = ½ (Total investment – scrap value) + (Scrap value)

= ½ (75,000 – 2,000) + 2,000 = Rs. 38,500

Average rate of return = $\frac{3500}{38,500} \times 100$

= 9.09%

Problem 6

Calculate the net present value of the two projects and suggest which of the two projects should be accepted assuming a discount rate of 10%.

Initial investment	Rs. 80,000	Rs. 60,000
Estimated	5 years	5 years
Scrap value	Rs. 1,000	Nil

The profits before depreciation and after taxes are as follows:

Year	1	2	3	4	5
Project X	16,000	20,000	10,000	15,000	12,000
Project Y	50,000	35,000	45,000	55,000	70,000

The present value of Re. 1 at 10% for 1st year 0.909

The present value of Re. 1 at 10% for 2nd year 0.826

The present value of Re. 1 at 10% for 3rd year 0.751

The present value of Re. 1 at 10% for 4th year 0.683

The present value of Re. 1 at 10% for 5th year 0.621

Solution:

Project X :

Year (1)	Cash inflows (2) Rs.	Present value of Re. 1 at 10% (3)	Present value of cash inflows (2) × (3)
1	16,000	0.909	14,544
2	20,000	0.826	16,520
3	10,000	0.751	7,510
4	15,000	0.683	10,245
5	12,000	0.621	7,452
5 (Scrap)	1,000	0.621	621
		Total	**56,892**

Present value of cash inflow = 56,892

(-) Present value of initial investment = 80,000

Net present value = – 23,108

Project Y :

Year (1)	Cash inflows (2) Rs.	Present value of Re. 1 at 10% (3) (Rs.)	Present value of cash inflows (2) × (3) (Rs)
1	50,000	0.909	45,450
2	35,000	0.826	28,910
3	45,000	0.751	33,795
4	55,000	0.683	37,565
5	70,000	0.621	43,470
		Total	**1,89,190**

Present value of cash inflow = Rs. 1,89,190

(-) Present value of initial investment = 60,000

1,29,190

Hence project Y is selected which has positive net present value.

Problem 7

The cash inflow and outflow of a particular project is given below.

Year	Cash outflow in Rs.	Cash inflow in Rs.
0	2,00,000	—
1	60,000	30,000
2		50,000
3		70,000
4		1,00,000
5		60,000

The salvage value at the end of 5th year is Rs. 20,000. The cost of capital is 12%. Calculate the net present value.

Solution :

Present value of initial investment = Rs. 2,00,000

(+) Present value of additional investment = 60,000 × 0.893

= Rs. 53,580

Present value of total investment = Rs. 2,53,580

Year (1)	Cash inflows (2) Rs.	Present value of Re. 1 at 12% (3)	Present value of cash inflows (2) × (3) Rs.
1	30,000	0.893	26,790
2	50,000	0.797	39,850
3	70,000	0.712	49,840
4	1,00,000	0.635	63,500
5	60,000	0.567	34,020
5 (scrap)	20,000	0.567	11,340
		Total	**1,89,190**

Net present value = 2,25,340 – 2,53,580

= Rs. –28,240

Problem 8

Give ranks to the projects P and Q in order of profitability according to (a) pay back period and (b) net present value assuming 10% capital cost.

Project	Initial Outlay Rs.	Annual cash inflow Rs.	Life (in years)
P	50,000	10,000	5
Q	10,000	5,000	6

Solution :

Pay back period :

Project P : Pay back period $= \frac{50{,}000}{10{,}000}$

= 5 years

Project Q : Pay back period $= \frac{10{,}000}{5{,}000}$

= 2 years

Net present value :

Project P : Present value of Rs. 10,000 received annually for 6 years = 10,000 × (0.909 + 0.826 + 0.751 + 0.683 + 0.621 + 0.564)

= 10,000 × (4.354) = 43,540

NPV = 43,540 – 50,000

Rs. = – 6,460

Project Q : Present value of Rs. 5,000 received annually for 6 years = 5,000 × 4.354

= Rs. 21,770

NPV = 21,770 – 10,000

= Rs. 11,770

(a) According to pay back period, project Q is given first rank.

(b) According to net present value also project Q stands first because of positive net present value.

Problem 9

The initial cash outlay of a project is Rs. 1,00,00 and it generates cash inflows of Rs. 20,000, Rs. 23,000, Rs. 25,000 and Rs. 18,000 in four years. Ascertain the profitability index of the proposed investment assuming 10% rate of discount.

Solution :

Year	Cash inflows Rs.	Discount factor at 10%	Present value of cash inflows
1	20,000	0.909	18,180
2	23,000	0.826	18,998
3	25,000	0.751	18,775
4	18,000	0.683	12,294
		Total	**68,247**

$$\text{Profitability Index} = \frac{\text{Present value of cash inflow}}{\text{Initial cash outlay}}$$

$$= \frac{68,247}{1,00,000}$$

$$= 0.68247$$

$$= 0.7$$

If PI is greater than 1 then only the project is accepted.

10. The project requires an investment of Rs.200,000.It yields an annual cash flows of Rs.40,000 for 9 years.Find out the payback period(PBP) of project.

    Solution :

    Pay back period = 200000/40000 = 5 years

11. A project requires Rs.20,000/- as initial investment and will generate an annual cash inflows (CIF's)of Rs.5000/-for 10 years.Calculate pay back period .

    Solution :

    Given:

    Initial investment = Rs.20000/-

    Annual CIF's = Rs.5000/-

    Initial investment

    PBP = Avg. Annual cash flows

    Avg. Annual cash flows = Rs.5,000/-

    Rs.50000

    (i.e., Rs.5,000 × 10 yrs = 10yrs.

    $$\text{PBP} = \frac{20,000}{5,000} = 4 \text{ Yrs.}$$

12. A project requires an initial investment of Rs.20000/- and generates the following cash flows CFs for 5 years.

Year	1	2	3	4	5
CFs(Rs. '000)	6	8	5	4	4

Calculate Payback period of the project.

Solution:

Calculation of PBP :

Year	CFs	Cummulative CFs
1	6000	6000
2	8000	(i.e. 6000 + 8000) = 14000
3	5000	14000 + 5000 = 19000
4	4000	19000 + 4000 = 23000
5	4000	23000 + 4000 = 27000

$$PBP = 3years + \frac{1000}{4000}$$

$= 3 + 0.25$

$=$ 3yrs and 3months

13. Determine Accounting Rate of Return from the following information:

    Cost of machine = Rs.56125/-

    Working capital required = Rs.5000/-

    Estimated life = 5 years

    Salvage value = 3000

    Income tax = 55%

    Method of depreciation = Straight line method (SLM)

    CFATs: (Cash Flow After Taxes)

Year	1	2	3	4	5
CFATs Rs.	3375	5375	7375	9395	11375

Solution :

$$ARR = \frac{\text{Avg.CEAT} \times 100}{\text{Avg.Investment}}$$

$$\text{Avg. CFAT} = \frac{\Sigma \text{CFAT}}{\text{no.of years}}$$

(Σ CFAT = 3375 + 5375 + 7375 + 9375 + 11375 = Rs. 36875)

Avg. CFAT = 36875/5 = Rs. 7375

Avg. investment = Net working capital + Salvage value +1/2(cost-salvage value)

= 5000 + 3000 + 1/2(56125 – 3000)

= 8000 + 1/2(53125)

= 8000 + 26563

= 34563 (Rs.)

$$ARR = \frac{7375 \times 100}{34563}$$

= 21.34%

14. Determine the average rate of return from the following date of two machines A and B.

	Machine A	Machine B
Original cost	Rs. 56125	Rs. 56125
Addl. Investment in net working cap.	5000	6000
Estimated life in years	5	5
Estimated salvage value	3000	3000
Avg. Income tax rate	50%	50%

Annual estimated income after dep. And tax:

Rs.

1st year	3375	11375
2nd year	5375	9375
3rd year	7375	7375
4th year	9375	5375
5th year	11375	3375
Total	36875	36875

Depreciation has been charged on straight line basis :

Solution :

$$\text{ARR} = \frac{\text{Avg.earnings} \times 100}{\text{Avg.investment}}$$

$$\text{Avg. income} = \frac{\text{Total income}}{\text{no of years}}$$

Machine A:

Avg income = 36875/5 = Rs.7375

Machine B:

Avg.income = 36875/5 = Rs.7375

Avg. investment = ½ (original investment-scrap value) + addl.net working capital + Scrap value

Machine A = 1/2(56125 – 3000) + 5000 + 3000

= 26562.5 + 8000

= Rs. 34562.5

Machine B = 1/2(56125 – 3000) + 6000 + 3000

= 35562.5

ARR for machine A $= \dfrac{(7375 \times 100)}{34562.5} = 21.34\%$

ARR for machine B $= \dfrac{(7375 \times 100)}{35562.5} = 20.74\%$

15. A project requires an initial investment of Rs. 25000 and is likely to generate the following CFATs.

Year		1	2	3
CFATs	Rs.	10000	15000	10000

Assume cost of capital to be 10%.compute NPV of the project.

Solution:

Given:

Initial investment = Rs. 25000

NPV = ΣPVCIF – 11101 Σ PVCOFs

ΣPVCIFs = $CF_1 / (1 + x)^n + CF_2 / (1 + x)^n + CF_2 /(1 + x)^n$

where n = year

x = cost of capital = 0.1(given)

ΣPVCIFs = (10000/1.1) + (15000/1.21) + (10000/1.331)

= 9091 + 12397 + 7513

= 29001

NPV = 29001 – 25000

= 4001

Decision :

Since NPV is positive we accept the project.

16. Compute NPV of a project whose cost of capital is 12% and is expected to generate the following cash flows :

Year	0	1	2	3	4	5
CFs ('000)	(10)	7	5	(2)	4	5

NPV = å PVICFs – å PVCOFs

Year	PVCIFs (a)	Year	PVCOFs (b)
1	6250	0	10000
2	3986	3	1423
4	2542		11423 åPVCOFs
5	2837		
	15615 å PVCIFs		

(year 0 and 3rd year have negative cash flows so, they are considered as cash out flows).

NPV = 15615-11423

= Rs.4129/-

Working notes(a):

ΣPVCIFs = $CF_1 / (1 + x)^n + CF_2 / (1 + x)^n + CF_4 / (1 + x)^n + CF_5 / (1 + x)^n$

where n = year

x = cost of capital =0.12

ΣPVCIFs = 7000/1.12 +5000/1.25 + 4000/1.57 + 5000/1.76

= 6250 + 3986 + 2542 + 2837 = 17615

Working notes(b) :

ΣPVCOFs = $CF_0 / (1 + x)^n + CF_3/(1 + x)^n$

= 10000/1 + 2000/1.41

= 10000 + 1423 = 11423

Decision :

Since NPV is positive, the project has to be accepted.

17. Beetron castings Ltd. Hyderabad wishes to install machinery in rented premises for the production of a component the demand for is expected to last for only 5 years.

Initial outlay will be :	Rs.
Plant and machinery	270000
Working capital	40000
Total	**310000**

The working capital will be fully realized at the end of 5th year is Rs.5000 The expected cash inflows from business operations and PV factor at 15% (cost of capital) are given. Calculate the NPV of the project.

Year	Cash inflows Rs.	PV factor at 15%
1	70000	0.8996
2	100000	0.7561
3	130000	0.6575
4	90000	0.5718
5	15000	0.3972

Solution :

Calculation of present value of inflow :

Year	Cash inflows Rs.	PV factor at 15%	Present value of cash inflow Rs.
1	70000	0.8996	62972
2	100000	0.7561	75610
3	130000	0.6575	85475
4	90000	0.5718	51462
5	15000 + (40000 + 5000)	0.3972	23832
		Total	299351

NPV = Total PV of cash inflow – original investments

= 299351 – 310000

= –10,649

Decision :

The project shall be rejected since NPV is negative.

18. The Sundar co.Ltd. is considering the purchase of a new machine. Two alternative machine (P andQ) have been

Suggested, each having an initial cost of Rs.400000 and requiring Rs.20000 as additional working capital at the end of the 1st year .Earning after taxation are expected to be as follows:

Cash inflows :

Year	Machine P	Machine Q
1	Rs.40000	Rs.120,000
2	120000	160000
3	160000	200000
4	240000	120000
5	160000	80000

The company has a target of return on capital of 10% and on this basis, you are required to compare the profitability of the machines as state which alternative you consider financially preferable.

Solution :

Computation of Net present value of the two machines:

		Machine P		Machine Q	
Year	Discount factor @10%	Cash inflow Rs.	Present value	Cash inflow Rs.	Present value
1	0.91	40000	36400	120,000	109200
2	0.83	120000	99600	160000	132800
3	0.75	160000	120000	200000	150000
4	0.68	240000	163200	120000	81600
5	0.62	160000	99200	80000	49600
	Totals		518400		523200
Total present value of cash out flows (Rs.400000 + 20000 × 0.91)			418200		418200
Net present value			100200		105000

Recommendations.

Machine Q is preferable to Machine P. Since the NPV of machine Q is greater than of machineP.

19. After conducting a survey that cost Rs.200000 Karnataka electronics Ltd.,decide to undertake a project for placing a new product in the market. The companies cut-off rate is 12% it was estimated that the project would have a life of 5 years

The project would cost Rs. 4000000 in plant and machinery in addition to working capital of Rs. 1000000. The scrap value of the machinery at the end of 5 years was estimated as Rs. 500000 after providing depreciation on straight line basis.

Profit after tax were estimated as follows :

Year	Profit Rs.	Present value factors at 12% per annum are given below :
1	500000	1st year-0.8929
2	800000	2nd year-0.7972
3	1000000	3rd year-0.7118
4	600000	4th year-0.6355
5	500000	5th year-0.5674

Ascertain the next present value of the project.

Solution :

Calculation of Net present value :

Year	Profit Dep.after tax	Cash Rs.	PV factor inflows Rs.	Present at 12 %	Value inflows of cash
1	500000	740000	1240000	0.8929	1107196
2	800000	740000	1540000	0.7972	1227688
3	1000000	740000	1740000	0.7118	1238532
4	600000	740000	1340000	0.6355	851570
5	500000	740000	1240000	0.5674	703576

Total PV of cash inflow 5128562

Add : PV of scrap value at the end of 5th year

Rs. 500000 × 0.5674

283700

Add : PV of working capital at the end of the 5th year

Rs. 1000000 × 0.5674
567400

Total PV of cash inflows
5979662

Less present values of out flows
5200000

Net present value
779662

Note : 1. Depreciation calculation

Cost of survey	200000
Plant and Machinery	4000000
Total	4200000
Less:Scrap	500000
Total Depreciation for 5 years	3700000

Depreciation per year = 3700000/5 = 740000

2. Initial Investment :

Cost of the survey	200000
Cost of the Plant and Machinery	4000000
Working capital provided total investment	1000000
Present value of outflow	5200000

20. A decision is to be made between two competing projects which require an equal investments of Rs.50000.

and are expected to generate net cash flows as under:

End of year 1	25000	10000
End of year 2	15000	12000
End of year 3	10000	18000
End of year 4	Nil	25000
End of year 5	12000	8000
End of year 6	6000	4000

The cost of capital of the company is 10 percent.Which project proposal should be chosen and why? Evaluate the project proposals under:

(a) Pay back period,and

(b) Net present value methods.

Solution :

Pay back period method :

	Project 1		Project 2	
	Cash inflows	Cumulative Cash inflows	Cash inflows	Cum.cash inflows
End of year 1	25000	25000	10000	10000
End of year 2	15000	40000	12000	22000
End of year 3	10000	50000	18000	40000
End of year 4	Nil	50000	25000	65000
End of year 5	12000	62000	8000	73000
End of year 6	6000	68000	4000	77000

Project 1 has the payback period of 3 years while project 2 has a payback period of 3.4 years.

Thus, project 1 has to be preferred because it has a shorter payback period.

Net present value method:

YEAR	Project 1	Project 2	Discount factor	PV of cash flow	PV of cash flow
	Cash inflow	Cash inflow	At 10% p.a.	Project 1	Project 2
1	25000	10000	0.909	22725	9090
2	15000	12000	0.826	12390	9912
3	10000	18000	0.751	7510	13518
4	Nil	25000	0.683	———	17075
5	12000	8000	0.621	7452	4968
6	6000	4000	0.564	3384	2256
Total present value of future cash inflows				53461	56819
Initial investments				50000	50000
Net present value(NPV)				3461	6819

Both projects need the same investment of Rs.50000. However,in case of project 1, there is a surplus of Rs.3,461, while in case of project 2, there is a surplus of Rs.6819. Hence project 2 is to be preferred.

21. A company is considering an investment proposal which will cost Rs.5000 with a life of 5 years. The estimated CFATs from the proposals are as follows:

Year	1	2	3	4	5
Cf's (Rs. '000)	1000	1045	1180	1225	1675

Determine IRR.

Solution:

Calculation of IRR:

Step 1 :

Calculation of FPBP:

FPBP = Initial investment

Avg. CFATs

Initial investment (given) = 5000

Avg. CFATs = åCFATs / no.of years

= 1/5(1000 + 1045 + 1180 + 1225 + 1675)

= 6125/5 = 1225

therefore FPBP = 5000/1225 = 4.0816 years

Step 2 :

PVAT table indicate that PVAF closest to 4.0186 against 5 years is 4.1 at 7%.

Step 3 :

Determine NPV at 7%.

Year	CFAT	PVIF @ 7%	PVs (Rs.)
1	1000	0.935	935
2	1045	0.873	912
3	1180	0.816	963
4	1125	0.763	935
5	1675	0.713	1194
			Σ PV 4939
		Initial investment	5000
		NPV	(61)

Since NPV is –ve, therefore calculate NPV at lower rate.

Step 4 :

Year	CFAT	PVIF @ 6%	PV (Rs)
1	1000	0.943	943
2	1045	0.890	930
3	1180	0.84	991
4	1125	0.792	970
5	1675	0.747	1251
			ΣPVs 5085
		Initial investment	5000
		NPV	85

Step 5 :

Interpolation :

$$\text{IRR} = \frac{\text{NPV at lower rate} \times \text{A Rate}}{\Delta\text{PVCIFs}}$$

$= 6\% + 85 \times 1/146$

$= 6 + 0.58$

$= 6.58\%$

(note : 146 = 85 + (-61))

22. A firm has to make a selection between two projects A and B which are mutually exclusive. The cash flows are as follows :

Year	Project A	Project B
0	5000	7500
1	6000	8800

The cost of capital is 10 %,Suggest which project should be taken up using (i) NPV method and (ii) IRR method.

Solution :

NPV method

Project	A	B
Present value of cash inflows	(6000 × 0.909)5454	(8800 × 0.909)7999
Initial investment	5000	7500
NPV	454	499

IRR method

Project	A	B
Internal Rate of return	20%	17.33%

Thus, according to NPV method, project B is superior to project A since its NPV is higher than that of B. But according to IRR method Project A is superior to project B since it has a higher IRR.

Since acceptance of project B would result in maximization of wealth of the shareholders as indicated by NPV,

It will be appropriate to reject project A. It must be noted that IRR has been calculated as reciprocal of pay back period.

23. A firm whose cost of capital is 10% is considering two mutually exclusive projects X and Y. The details of which are:

Investment (Rs.) 70,000 each CIFs: years	Project X	Project Y
1	10000	50000
2	20000	40000
3	30000	20000
4	45000	10000
5	60000	10000

Compute NPV at 10% and IRR and suggest.

Solution: Determination of NPV:

CFAT (Rs.)		PVs			
Year	P_x	P_y	PVIF @10%	P_x	P_y
1	10000	50000	0.909	9090	45450
2	20000	40000	0.826	16250	33040
3	30000	20000	0.751	22530	15020
4	45000	10000	0.683	30735	6830
5	60000	10000	0.621	37260	6210
				116130	106550
		Less:	Initial investment	70000	70000
			NPV	46130	36550

Determination of IRR :

Step 1 :

Fake payback period (FPBP) = Initial investment

Avg. cash inflows

Initial investment (given):

P_x = 70,000/-

P_y= 70,000/-

$$\text{Avg. cash inflows} = \frac{\Sigma \text{CFATs}}{\text{No.of years}}$$

Avg. cash inflows (P_x) = 165000/5 = 33000/-

Avg. cash inflows (P_y) = 130000/5 = 26000/-

Therefore FPBP (P_x) = 70000/33000 = 2.121years.

FPBP (P_y) = 70000/26000 = 2.692years.

Step 2 :

PVAF table indicates that PVF closest to 2.121 against 5 years is 2.143 at 37% but since CFATs in the initial years are considerable, smaller the avg. CIFs and hence IRR is likely to be much smaller.

Therefore let us try at 28% and 27%

Year	CFAT	PVF@ 27%	PVF@ 27%	PVs@ 27%	PVs@ 28%
1	10000	0.787	0.781	7870	7810
2	20000	0.620	0.61	12400	12200
3	30000	0.488	0.477	14640	14310
4	45000	0.384	0.373	17280	16785
5	60000	0.303	0.291	18180	17460
			70370	68565	
		Less initial investment	70000	70000	
		NPV		(1435)	

Therefore $IRR_{(x)}$ = LR + NPV at LR × DR

ΔPVs

= (27) + 370 × 1/1805

= 27 + 0.2

= 27.2%

24. A co. is considering to invest into a project that cost of Rs.50,000.The project is likely to generate the following expected CFs.

Year	1	2	3	4	5
CFs (Rs. '000)	10000	10000	15000	15000	20000

Assume cost of k to be 15% .Determine NPV and profitability index of the project and comment:

Solution :

NPV = Σ PVCIFs – å PVCOFs

Year	CFs	PVIF @ 15%	PVs
1	10000	0.8696	8696
2	10000	0.7561	7561
3	15000	0.6575	9863
4	15000	0.5718	8577
5	20000	0.4972	9944
			44641
		(-) Initial investment	50000
		NPV	(5359)

Therefore NPV = (5359)

Calculation of profitability index /BCR

$$BCR = \frac{\Sigma PVCIFs}{\text{Initial Investment}}$$

$$= 44641/50000 = 0.8928$$

Comment :

The project has to be rejected as it is yielding a –ve NPV and BCR is less than 1.

25. A chemical co is considering to investment into a project that cost Rs.500000/-.The estimated salvage value is zero.

The co is under 50% tax bracket and uses SLM method of depreciation. The project is expected to generate the following

CFs before taxes.

Year	1	2	3	4	5
CFs (Rs.)	100000	100000	150000	150000	200000

Determine the following (a) PBP (b) ARR (c) NPV @15% (d) IRR (e) Profitability index@ 10%

Solution :

Calculation of CFATs:

Year	CFBTs	Deprn. PBT	(CBT deprn) on PBT	Tax @50%	EAT CFAT	(EAT + deprn)
1	100000	100000	Nil	Nil	Nil	100000
2	100000	100000	Nil	Nil	Nil	100000
3	150000	100000	50000	25000	25000	125000
4	150000	100000	50000	25000	25000	125000
5	200000	100000	100000	50000	50000	150000

$$\text{Deprn} = \frac{\text{Cost} - \text{Salvage Value}}{\text{Life of project}}$$

= 500000 – 0

= Rs.1,00,000/-

(a) Calculation of Payback period :

Year	CFAT	Cumulative CFATs
1	100000	100000
2	100000	200000
3	125000	325000
4	125000	450000
5	150000	600000

PBP = 4year + 50000/150000 = 4.33years

(b) ARR = Avg. annual EATs/Avg. Investments

Avg. Annual EATs = 100000/5 = 20000

Avg. investment = Net working capital + S.V + 1/2 (cost-S.V)

= 0 + 0 + 1/2(500000 – 0) = 2,50,000

$$\text{ARR} = \frac{20,000}{2,50,000} \times 100$$

= 8%

(c) NPV at 15 %

Year	CFATs	PVIF@15%	PVs
1	100000	0.8696	86960
2	100000	0.7561	75610
3	125000	0.6575	82188
4	125000	0.5718	71475
5	150000	0.4972	74580
		390813	
	(-) initial investment	500000	
	NPV	(109187)	

Therefore NPV = (109187)

(d) *IRR Calculation :*

Step 1 :

Calculation of Fake pay back period:

$$FPBP = \frac{\text{Initial Investment}}{\text{Avg. CFATs}}$$

Avg. CFATs = 600000/5 = 120000

FPBP = 500000/120000 = 4.1667 Years.

Step 2 :

PVAF table indicates that value closes to 4.1667 against 5years is 4.2124 at 6%

Step 3 :

Calculation of NPV at 6%.

Year	CFATs	Pvif @ 15%	PVs
1	100000	0.9434	94340
2	100000	0.8900	89000
3	125000	0.8396	104950
4	125000	0.7921	99013
5	150000	0.7473	112095
			499398
		(-)initial investment	500000
		NPV	(602)

Calculation of NPV at 3%

Year	CFATs	PVIF @15%	PVs
1	100000	0.9709	97090
2	100000	0.9426	94260
3	125000	0.9151	140388
4	125000	0.8885	111063
5	150000	0.8626	129390
			546191
		(-)initial investment	500000
		NPV	(46191)

$$\text{IRR} = \text{LR} + \frac{\text{NPV at LR} \times \Delta\text{R}}{\Delta\text{PVCIFs}}$$

$= 3 + 46191 \times 3/46793$

$= 5.96\%$

(e) *BCR calculation :*

Year	CFATs	PVIF @15%	PVs
1	100000	0.9091	97910
2	100000	0.8264	82640
3	125000	0.7513	93913
4	125000	0.6830	85375
5	150000	0.6209	93135
		445973	
	(-)initial investment	500000	
	NPV	(54027)	

Summary

1. ***Working Capital :*** For every busines what ever amount of money utilising for the purpose of starting of the business or establing of business is known as 'working capital'.
2. Working capital, also known as short-term capital largely deals with the management and control of current assets and current liabilities. Two distinct views may be noted as regards the definition of working capital.

   1. Net working capital 2. Gross working capital
3. ***Net working Capital :*** According to this concept working capital means total current assets less the total current liabilities. This concept is supported by authorities like Lincoln, Saliers and Stevens.
4. ***Gross working capital :*** In its broad sense, the term working capital refers to the gross working capital and represents the amount of funds invested in current assets. This view is supported by Field, Baker, Malott and Mead.
5. **Need of Working Capital:**
   1. For the purchase of raw materials.
   2. To pay wages, salaries and incur day-to-day expenses.
   3. To provide credit facilities to the customers.
   4. To meet the selling costs as packing, advertising etc.
   5. To maintain the inventories of raw material, work-in-progress.
6. The classification of working capital

   (a) fixed, regular or permanent, and (b) variable, seasonal or special
7. Importance of Working Capital

   (i) Good running of the Business (ii) Good Will

   (iii) Increases credit worthiness (iv) Uninterrupted supply of raw materials

   (v) Regular day-to-day Commitment (vi) Cash discount

   (vii) Exploitation of favourable market conditions

   (viii) Increase the confidence of investors (ix) Ability to face crisis

   (x) High morale
8. Working Capital Cycle Concept

   The operating cycle refers to the average time that elapses between the acquisition of raw materials and the final cash realisation. This concept is new and is gaining more and more importance in recent years.

9. Determinants of Working Capital
   - (i) Nature of Business
   - (ii) Production Policy
   - (iii) Manufacturing Process
   - (iv) Growth and expansion of business
   - (v) Seasonal variations
   - (vi) Turn of circulating capital
   - (vii) Terms of purchase and sales
   - (viii) Business cycle
   - (ix) Scale of operations
   - (x) Rate of stock turnover
   - (xi) Dividend Policy
   - (xii) Other factors
10. Financing of Working Capital

    The working capital requirements of a concern can be classified as:
    - (i) Permanent or fixed working capital requirements.
    - (ii) Temporary or variable working capital requirements.
11. Sources of Working Capital

FIXED	VARIABLE
1. Shares	1. Commercial banks
2. Debentures	2. Indigenous bankers
3. Public Deposits	3. Accruals
4. Ploughing back of profits	4. Trade credits
5. Loans from financial institutions	5. Advances.
	6. Accounts Receivable
	7. Instalment Credit
	8. Commercial paper.

12. Finance Mix of Working Capital
    - (i) Retained earnings
    - (ii) Share capital
    - (iii) Debentures
    - (iv) Public Deposits
    - (v) Term loans.
13. ***Capital Budgeting:*** The planning and control of capital expenditure is termed as 'capital budgeting'. In otherwords capital budgeting is the art of finding assets that are worth more than they cost, to achieve a predetermined goal, i.e., optimising the wealth of a business enterprise. Thus, the capital budgeting decisions are decisions as to whether or not money should be invested in long – term projects.
14. Importance of Capital Budgeting
    - (i) Long-Term effect on business operations
    - (ii) Large amount as investments
    - (iii) Irreversible
    - (iv) Difficulties of investment decisions
    - (v) Ability to compete
    - (vi) National importance

15. ***Capital Budgeting Process:*** Capital budgeting process is very complex as it involves decisions relating to the investment of current funds for the benefit to be achieved in capital budgeting process are as follows:
    (i) Project generation
    (ii) Project evaluation
    (iii) Project selection
    (iv) Project execution
    (v) Performance review.

16. ***Capital Budgeting Appraisal Techniques:*** There are many methods of evaluating profitability of capital investment proposals. The criterea for the appraised of investment proposals are grouped into two types, viz.,
    1. *Traditional Methods :*
        (a) Pay back period method
        (b) Improvement of Traditional Approach to Pay Back Period Method.
        (c) Accounting Rate of Raturn.
    2. *Time-Adjusted method / Discounted cash Flow Mehtod :*
        (a) Net Present Value (NPV)
        (b) Internal Rate of Return (IRR)
        (c) Profitability Index (PI)

17. ***Traditional Methods:*** These methods determine the desirability of an investment project on the basis of its useful life and expected returns. These methods will not take into consideration the concept of 'time value of money' and depend upon the accounting information available from the books of accounts of the company.

18. ***Pay – Back Period Method:*** This is the most popular and widely recognised traditional method of evaluating the investment proposals. It is based on the principle that every capital expenditure pays itself back within a certain period out of the additional earning generated from the capital assets. The pay back period may be defined as "as the number of years required to recover the original cash outlay invested in a project". It can be calculated with the help of the following formual:

$$\text{Pay back period} = \frac{\text{Cash outlay}}{\text{Annual cash inflows}}$$

19. ***Accounting Rate of Return (ARR) Method:*** This is known as Rate of Return method for the reason that under this method, the account concept of profit is used rather than cash inflows. According to this method, capital projects are ranked in order of earnings. This method employs the normal accounting technique to measure the profitability of the investment proposal. It can be determined by dividing average income less taxes by the average investment i.e., average book value after depreciation.

$$\text{Average Rate of Return} = \frac{\text{Average net income}}{\text{Average investment}}$$

20. ***Discounted Cash Flow Techniques or Modern Techniques:*** The method of computing expected rates of return is the present value method, popularly known s DCF Method. It involves the present value of the cash benefits at a rate equal to the firm's cost of capital. These methods consider the magnitude and timing of cash flows in each period of a projects life. To determine the desirability of the project the financial executive compares the peresent value with the cost of the proposal.

21. ***Net Present Value Method:*** This is the modern method of evaluating investment proposals and takes into consideration the time value of money. We know, the objective of the firm is to create wealth by existing and future resources to produce goods and service. To create wealth, the cash inflows must exceed the present value of all anticipated cash outflows. The net present values of all inflows and outflows of cash occuring during the entire life of the project is determined separately for each year by discounting these flows by the firm's cost of capital or at a predetermined rate. The method discounts the net cash flows from the investment by the minimum required rate of return and deducts the initial investment to give the yield from the funds invested.

22. ***Internal Rate of Return Method:*** This method is popularly known as time adjusted rate of return method discounted rate of return method. The internal rate of return is defined as the rate of return which equates the present value of anticipated net cash flows with the initial outflow. The Internal Rate of Return is also defined as the rate at which present value is zero. The internal rate of return is found by trial and error method.

23. ***Profitability Index Method:*** It is also time – adjusted method of evaluating the investment proposals and is sometimes called the Benefit – Cost ratio. The profitability Index is the present value of an anticipated net future cash flows divided by the initial out lay.

$$\text{Profitability Index} = \frac{\text{Present value of cash inflows}}{\text{Present value of initial cash outflows}}$$

$$\text{or} \qquad = \frac{\text{Present value of cash inflows}}{\text{Initial cash outlay}}$$

Essay Questions

1. What are the objectives of working capital?
2. What are the types of working capital?
3. Expiain the working capital cycle.
4. What is the impact of current assets on working capital?
5. What is meant by time value of money.?
6. What is the importance capital budgeting?
7. What is the impact of depreciation on Accounting Rate of Return.(ARR).
8. Explain advantages and limitations of Net Present Value.(NPV) technique in capital budgeting.
9. Explain the advantages and limitations of IRR in capital budgeting.
10. Give various examples of capital budgeting decisions. Classify them into specific kinds.
11. What are the merits and limitations of pay back period ? How does discounting approach overcome the limitations of pay back method ?
12. Give various examples of capital budgeting decisions. Classify them into specific kinds.
13. "The return on investment is a single comprehensive measure that is influenced by everything happening within the organisation". Explain the statement and illustrate its computation with imaginary figures.
14. Explain tradional and modern techniques of capital budgeting.

Short Questions

1. What are the major sources of short term finance ?
2. What is meant by discounting and time value of money? How is it useful in capital budgeting?
3. What is the importance of capital budgeting ? Explian the basic steps involved in evaluating the capital budget proposals.
4. What are the traditional and discount cash flow techniques of capital budgeting.?
5. Explain working capital cycle. How does it affect the profit of the business.?
6. Explain the important factors affecting the requirement of working capital?
7. What are the sources of financing working capital?
8. Discuss the modern techniques of capital budgeting.
9. What is meant by capital? State the factors determining the capital requirements of a business undertaking.
10. Explian the capital budgeting in a business enterprise. Evaluate capital budgeting process.
11. Describe the institutions providing long-term finances.
12. What is meant by working capital cycle ?
13. What are the determinants of working capital ?
14. What is the importance of IRR method ?
15. Explain briefly net present value method.

CHAPTER 7

Introduction to Financial Accounting

7.1 Introduction

Nikhil, after his engineering graduation,was not interested to get into any white collared job.He wanted to start his own business. His father agreed to provide him with the seed capital of Rs.2,50,000 and his friends Vamsi and Balu volunteered to advance Rs.1,50,000 and Rs.1,00,000.respectively at 18% interest. With the fund of Rs.5,00,000. Nikhil hired a place of business in a busy locality at a monthly rent of Rs.3,000 and employed two helpers at a salary of Rs.1,500 per month. On 1st June 2001 ,he started his business activities. For the first few days ,he was able to remember all his business activities .But , as the business improved briskly and the number of his business activities increased ,he could not remember every thing. He therefore, noted all his dealings of his business activities for the month of June 2001 in chronological manner. When he went through the list, he could not make head or tail of it. Answers were not available to many of the questions that have been cropping up in his mind now-a-days, such as

1. what happened to his seed capital and the borrowed money?
2. who are the parties that owe money to him and to what extent ?
3. Who are the parties to whom he owes and how much?
4. What is the cash balance, bank balance in his hand on particular date?
5. What is the long term debt expanded on each head of expenditure?
6. He also found it difficult to identify or remember the date of transactions incurred.
7. Ultimately we cannot find out the original values of assets and liabilities and profit (or) loss made during the financial year.

The dilemma in which Nikhil and new business people like his are in, is due to their ignoring an important aspect of success in business, record of the business activities, known as the "Transactions" in accounting terminology, in an orderly manner. But the problem is not insurmountable. The system of recording business activities is known as book keeping.

Nikhil can easily learn the art of recording his business deals by going through any fundamental accounting literature. Once he acquaints himself with basic terms of accounting ,the rest is easy, the remaining things any accountant or auditor can prepare very easily. Otherwise as simple accounting packages like tally are available in the market. Or else, Nikhil can employ an accounting clerk to do the job at any affordable cost.

So , any business organizations are set up with profit motive or with service motive. What ever maybe the purpose with which they are set up they should posses the information about the resources they have ,allocations that are being made, result of such allocations and their financial standing in the society. This is necessary both from there own point of view and the point of number of people who are associated with it like the members, share holders, employees, creditors, debtors, government etc. Such business information is called accounting.

The dictionary meaning of accounting is "the art of keeping accounts in a regular and systematic manner in order to serve the information so recorded to the interested parties in the form in which they need".

The main purpose of accounting is to ascertain profit or loss during a specified period ,to show financial position of the business on the particular day.

The origin of business accounting is Kautilya's Artha Sastra. But the present practice which is called "Double Entry Book keeping" was first introduced in Italy in 1494 by Luca Pacioli.

Definitions

The American Institute of Certified Public Accounts (AICPA)has defined accounting as "The art of recording , classifying and summarizing in a significant manner and in terms of money , transactions and events which are in part, at least of financial character, and interpreting the result thereof".

American accounting Association defines accounting as "The process of identifying, measuring and communicating economic information to permit informed judgments and decisions by users of in formations".

7.1.1 Objectives of Accounting

1. To have systematic and permanent record of all financial transactions of the business.
2. To keep records of incomes and expenses in such a manner that the net profit or net loss for any period may be readily asserted.
3. To keep records of assets and liabilities in such a manner that the financial positions of the undertaking of business at any point of time may be readily asserted.
4. To keep track of all changes in the value of assets and liabilities.

5. To record and control all the expenses.
6. To serve the financial information like interested parties like owners, creditors, management , employees, government, trade unions, researchers, and public at large.
7. To provide information for meeting various legal requirements such as income tax returns, sales tax returns etc.
8. To make decisions concerning the acquisition, use and prevention of scarce resources.
9. To help in devising remedial measures for the deviation of actual performance from planned performance.

7.1.2 Book Keeping and Accounting

"Book keeping is a science and art of correctly recording in the books of accounts all those business transactions that result in the transfers of moneys worth".

A book keeper always keeps all financial records and his job is more routine in nature which can be done by mechanical or electronic equipment.

On the other hand 'Accounting is concerned with preparation of necessary information from the records maintained by the book keeper. An accountant should possess higher intellectual ability to analyze the records maintained by book keeper.

7.1.3 Accounting vs. Accountancy

The principles, postulates, assumptions, conventions, concepts, rules governing the science of recording ,classifying and analyzing financial transactions is accounting where as the practice of art of accounting is accountancy.

7.2 Basic Terminology in Accountancy

The dictionary meaning of accounting is "the art of keeping accounts in a regular and systematic manner in order to serve the information so recorded to the interested parties in the form in which they need."

In the words of AICPA (American Institute of Certified Public Association). "Accounting is the art of recording, classifying and summarising in a significant manner and in terms of money, transactions and events which are , in part atleast, of a financial character and interpreting the results there of".

Assets : Assets refer to tangible objects and intangible rights of an enterprise which carry probable future benefits.

Current assets : Current assets are those assets which are held (i) in the form of cash (ii) for their conversion into cash, (iii) for their consumption in the production of goods or rendering of services in the course of business. For example, cash in hand, Stock of finished goods, Debtors, Bills receivable, Stock of raw materials, Stock of work in progress etc.

Fixed Assets : Fixed assets refer to those assets which are held for the purpose of providing or producing goods or services and those that are not held for resale in the normal course of business .For example, Land and buildings, Plants and machinery, Furnitures and fixtures.

Liabilities : Liabilities refer to the financial obligations of an enterprise other than owners funds. Broadly liabilities can be classified as follows.

Current liabilities : Current liabilities refer to those liabilities which do not fall due for payment in a relatively short period, normally in a period of not more than 12 months. For example, Long term loans, Debentures etc.

Capital : Capital refers to the amount invested by the proprietor .It is the excess of assets over external liabilities.

Revenue : The term revenue refers to the amount charged for the goods sold or services rendered, or permitting others to use enterprises resources yielding interest, royalty and dividend.

Expense : The term expense refers to the amount incurred in the process of earning revenue.

Purchase : The term 'Purchase' refers to the total amount of goods obtained by an enterprise for resale or for reuse in the production of goods or rendering services in the normal course of business.

Sales : The term sales refers to the amount for which the goods are sold and services are rendered.

Stock : The term stock refers to the tangible property held for sale in the ordinary course of business or for consumption in the production of goods or services for sale.

Debtor : The term 'Debtor' refers to the person from whom the amounts are due for goods sold or services rendered or in respect of contractual obligations.

Equity : Any right to claim over the assets of the business is called equity.If such equity is held by owners, it is called as owners equity and if it is held by others then it is called as creditors equity.

Creditor : The term 'Creditor' refers to the person to whom the amounts are due for:

(i) ***Dual aspect concept :*** According to this concept every transaction has two aspects : the benefit receiving aspect(debit) and benefit giving aspect (credit). These two aspects are to be recorded in the books of account.

(ii) ***Realization concept :*** This concept speaks about recording only those transactions which are actually realized.For example sale or profit on sales will be taken in to account only when money is realized i.e, either cash is received or legal obligations from debtors is created.

(iii) ***Accrual concept :*** According to this concept accrued items also are to be recorded if they accrue in the year in which they are to be accounted for .For example , expenditure incurred during the period but not paid and income earned but not received are called accrued items.

Accounting Conversions

These are the traditions in usages and customs to be followed while recording and presenting accounting information.

(i) ***Conservatism :*** According to this convention all the losses are provided for but not all anticipated profits to workout the profits of business. Similarly while working out the value of stock, least of the two values i.e: market price or cost price, is to be taken in to account.

(ii) ***Consistency :*** Accounting practices should not be changed or must remain unchanged over a period of several years . For example , if straight line method is followed to write off depression, same method is to be followed for several years to come to work out depreciation.

(iii) ***Disclosure :*** This conversion speaks about presenting every vital information through the financial statements without concealing any fact/piece of information.

(iv) ***Materiality :*** The term 'materiality ' refers to the material facts capable of influencing decisions .As per this convention only the material or important facts about the commercial activities are to be presented through *the financial statements.*

7.3 Classification of Accounts

An account is a summary of the relevant transactions at one place relating to a particular head. The accounts are classified in to three groups viz., Personal accounts , Real accounts and Nominal accounts.

(i) ***Personal accounts :*** These accounts related to natural persons , artificial persons and representative persons. For example, Ram account, Ram and company account, Outstanding salary account etc.

(ii) ***Real accounts :*** These accounts relate to the tangible or intangible real assets. For example , Machinery ,Goodwill etc.

(iii) ***Nominal accounts :*** These accounts relate to expenses, Losses, Profits and gains .For example, purchases account, Salaries account, Loss by fire account, Sales account, Discount received account.

Double entry system

According to this concept "Every debit has its corresponding credit".

The most scientific system of accounting is double entry system .According to this system both the aspects of a transaction, viz., benefit giving and benefit receiving , are recorded in the books of accounts. These aspects may relate to Personal, Real, and Nominal Accounts.

7.3.1 Golden Rules of Debit and Credit

The various aspects of a transaction, depending upon their nature, are accounted for as debit or credit as follows.

Types of accounts (to which the aspects belong to)	Rules for Debit	Rules for .Credit
(a) For personal accounts	Debit the receiver	Credit the giver
(b) For Real Accounts	Debit what comes in	Credit what goes out
(c) For Nominal Accounts	Debit all expenses and losses	Credit all gains and profits.

7.3.2 Books of Account

The books used in book-keeping are mainly of two types.The following chart illustrates it more clearly.

Table 7.1 Books of account

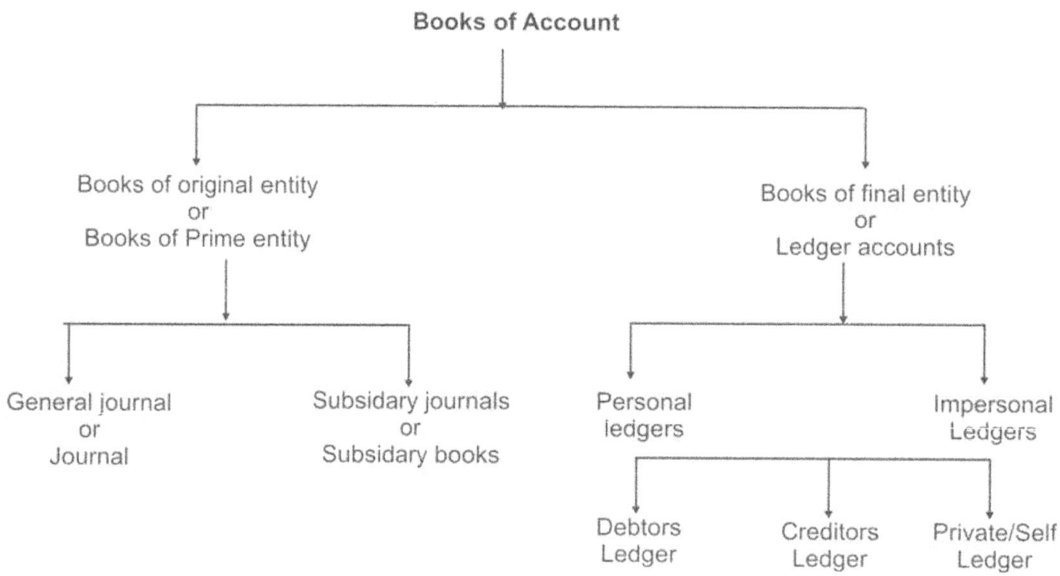

7.4 Journal

In the double entry system of book keeping both the aspects of the transaction the receiving aspect and giving aspect are recorded. Every business transaction affects two accounts. One account receives the benefit of the transaction and the other gives the benefit of the transaction. The transaction so recorded that the entry is made in both the accounts.

Journal is a daily record. It is a book of original entry in which all transactions are recorded in the form of entries.

For running any business, a trader requires (i) persons from whom he purchases goods and to whom he sells goods and (ii) goods intended for resale and some other assets such as furniture, machinery etc. Further in the course of his business, he has to incur some expenditure, for example, rent, wages to workers, salaries to office staff, insurance, stationery etc. It is clear form the above that the accounts maintained by him must relate to all the above categories. The accounts maintained by a trader are therefore of the following types.

(i) ***Personal Accounts :*** Personal accounts are those account, which relate to persons or firms with whom the trader deals.

Ex : Rama account; Kumar account; Venkat & Co, Indian Bank account; Insurance company account etc.

(ii) ***Impersonal accounts :*** Accounts which do not relate to persons, but which affect the business in general are called impersonal accounts. These impersonal accounts further divided into two types 1. Real Accounts, 2. Nominal Accounts.

1. ***Real Accounts :*** Real accounts are also called as property or Assets Accounts. These accounts are impersonal, tangible (i.e. things that can be touched) and visible (i.e. those which can be seen).

   Ex : Goods account, Furniture account, Machinery account, Instruments account, Plant account, Goodwill account, Patent rights account. These assets may be those in which the trader deals or they may be those with the help of which he conducts his business.

2. ***Nominal Accounts :*** These accounts are also called as Fictious Accounts. Nominal account relate to expenses or losses or gains or profits.

   Ex : Wages account, Salaries account, Rent account, Discount account, Commission account etc.

Now every transaction necessarily affects two accounts. Each one of these two accounts falls into one of the above three categories. One of these three accounts receives the benefit, and the other gives the benefit of the transaction. The account, which receives the benefit of the transaction, must be debited; i.e. the entry must be made on the debit side of the account. The account which gives the benefit of the transaction must be credited i.e. the entry must be made on the credit side of the account.

7.4.1 Form of the account

An account is defined as "a summarized statement of day to day transactions. It is divided into two halves, the left hand side and the right hand side. The left hand side is called debit side (Dr.side) and the right hand side is called credit side. (Cr. Side). When an account is to be debited the entry is made on the debit side, when it is to be credited the entry is made on the credit side, The form of an account is as follows.

Dr. Account Cr.

Date	Particulars	L.F.	Amount	Date	Particulars	L.F.	Amount

7.4.2 Rules of Debit and Credit

Whether an account has to be debited or credited has to be decided with reference to the following rules.

1. ***Personal Accounts :*** In the case of personal accounts the rule is debit the receiver and Credit the giver.
2. ***Nominal Accounts :*** In the case of Nominal Accounts the rule is Debit all expenses and losses and Credit all incomes and gains.

The following examples if carefully studied by the student will enable him to find out how the above rules are to be applied.

(i) ***Sold goods for Cash Rs. 18000-/***

The two accounts affected here are the goods account and cash account. Both are real accounts. Since cash is coming in cash account must be debited and since goods are going out, goods account must be credited.

(ii) ***Purchased furniture for cash Rs. 12000-/***

The two accounts affected here are the furniture account and cash account. Both are real accounts. Since furniture is coming in, Furniture account must be debited and since the cash is going out, cash account must be credited.

(iii) ***Sold goods for cash Rs. 1700-/***

This is a cash transaction and it is immaterial whether goods are sold to X or Y, or Z. The two accounts affected here are goods account and cash account. Both are real accounts. Since cash is coming in, cash account must be debited. Since goods are going out goods account must be credited.

(iv) ***Purchased goods for cash rs. 12000-/***

The two accounts affected here are goods account and cash account. Both are real accounts. Since goods are coming in, goods account must be debited. Since cash is going out cash account must be credited.

(v) ***Purchase goods form M Rs. 15000-/.***

The two accounts affected here are goods account and M's account. Goods account is a real account, since goods are coming in goods account must be debited. M's account is a personal account. Since M is giving the benefit of the transaction M's account must be credited.

(vi) ***Bought goods from Narayana on Credit of Rs. 12500-/.***

The two accounts affected here are goods account and Narayana's account. Goods account is real account. Since goods are coming in goods account must be debited. Narayana's account is a personal account. Since Narayana is giving the benefit of the transaction Narayana's account must be credited.

(vii) ***Received from Mohan Rs. 18000/- on account***

The two accounts affected here are cash account and Mohan's account. Cash account is a Real account. Since cash is coming in Cash account must be debited. Mohan's account is a personal account. Since Mohan is giving the benefit of the transaction, Mohan's account must be credited.

(viii) ***Paid to 'Z' Rs. 1200/- on account.***

The two accounts affected here are Z's account and cash account. R's account is a personal account. Since Z is receiving the benefit his account must be debited. Cash is a real account. Since cash is going out, cash account must be credited.

(ix) ***Paid Rent to Land Lord Rs. 1300/-.***

The two accounts affected here are Rent account and Cash account. Since Rent is an item of expenditure, rent account must be debited; since cash is being paid (going), cash account must be credited.

(x) ***Paid wages Rs. 1115/-.***

The two accounts affected here are wages account and cash account. Since wages are an item of expenditure, wages account must be debited. Sine cash is being paid (going) cash account must be credited.

(xi) ***Paid Interest on Loan Rs. 1100/-***

The two accounts affected here are Interest account and Cash account. Since Interest is an item of expenditure it must be debited. Since cash is going out, cash account must be credited.

(xii) ***Received Interest Rs. 1200/-***

The two accounts affected here are cash account and Interest account. Since cash is coming in cash account must be debited. Since interest is an item or Income it must be credited.

(xiii) ***Paid Rs. 1500/- into bank from office cash.***

The two accounts affected here are Bank account and cash account. Bank account is a real account. Since the Bank account is receiving the benefit, Bank account must be debited. Cash is a real account. Since cash is going out from the business it must be credited.

(xiv) ***Withdrawn form bank for office use Rs. 1100/-.***

The two accounts affected here are cash account and Bank account. Cash account is a real account. Since cash is coming in, cash account must be debited. Bank account is a personal account. Since the Bank account is giving the benefit it must be credited.

(xv) ***Paid 'Y' the Manager, his salary Rs. 1400/-.***

The two accounts affected here are the salaries account and cash account. The personal account of Y is not at all affected because the payment is made to him or services rendered. As such the transaction does not create any obligation on the part of Y to return the amount to the trader. Hence entry need not be made in Y's personal account. Cash account is a Real account. Salaries account is a Nominal account. Since salary in an item of expenditure this account must be debited. Since cash is going out, it must be credited.

From the above examples, the student must have seen that in case of every transaction one account is debited and another account is credited.

Every transaction must be recorded in the Journal i.e. a book of original entry. In the Journal the transactions are entered in the order in which they occur. Journal means a daily record. The following is the ruling of Journal:

Journal

Date of the transaction	Particulars of the transaction	Ledger Folio	Amount to be debited Rs.	Amount to be credited Rs.

In the first column the date of the transaction is entered. In the Second column the names of the two accounts, which the transaction affect, are entered. In the third column the number of the page in the ledger to which the entry is finally transferred or posted is entered. The fourth and fifth columns are used to record the amounts to be debited and credited.

Illustration No. 1

Journalise the following transactions in the books of Vasu.

2000	**Rs.**	
Jan.	1 Started business with cash	40,000
"	2. Purchased goods for cash	18,000
"	3. Sold goods for cash	17,000
"	5. Received cash from Mohan	11,000
"	8. Cash paid to Mohan	1,500
"	11. Purchased goods from Y	14,000
"	14. Goods sold to Z	16,000

Before entering the transactions in a Journal, students are advised first analyse them to decide the accounts to be debited or credited.

With the help of the last column of the analysis table we can now write the Journal as under.

Journal of Vasu

Date	Particulars		L.F.	Debit Rs.	Credit Rs.
2000 Jan 1	Cash account To Capital a/c (Being cash invested to start the business)	Dr.		40,000	40,000
2	Purchases a/c To Cash a/c (Being goods puchased for cash)	Dr.		18,000	18,000
3.	Cash a/c To sale account (Being goods sold for cash)	Dr.		17,000	17,000
5.	Cash a/c To Mohan's a/c (Being cash received from Mohan)	Dr.		11,000	11,000
8.	Mohan's a/c To Cash a/c (Being cash paid to Mohan)	Dr.		1,500	1,500
11.	Purchases a/c To Y's a/c (Being goods purchased from Y)	Dr.		14,000	14,000
14.	Z's a/c To sales a/c (Being goods sold to z)	Dr.		16,000	16,000

Analysis of Transactions

Date	Nature of transaction	Two accounts involved	Types of accounts	How each aspect is effected	Rules of entry	Accounts to be debited or credited	
2000	Step I	Step II	Step III	Step IV	Step V		
Jan. 1	Cash received from Vasu, the proprietor	Cash	Real	Cash come in	debit what comes in	Cash a/c.	
	of the business as Capital	Capital	Personal	Vasu is giver	Credit the giver	Capital a/c.	
" 2	Cash purchases of goods	Goods	Real	goods comes	debit what	goods a/c.	
		Cash	Real	Cash goes goesout	Credit what goesout		Cash a/c.
" 3	Cash received for sale of goods	Cash	Real	Cash comes in	debit what comes in	Cash a/c.	
		Goods	Real	goods goes Out	Credit what goes out		goods a/c.
" 5	Cash received from Mohan	Cash A/c.	Real	Cash comes in	debit what comes in	Cash a/c.	
		Mohan's A/c.	Personal	Mohan is the giver	Credit the giver		Mohan a/c.
" 8	Cash paid to Mohan	Mohan's A/c.	Personal	Mohan is the receiver	Debit the receiver	Mohan a/c.	
		Cash A/c.	Real	Cash goes Out	Credit what goes out		Cash a/c.
" 11	Goods Purchased from Y	Goods A/c.	Real	goods comes in	Debit what come in	goods a/c.	
		Y's A/c.	Personal	Y is the giver	Credit the giver		Y's a/c.
" 14	Goods sold	Z's A/c	Personal receiver	Z is the receiver	Debit the receiver	Z's a/c.	
		Goods	Real	goods goes out	Credit what goes out		goods a/c.

Illustration No. 2

Journalise the following transaction in the books of Sagar.

2002

March 1 Started business with Rs. 4,000 in cash
" 3 Bought goods from Prasad Rs. 3,271.
" 6 Sold goods to Hari Krishna Rs. 1,293.
" 9 Cash sales Rs. 372.
" 12 Sold goods to Babulal Rs. 631.
" 15 Paid to Prasad on Account Rs. 1,500.
" 18 Paid Salary to Manager Rs. 500.
" 29 Office rent paid to Land Lord Kumar Rs. 400.

Journal entries is the books of Sagar

Date	Particulars		L.F.	Debit Rs.	Credit Rs.
2002 Jan. 1	Cash a/c. To Capital a/c (Being cash invested to start the business)	Dr.		4,000	4,000
3	Purchases a/c To Prasad a/c (Being goods purchased for credit)	Dr.		3,271	3,271
6	Hari Krishna a/c To sales account (Being goods sold for credit)	Dr.		1,293	1,293
9	Cash a/c To sales a/c (Being goods sold for cash)	Dr.		372	372
12	Babulal a/c To sales a/c (Being goods sold on credit)	Dr.		631	631
15	Prasad a/c To Cash a/c (Being cash paid on a/c)	Dr.		1,500	1,500
18	Salary a/c To Cash a/c (Being salary paid)	Dr.		500	500
29	Rent a/c To Cash a/c (Being rent paid)	Dr.		400	400

Illustration No. 3

Journalise the following transactions in the books of Srinadh.

2001			Rs.
Jan.	1	Srinadh commenced business with cash	20,000
"	2	Purchased goods form Ramu for	15,000
"	3	Purchased goods for cash	500
"	3	Cash paid to Gopal on account	1,075
"	4	Received cash form Murthy	1,500
"	5	Purchased office furniture for office use	400
"	6	Wages paid	200
"	7	Paid cash to Kumar	250
"	9	Discount received	100
"	10	Postage 50	
"	13	Goods returned to Ramu 100	
"	16	Goods sold to Johnson5,000	
"	19	Goods returned by Johnson 145	
"	24	Paid for stationery 100	
"	25	Paid into Bank 400	
"	27	Goods sold for cash 250	
"	28	Bought goods from Prasad for cash 1,000	
"	29	Withdrawn from Bank 100	
"	31	Draw for Personal use 200	
"	31	Paid rent 200	

Journal entries in the books of Srinadh

Date	Particulars	L.F.	Debit Rs.	Credit Rs.
2001 Jan. 1	Cash a/c. Dr. To Capital a/c (Being cash invested to start the business)		20,000	20,000
2.	Purchases a/c Dr. To Ramu a/c (Being goods purchased on credit)		15,000	15,000
3	Purchases a/c Dr. To cash account (Being goods Purchased for cash)		500	500

Table Contd...

Date	Particulars		L.F.	Debit Rs.	Credit Rs.
3	Gopal a/c To Cash a/c (Being cash paid on a/c)	Dr.		1,075	1,075
4	Cash a/c To Murthy a/c (Being cash received)	Dr.		1,500	1,500
5	Office furniture a/c To Cash a/c (Being office furniture purcased)	Dr.		400	400
6	Wages a/c. To Cash a/c (Being wages paid)	Dr.		200	200
7	Kumar a/c To Cash a/c (Being cash paid on a/c)	Dr.		250	250
9	Cash a/c To Discount a/c (Being discount received)	Dr.		100	
10	Postage a/c To Cash a/c (Being postage paid)	Dr.		50	50
13	Ramu a/c To Purchase Returns a/c (Being goods returned)	Dr.		100	100
16	Johnson a/c. To sales a/c (Being goods sold on credit)	Dr.		5,000	5,000
19	Sales return a/c To Johnson a/c (Being goods returned for credit)	Dr.		145	145
24	Stationery a/c To Cash account (Being cash paid to stationery)	Dr.		100	100
25	Bank a/c To Cash a/c (Being cash paid into Bank)	Dr.		400	400

Date	Particulars		L.F.	Debit Rs.	Credit Rs.
27	Cash a/c To sales a/c (Being goods sold for cash)	Dr.		250	250
28	Purchases a/c To Cash a/c (Being goods bought for cash)	Dr.		1,000	1,000
29	Cash a/c To Bank a/c (Being cash drawn from Bank)	Dr.		100	100
31	Drawing's a/c To Cash a/c (Being cash drawn for personal use)	Dr.		200	200
31	Rent a/c To Cash a/c (Being rent paid)	Dr.		200	200

In recording the transactions in the Journal the following points must be kept in mind:

1. The transactions must be recorded in the Journal in the order of date i.e. in the cronological order.
2. In deciding which account is to be debited and which account is to be credited the rules of debit and credit must be carefully followed. It must be remembered that rules never vary.
3. In particulars column of the Journal the names of the two accounts affected must be entered. Debit aspect will be written in the first line and the credit aspect will be written in the second line.
4. The letters 'Dr' must be written after the name of the account to be debited.
5. Every entry in the Journal must be followed by a brief description of the transaction called 'narration'. Narration provided us with a record of the details of the transaction, which can be used in future for reference.
6. The letters of 'Rs' must be written at the top of the amount columns.

EXERCISES

Exercise No. 1

What do you understand by (a) a personal account (b) a Real account and (c) a nominal account? Determine the nature of the following accounts.

1. Machinery account.
2. Prasad account.
3. Bank account.

4. Cash account.
5. Rent account.
6. Outstanding expenses account.
7. Insurance account.
8. Prepaid expenses account.
9. Audit fee account.
10. Postage account.
11. Drawings account.
12. Capital account.
13. Advertisement account.
14. Stationery account.
15. Commission account.
16. Landlord's account.
17. Salaries account.

***Exercise No.* 2**

Fill up the blanks by placing against each of the following item, the correct nature of accounts (Personal, Real or Nominal).

1. Prasad's account is a ___________
2. Goods is a ________________
3. Machinery is a _____________
4. Drawings is a _____________
5. Cash is a ______________
6. Stock of goods is a ___________
7. Rent is a ____________
8. Commission is a ______________
9. Trade expenses is a __________
10. Buildings is a ____________
11. Repairs is a ____________
12. Interest is a _____________

***Exercise No.* 3**

Journalise the following transactions.

2000			Rs.
Mar.	1.	K commenced business with	40,000
	3.	Purchased goods for cash	17,500

4.	Purchased goods for cash from Raju	1,000
6.	Goods sold to Deepthi	8,000
7.	Bought goods from R.K.P. Sharma	10,000
13.	Goods returned to R.K.P. Sharma	100
15.	Sold goods for cash	6,000
16.	Sold goods for cash to X	500
17.	Paid Cash to Govind & Co., on account	1,000
24.	Received cash from Nalini on account	1,000
27.	Sold goods to Murali	750
29.	Received cash from Murali on account	200
31.	Paid Rent to Land Lord postage	100

***Exercise No.* 4**

On being asked by a Asst. Professor, one student submits the following list of accounts duly arranged under three heads listed below. Do you agree with him? If not give a revised list.

Nominal Account	Real Account	Personal Account
Discount Account	Capital Account	Debtors Account
Machinery Account	Bank Account	Creditors Account
Furniture Account	Loose Tools a/c.	Purchase a/c.
Mohan's account	Rent Account	
Bank Overdraft a/c.	Stationery Account	
Cash Account	Goodwill Account	
Drawings	Account	

7.5 Ledger

We have studied in the earlier chapter how entries are recorded in the Journal and the rules that are to be followed for passing entries in the Journal.

A number of transactions take place daily in a business. All these transactions are entered in the Journal in a chronological order. Transactions relating to particular account may take place in different dates and hence they are entered in different pages of the Journal. By referring to the Journal, it will not be possible to find out the position relating to any particular account on a given date. To overcome this, the necessity arises, for classifying the various transactions relating to a particular account to one place. Posting them into Ledger does this.

Ledger is the chief book of accounts in which all the accounts of personal, properties, expenses and gains are kept, to which the entries made in the Journal are transferred. Ledger contains classified summary of the transactions, which are recorded in the Journal.

Personal accounts will reveal the amounts that the businessman owes or has to pay to his creditors and amounts he has to recover from his debtors. Real accounts reveal his assets. The nominal accounts will reveal the sources of his income and expenditure incurred by him to rum the business.

The accounts, which receive the benefit of the transaction, must be debited and accounts, which give the benefit of the transactions, must be credited.

Dr. **Form of Ledger Account** **Cr.**

Date	Particulars	L.F.	Amount (Rs)	Date	Particulars	L.F.	Amount (Rs)

We have already studied that every accounts is divided into two equal parts by drawing a thick vertical line in the center. The left hand side is called debit side and the right hand side is called credit side. On each side there will be four columns to record date, particulars, ledger folio and amount.

7.5.1 Steps in ledger posting

1. ***Date column :*** Write here the date of the transaction as noted in Journal.
2. ***Particulars column :*** Every entry on the debit side of this column must begin with the word 'To' and on credit side with the word 'By'.
   - **(i)** On the debit side of the account after the word 'To' write "Name of the Credit Part of the Journal entry.
   - **(ii)** On the credit side of the account, after the word 'By' write 'Name of the Debit Part of the Journal entry'.
3. ***Ledger Folio column :*** Write here the page number of the Journal from where the entry is posted.
4. ***Amount Column :*** Write here the amounts of the transaction. The amount in the debit column of the Journal is entered on the debit side. The amount in the credit column of the Journal is entered on the credit side.

Illustration No. I

Enter the following transactions in the Journal of Kumar Swamy and post them into ledger accounts.

1999			Rs.
March	1.	Commenced Business with cash	28,000
	2.	Bought goods for cash	18,000
	3.	Paid Wages	200
	5.	Paid for stationery	100
	8.	Purchased goods from Rama	16,000
	9.	Goods returned to Rama	1,500
	11.	Goods sold to Bhaskar	4,000
	13.	Received cash from Bhanu on account	4,000
	16.	Cash paid to Tarun	1,000
	18.	Purchased goods from Sharma	4,000
	21.	Cash paid into Bank	3,000
	24.	Kumar withdraw for personal use	1,250
	31.	Paid office rent	200
	31.	Paid Salaries	400

Journal entries is the books of Kumar Swamy

Date	Particulars	L.F.	Debit Rs.	Credit Rs.
1999 Mar.1	Cash a/c. To Capital a/c Dr. (Being cash invested to start the business)		48,000	48,000
2	Purchases a/c Dr. To Cash a/c (Being goods purchased for cash)		18,000	18,000
3	Wages a/c Dr. To Cash account (Being wages paid)		200	200
5	Stationery a/c Dr. To Cash a/c (Being cash paid to stationery a/c)		100	100
8	Purchases a/c Dr. To Rama's a/c (Being goods purchased from Rama)		16,000	16,000
9	Rama a/c Dr. To Purchases returns a/c (Being goods returned to Rama)		1,500	1,500

Table Contd...

Date	Particulars	L.F.	Debit Rs.	Credit Rs.
11	Bhaskar a/c Dr. To Sales a/c (Being goods sold to Bhaskar)		4,000	4,000
13	Cash a/c Dr. To Bhanu a/c (Being cash received from Bhanu a/c)		4,000	4,000
16	Tarun a/c Dr. To Cash a/c (Being Cash paid to Tarun)		1,000	1,000
18	Purchases a/c Dr. To Sharma a/c (Being goods purchased)		4,000	4,000
21	Bank a/c Dr. To Cash a/c (Being goods returned)		3,000	3,000
24	Drawing's account Dr. To Cash a/c (Being Cash withdrawn personal use)		1,250	1,250
31	Rent a/c Dr. To Cash a/c (Being Rent paid)		200	200
31	Salaries account Dr. To Cash a/c (Being salaries paid)		400	400

Dr. **Cash Account** **Cr.**

Date	Particulars	L.F.	Amount	Date	Particulars	L.F.	Amount
1999			Rs.	1999			Rs.
Mar. 1	To			Mar. 2	By Purchases a/c		18,000
	Capital a/c		28,000	3	" Wages a/c		200
13	" Bhanu a/c		4,000	5	" Stationery a/c		100
				16	" Tarun a/c		1,000
				21	" Bank a/c		3,000
				24	" Drawings		1,250
				31	" Rent a/c		200
				31	" Salaries a/c		400

Table Contd...

Dr. **Capital Account** Cr.

Date	Particulars	L.F.	Amount (Rs)	Date	Particulars	L.F.	Amount (Rs)
				1999			
				Mar.	By Cash a/c		48,000

Dr. **Purchase Account** Cr.

Date	Particulars	L.F.	Amount (Rs)	Date	Particulars	L.F.	Amount (Rs)
1999				1999			
Mar.2	To Cash a/c		18,000				
8	"Rama a/c		16,000				
18	"Sharma a/c		4,000				

Dr. **Sales A/C** Cr.

Date	Particulars	L.F.	Amount (Rs)	Date	Particulars	L.F.	Amount (Rs)
				1999			
				Mar.9	By Rama a/c		1,500
				Mar.9	By Bhaskar a/c		4,000

Dr. **Wages Account** Cr.

Date	Particulars	L.F.	Amount (Rs)	Date	Particulars	L.F.	Amount (Rs)
1999							
Mar.3	To Cash a/c		200				

Dr. **Stationary Account** Cr.

Date	Particulars	L.F.	Amount (Rs)	Date	Particulars	L.F.	Amount (Rs)
1999							
Mar.5	To Cash a/c		100				

Dr. **Rama Account** Cr.

Date	Particulars	L.F.	Amount (Rs)	Date	Particulars	L.F.	Amount (Rs)
1999	Sales			1999			
Mar.9	To a/c		1,500	Mar.8	By Purchase A/c		16,000

Dr. **Bhaskar Account** Cr.

Date	Particulars	L.F.	Amount (Rs)	Date	Particulars	L.F.	Amount (Rs)
1999							
Mar. 11	To Sale a/c		4,000				

Table Contd...

Dr. **Bhanu Account** Cr.

Date	Particulars	L.F.	Amount (Rs)	Date	Particulars	L.F.	Amount (Rs)
				1999			
				Mar. 18	By Cash a/c		4,000

Dr. **Tarun Account** Cr.

Date	Particulars	L.F.	Amount (Rs)	Date	Particulars	L.F.	Amount (Rs)
1999							
Mar. 16	To Cash a/c		1,000				

Dr. **Sharma Account** Cr.

Date	Particulars	L.F.	Amount (Rs)	Date	Particulars	L.F.	Amount (Rs)
				1999			
				Mar. 18	By Purchases a/c		4,000

Dr. **Bank Account** Cr.

Date	Particulars	L.F.	Amount (Rs)	Date	Particulars	L.F.	Amount (Rs)
1999							
Mar. 21	To Cash a/c		3,000				

Dr. **Drawings Account** Cr.

Date	Particulars	L.F.	Amount (Rs)	Date	Particulars	L.F.	Amount (Rs)
1999							
Mar. 24	To Cash a/c		250				

Dr. **Rent Account** Cr.

Date	Particulars	L.F.	Amount (Rs)	Date	Particulars	L.F.	Amount (Rs)
1999							
Mar. 31	To Cash a/c		200				

Table Contd...

Dr. **Salaries Account** Cr.

Date	Particulars	L.F.	Amount (Rs)	Date	Particulars	L.F.	Amount (Rs)
1999							
Mar. 31	To Cash a/c		400				

7.5.2 Balancing of Accounts

We have studied earlier that an account is debited whenever it receives the benefit of the transaction and credited when ever it yields the benefit of the transaction. On any given date the total of the benefits on the debit side may not be equal to the total of the credit side. Some times the debit side of the account may show heavier balance than the credit side total. Similarly sometimes the credit side of the account may show heavier balance than the debit side total. The difference between the two sides of the account is called 'balance'. It is said to show a debit balance if the debit side is heavier than the credit side; it is said to show a credit balance if the credit side is heavier than the debit side. The process of calculating the debit or credit balance of a particular account on a given date is known as 'Balancing the account' or striking balance'. Balancing of Accounts helps the trader to know the position of accounts at any time.

7.5.3 Procedure to be followed for balancing of Accounts

While balancing an account, follow the procedure given below for easy understanding.

1. Take up the totals of both the sides of the account on a rough sheet.
2. Calculate the difference between the bigger total and the smaller total again on rough sheet. The difference is called 'Balance'.
3. Write the above balance as a last column on the side, having a smaller total. The date should be the last date of the period.
4. Write 'To balance carried down' (c/d) in the particulars column if the balance is written on the debit side; Write 'By balance carried down' (c/d) in the particulars column if the balance is written on the credit side.
5. Write the total of each side in the account. These totals, which are now similar, must be noted on both the sides of the account on equal line, i.e., on the same horizontal line on both the sides.
6. The amount recorded as a closing balance should be brought down as the opening balance at the beginning of the next day. Please keep in mind that if the brought down balance (b/d) (opening) is not written after next day of the closing day, the balancing is incomplete.

The following illustration illustrate the above rules.

Illustration No. 2

Enter the following transactions in Prabhakar's account and bring down the debit balance or credit balance as the case may be.

2000			Rs.
April	1.	Sold goods to Prabhakar	13,000
	2.	Purchased goods from Prabhakar	6,000
	3.	Paid cash to Prabhakar	3,000
	14.	Received cash from Prabhakar	2,000
	30.	Sold goods to Prabhakar	1,000

Ledger

Dr. **Prabhakar Account** Cr.

Date	Particulars	L.F.	Amount	Date	Particulars	L.F.	Amount
2000			Rs.	1999			Rs.
Apr. 1	To Sales a/c		13,000	Apr. 2	By Purchases a/c		6,000
3	" Cash a/c		3,000	14	" Cash a/c		2,000
30	" Sales a/c		1,000	30	"Balance c/d		9,000
			17,000				17,000
June. 1	To Balance b/d		9,000				

Illustration No. 3

On 1-1-2001 a trader has the following opening balances. Stock Rs. 27,000; furniture Rs. 24,000; Buildings Rs. 1,14,000; Sundry debtors Rs. 12,000; Cash on hand Rs. 10,000; Cash at Bank Rs. 12,500; Sundry Creditors Rs. 33,000; Bills payable Rs. 11,500; Capital Rs. 2,16,000.

Give the necessary opening entry and post in the ledger.

Journal entry

Date	Particulars		L.F.	Debit Rs.	Credit Rs.
2001					
Jan.1	Stock a/c.	Dr.		27,000	
	Furniture a/c	Dr.		24,000	
	Buildings a/c	Dr.		1,14,000	
	Sundry debtors a/c	Dr.		12,000	

Date	Particulars		L.F.	Debit Rs.	Credit Rs.
	Cash a/c	Dr.		10,000	
	Bank a/c	Dr.		12,500	
	To Sundry Creditors a/c			33,000	
	To Bills Payable a/c				11,500
	To Capital a/c				216,000
	(Being the entry to bring into account the opening balances)				

Ledger

Dr. **Stock Account** **Cr.**

Date	Particulars	L.F.	Amount (Rs)	Date	Particulars	L.F.	Amount (Rs)
2001							
Jan. 1	To balance b/d		27,000				

Dr. **Furniture Account** **Cr.**

Date	Particulars	L.F.	Amount (Rs)	Date	Particulars	L.F.	Amount (Rs)
2001							
Jan. 1	To balance b/d		24,000				

Dr. **Building Account** **Cr.**

Date	Particulars	L.F.	Amount (Rs)	Date	Particulars	L.F.	Amount (Rs)
2001							
Jan. 1	To balance b/d		14,000				

Dr. **Sundry Debtors Account** **Cr.**

Date	Particulars	L.F.	Amount (Rs)	Date	Particulars	L.F.	Amount (Rs)
2001							
Jan. 1	To balance b/d		12,000				

Dr. **Cash Account** Cr.

Date	Particulars	L.F.	Amount (Rs)	Date	Particulars	L.F.	Amount (Rs)
2001							
Jan. 1	To balance b/d		10,000				

Dr. **Bank Account** Cr.

Date	Particulars	L.F.	Amount (Rs)	Date	Particulars	L.F.	Amount (Rs)
2001							
Jan. 1	To balance b/d		12,500				

Dr. **Sundry Creditors Account** Cr.

Date	Particulars	L.F.	Amount (Rs)	Date	Particulars	L.F.	Amount (Rs)
				2001			
				Jan. 1	By balance b/d		33,000

Dr. **Bills Payable Account** Cr.

Date	Particulars	L.F.	Amount (Rs)	Date	Particulars	L.F.	Amount (Rs)
				2001			
				Jan. 1	By balance b/d		11,500

Dr. **Capital Account** Cr.

Date	Particulars	L.F.	Amount (Rs)	Date	Particulars	L.F.	Amount (Rs)
				2001			
				Jan. 1	By balance b/d		26,000

Significance of debit and credit balances

Personal account : If the personal account shows a debit balance, it means that the person under consideration has received more benefit than what he has given and thereby he is a debtor to the trader. On the other hand, if a personal account shows a credit balance, it indicates that he has given more benefit to the trader than what he has received and as such he is a creditor to the trader. Thus by balancing the personal accounts one can ascertain the total debtors and total creditors.

Real accounts : Furniture, Machinery, Land and Buildings, Cash are some of the examples of real accounts. Real accounts always show a debit balance. Very rarely Real accounts show credit balance. If they are sold for a higher price than the purchase price, they may show credit balances. If the asset account shows a credit balance it represents profit on sale of asset. Such profit on sale of asset should be transferred to profit and loss account.

(i) ***Cash account :*** This account is intended to record all the cash transactions. Cash account is a real account and it is debited whenever cash comes in and it is credited whenever cash goes out. The cash account always shows a debit balance and never a credit balance, because it is not possible to spend more cash than he has received. This account is always closed by balance, the balance indicating the cash on hand.

Nominal accounts : If a nominal account shows a debit balance it indicates an expense or loss to the business. If the nominal account shows a credit balance, it indicates a gain or profit to he business, one of the objects of Bookkeeping is to find out whether the trader has made profit or loss. For achieving this, the trader has to prepare profit and loss account. The nominal accounts also must be transferred to the profit and loss account, which then shows the net profit or loss of the trader during a period. Transfer to profit and loss account closes the nominal accounts.

Capital account : The position of the trader in relation to the business is shown by his personal account. When a trader commences his business with certain amount of cash, cash account is debited and his personal account is credited. Personal account always shows a credit balance except when the trader has withdrawn more cash than the capital he has invested.

Drawings account : The trader may take goods or cash from his business for his personal use. In such cases the drawings account is debited and the cash account or the goods account is credited. At the end of the financial period, drawings account is closed by transfer to the capital account.

Exercise No. 1

Journalise the following transactions and post them into the ledger. Also balance the accounts.

2000			Rs.
Jan.	1	Mohan commenced business with a capital of	80,000
	4	Goods purchased from Krishna on credit for	24,000
	5	Goods purchased for cash	6,000
	6	Paid Wages	2,000

17	Goods sold to Swamy	14,000
18	Goods sold for cash	13,000
21	Cash paid to X on account	2,000
31	Paid salaries	4,000

Exercise No. 2

Journalise the following transactions of Prasad. Post them into ledger and Balance the accounts on 31-3-2002.

2002			Rs.
Mar,	1	Prasad commenced business with	48,000
	3	Goods purchased form Sagar Agencies	9,000
	8	Purchased goods for cash	6,000
	11	Bought goods from Murthy & Co.,	4,000
	13	Goods returned to Sagar Agencies	1,000
	15	Paid brokerage	100
	17	Paid cash for purchase of office furniture	300
	18	Paid sager on account	5,000
	20	Goods sold to Nagini & Co.,	8,000
	21	Received cash on account from Nagini & Co.,	4,000
	24	Goods returned by Nagini & Co.,	250
	25	Bought stationary	330
	28	Cash sales	350
	29	Paid into Bank	1,000
	30	Withdrew from Bank	250
	31	Paid Rent	300
	31	Paid salaries by cheque	500
	31	Received commission	300

1. Prepare Journal in the books of Rao & Co., from the following transactions.

Date 2000	Particulars	Amount Rs.
Apr 1	Started business with capital	1,00,000
Apr 5	Paid into bank	50,000
Apr 8	Purchased goods for cash	15,000
Apr 9	Paid to Shyam	5,000
	Discount allowed by him	1,000

Table Contd...

Date 2000	Particulars	Amount Rs.
Apr 10	Cash sales	5,000
Apr 11	Sold to Krishna for cash	15,00
Apr 12	Purchased goods from Shyam	2,500
Apr 13	Paid wages to workers	10,000
Apr 20	Received from Pankaj allowed him discount Rs.50	2,000
Apr 21	Withdrawn form bank	4,000
Apr 23	Paid Shyam by cheque	3,000
Apr 30	Withdrawn for personal use.	1,000

Solution :

Date 2000	Particulars		L.F.	Debit Rs.	Credit Rs.
2000					
Apr. 1	Cash a/c	Dr.		100,000	
	To Capital a/c				100,000
	(Being business started with capital)				
5	Bank a/c	Dr.		50,000	
	To Cash a/c				50,000
	(Being cash paid into bank)				
8	Purchases a/c	Dr.		15,000	
	To Cash account				15,000
	(Being goods Purchased for cash)				
9	Shyam a/c	Dr.		6,000	
	To Cash a/c				5,000
	To Discount received a/c				1,000
	(Being cash paid to Shyam a/c)				
10	Cash a/c	Dr.		5,000	
	To Sales a/c				5,000
	(Being goods sold for cash)				
11	Cash a/c	Dr.		15,000	
	To Sales a/c				15,000
	(Being goods sold for cash)				
12	Purchases a/c	Dr.		2,500	
	To Shyam a/c				2,500
	(Being goods purchased from Shyam)				

Table Contd...

Date 2000	Particulars		L.F.	Debit Rs.	Credit Rs.
13	Wages a/c	Dr.		10,000	
	To Cash a/c				10,000
	(Being Wages paid)				
20	Cash a/c	Dr.		2,000	
	Discount allowed a/c			50	
	To Pankaj a/c				2,050
	(Being cash received from Pankaj)				
21	Cash a/c	Dr.		4,000	
	To Bank a/c				4,000
	(Being cash withdrawn form bank)				
23	Shyam a/c	Dr.		3,000	
	To Bank a/c				3,000
	(Being with drawn for personal use)				
30	Drawings a/c	Dr.		1,000	
	To Bank a/c				1,000
	(Being withdrawn for personal use)				

2. Journalise the following transactions done in year 2001.

Date 2001	Particulars	Amount Rs.
Nov 1	Commenced business with cash	15,000
Nov 2	Paid into bank	8,000
Nov 3	Bought goods for cash	5,00
Nov 4	Bought furniture for office use by cheque	5,00
Nov 10	Withdrawn form bank for office use	900
Nov 13	Goods sold to Paul	1,000
Nov 15	Bought goods from Ram	1,000
Nov 18	Paid trade expenses	500
Nov 19	Received cash from Paul & allowed discount of Rs. 10	500
Nov 25	Paid wages	100
Nov 28	Paid Ram in full settlement of received discount of Rs. 10	700
Nov 30	Paid Interest on capital	700
Nov 30	Paid rent	300

Table Contd...

Solution:

Date 2000	Particulars	L.F.	Debit Rs.	Credit Rs.
Nov.1	Cash a/c Dr. To Capital a/c (Being business started with capital)		15,000	 15,000
2	Bank a/c Dr. To Cash a/c (Being cash paid into bank)		8,000	 8,000
3	Purchases a/c Dr. To Cash account (Being goods Purchased for cash)		500	 500
4	Furniture a/c Dr. To Bank a/c (Being cash paid to Ram & Discount a/c)		500	 500
10	Cash a/c Dr. To Bank a/c (Being cash withdrawn form bank for office)		900	 900
13	Paul a/c Dr. To Sales a/c (Being goods sold to Paul on credit)		1000	 1000
15	Purchases a/c Dr. To Ram a/c (Being goods purchased form Ram on credit)		1000	 1000
18	Trade expenses a/c Dr. To Cash a/c (Being trade expenses paid in cash)		500	 500
19	Cash a/c Dr. Discount allowed a/c To Paul a/c (Being cash received from Paul)		500 10	 510
25	Wages a/c Dr. To Cash a/c (Being Wages paid in cash)		100	 100
28	Ram a/c Dr. To Cash a/c To Discount received a/c (Being cash paid to Ram and discount received)		710	 700 10
30	Interest on capital a/c Dr. To Cash a/c (Being interest on capital paid in cash)		700	 700
30	Rent a/c Dr. To Cash a/c (Being rent paid)		300	 300

Table Contd...

3. Pass necessary journal entries for the following transactions and post them in appropriate ledger accounts of srinivas in the year 1998.

Date	Particular
Mar 1	Started business with Rs. 2,50,000 bank balance and Rs. 40,000 with cash.
Mar 1	Bought shop fitting Rs. 40,000 and Vans Rs. 50,000 both paid by cheque.
Mar 2	Paid rent by cheque Rs. 5,000
Mar 3	Bought goods for resale on credit from Zaheer & co Rs. 50,500
Mar 5	Cash sales Rs. 5,000
Mar 8	Paid wages of assistant in cash Rs. 1,500
Mar 10	Paid insurance by cheque Rs. 500
Mar 12	Cash sales Rs. 8,500
Mar 15	Paid wages of assistant in cash Rs. 1,000
Mar 17	Paid Zaheer & co Rs. 35,000 by cheque
Mar 19	Bought goods for resale on credit from Rao & Co. Rs. 30,000
Mar 19	Cash sales Rs. 8,000
Mar 22	Paid wages of assistant in cash Rs. 1,500
Mar 24	Bought stationary paid in cash Rs. 1,000
Mar 25	Cash sales Rs. 15,000
Mar 27	Paid Rao & Co. Rs. 14,500 by cheque
Mar 29	Paid wages of assistant in cash Rs. 2,000
Mar 31	Paid Rs. 20,000 into the bank.

Solution :

Date 2000	Particulars		L.F.	Debit Rs.	Credit Rs.
Mar.1	Bank a/c	Dr.		2,50,000	
	Cash a/c	Dr.		40,000	
	To Capital a/c				2,90,000
	(Being business started with capital)				
1	Furniture & fitting a/c	Dr.		40,000	
	Van a/c			50,000	
	To Cash a/c				90,000
	(Being the purchase of fitting and van)				
2	Rent a/c	Dr.		5,000	
	To Bank account				5,000
	(Being rent paid by cheque)				
3	Purchases a/c	Dr.		50,500	
	To Zaheer & Co. a/c				50,500
	(Being Goods purchased on credit)				

Table Contd...

Date 2000	Particulars		L.F.	Debit Rs.	Credit Rs.
5	Cash a/c	Dr.		5,000	
	To Sales a/c				5,000
	(Being Goods sold for cash)				
8	Wages a/c	Dr.		1,500	
	To Cash a/c				1,500
	(Being wages paid to assistant)				
10	Insurance a/c	Dr.		500	
	To Bank a/c				500
	(Being insurance paid by cheque)				
18	Trade expenses a/c	Dr.		500	
	To Cash a/c				500
	(Being trade expenses paid in cash)				
12	Cash a/c	Dr.		8,500	
	To Sales a/c				8,500
	(Being goods sold for cash)				
15	Wages a/c	Dr.		1,000	
	To Cash a/c				1,000
	(Being Wages paid in cash)				
17	Zaheer & Co. a/c	Dr.		35,000	
	To Bank a/c				35,000
	(Being paid by cheque)				
Mar 19	Purchase a/c	Dr.		30,000	
	To Rao & Co a/c				30,000
	(Being goods purchased on credit)				
19	Cash a/c	Dr.		8,000	
	To Sales a/c				8,000
	(Being goods sold for cash)				
22	Wages a/c	Dr.		1,500	
	To Cash account				1,500
	(Being wages paid to assistant)				
24	Stationary a/c	Dr.		1,000	
	To Cash a/c				1,000
	(Being purchases of stationary)				
25	Cash a/c	Dr.		15,000	
	To Sales a/c				15,000
	(Being goods sold for cash)				

Table Contd...

Date 2000	Particulars	L.F.	Debit Rs.	Credit Rs.
27	Rao & Co. a/c Dr.		14,500	
	To Bank a/c			14,500
	(Being paid by cheque)			
29	Wages a/c Dr.		2,000	
	To Cash a/c			2,000
	(Being wages to assistant paid in cash)			
31	Bank a/c Dr.		20,000	
	To Cash a/c			20,000
	(Being Cash paid into bank)			

Ledger Accounts in the Books of Srinivas

Dr. Cash account Cr.

Date	Particulars	L.F.	Amount (Rs)	Date	Particulars	L.F.	Amount (Rs)
Mar 1	To Capital a/c		40,000	Mar 8	By Wages a/c		1,500
Mar 5	To Sales a/c		5,000	Mar 15	By Wages a/c		1,000
Mar 12	To sales a/c		8,500	Mar 22	By Wages a/c		1,500
Mar 19	To Sales a/c		8,000	Mar 24	By stationary		1,000
Mar 25	To sales a/c		15,000	Mar 29	By Wages a/c		2,000
				Mar 31	By Bank a/c		20,000
				Mar 31	By Balance c/d		49,500
Total			**76,500**		**Total**		**76,500**
Apr. 1	To balance b/d		49,500				

Dr. Bank Account Cr.

Date	Particulars	L.F.	Amount (Rs)	Date	Particulars	L.F.	Amount (Rs)
Mar 1	To capital a/c		2,50,000	Mar 1	By furniture & fittings a/c		40,000
Mar 31	To cash a/c		20,000		By van a/c		50,000
Mar 2	By rent a/c		5,000				
Mar 10	By insurance a/c		500				
Mar 17	By Zaheer & co		35,000				
Mar 27	By Rao & Co a/c		14,500				
Mar 31	By balance c/d		1,25,000				
Total			**2,70,000**		**Total**		**2,70,000**
Apr. 1	To balance b/d		1,25,000				

Capital a/c

Date	Particulars	L.F.	Amount (Rs)	Date	Particulars	L.F.	Amount (Rs)
Mar 31	To balance c/d		2,90,000	Mar 1	By bank a/c		2,50,000
				Mar 1	By cash a/c		40,000
	Total		2,90,000		Total		2,90,000
				Mar 2	By balance b/d		2,90,000

Furniture Account

Date	Particulars	L.F.	Amount (Rs)	Date	Particulars	L.F.	Amount (Rs)
Mar. 1	To Bank a/c		40,000	Mar 31	By Balance c/d		40,000
	Total		40,000				40,000
Mar 1	To balance b/d		40,000				

Van Account

Date	Particulars	L.F.	Amount (Rs)	Date	Particulars	L.F.	Amount (Rs)
Mar. 1	To Bank a/c		50,000	Mar31	By balance c/d		50,000
	Total		50,000		Total		50,000
Mar.1	To balance b/d		50,000				

Rent Account

Date	Particulars	L.F.	Amount (Rs)	Date	Particulars	L.F.	Amount (Rs)
Mar. 2	To Bank a/c		5,000	Mar 31	By balance c/d		5,000
	Total		5,000		Total		5,000
	To balance b/d		5,000				

Purchase Account

Date	Particulars	L.F.	Amount (Rs)	Date	Particulars	L.F.	Amount (Rs)
Mar.3	To Zaheer a/c		50,500	Mar31	By balance c/d		80,500
Mar 19	To Rao & Co. a/c		30,000				
	Total		80,500		Total		80,500
	To balance b/d		80,500				

Sales Account

Date	Particulars	L.F.	Amount (Rs)	Date	Particulars	L.F.	Amount (Rs)
	To Balance c/d		36,500	Mar 5	By Cash a/c		5,000
				Mar 12	By cash a/c		8,500
				Mar 19	By cash a/c		8,000
				Mar 25	BY cash a/c		15,000
	Total		36,500		Total		36,500
					By balance b/d		36,500

Table Contd...

Dr. — Wages Account — Cr.

Date	Particulars	L.F.	Amount (Rs)	Date	Particulars	L.F.	Amount (Rs)
Mar 8	To cash a/c		1,500	Mar 5	By Balance c/d		6,000
Mar 15	To cash a/c		1,000				
Mar 22	To cash a/c		1,500				
Mar 29	To cash a/c		2,000				
	Total		6,000		Total		6,000
	To balance b/d		6,000				

Dr. — Zaheer & Co. a/c — Cr.

Date	Particulars	L.F.	Amount (Rs)	Date	Particulars	L.F.	Amount (Rs)
Mar 17	To Bank a/c		35,000	Jan 5	By Purchases a/c		50,500
	To Balance b/d		15,500				50,500
	Total		50,500	Total	By balance c/d		15,500

Dr. — Insurance — Cr.

Date	Particulars	L.F.	Amount (Rs)	Date	Particulars	L.F.	Amount (Rs)
Mar 10	To Bank a/c		500		By Balance c/d		500
	Total		500		Total		500
	To balance b/d		500				

Dr. — Rao & Co., a/c — Cr.

Date	Particulars	L.F.	Amount (Rs)	Date	Particulars	L.F.	Amount (Rs)
Mar 15	To bank a/c		14,500	Mar 19	By Purchases		30,000
	To balance c/d		15,500				
	Total		30,000		Total		30,000
					By balance b/d		15,500

Dr. — Stationary a/c — Cr.

Date	Particulars	L.F.	Amount (Rs)	Date	Particulars	L.F.	Amount (Rs)
Mar 24	To cash a/c		1,000	Mar 15	By balance c/d		1,000
	Total		1,000		Total		1,000
	To balance b/d		1,000				

Table Contd...

4. Prepare a trial balance for the month ending 31st August 2001

	Rs.
Cash a/c	50,500
Madhu capital a/c	30,000
Interest from bank	3,000
Discount (credit)	250
Sales	35,000
David a/c	3,000
Purchase returns a/c	500
Bank a/c	10,000
Rent a/c	2,500
Salaries a/c	500
Entertainment expenses	150
Purchase a/c	2,000
Sales returns a/c	100

Solution

LF	Particulars	Debit Rs.	Credit Rs.
	Cash a/c	50,500	—
	Madhu capital a/c	—	30,000
	Interest form bank	—	3,000
	Discount	—	250
	Sales	—	35,000
	David a/c	3,000	—
	Purchase returns a/c	—	500
	Bank a/c	10,000	—
	Rent a/c	2,500	—
	Salaries a/c	500	—
	Entertainment expenses	150	—
	Purchase a/c	2,000	—
	Sales returns	100	—
		68,750	68,750

5. Prepare trial balance as on 31st Dec 1998.

	Rs.
Purchases	43,000
Sales	72,500
Insurance premium	510
Drawings	6280

Plant and machinery	4500
Commission paid	1070
Opening stock	11,200
Repairs	880
Returns inwards (sales returns)	1,000
Discount allowed	1,150
Rent paid	3,000
Returns outwards (purchase returns)	400
Investments	2,500
Creditors	14,260
Debtors	1,430
Traveling expenses	2,850
Salaries	33,540
Cash at bank	1,090
Fire wood	1,770
Capital	30,000
Carriage	240
Bad debts	690
Petty expenses	460

Solution :

LF	Particulars	Debit Rs.	Credit Rs.
	Purchases	43,000	—
	Sales	—	72,500
	Insurance premium	510	—
	Drawings	6,280	—
	Plant and machinery	4,500	—
	Commission paid	1,070	—
	Opening stock	11,200	—
	Repairs	880	—
	Return in wards	1,000	—
	Discount allowed	1,150	—
	Rent paid	3,000	—
	Return outwards	—	400
	Investments	2,500	—
	Creditors	—	14,260
	Debtors	1,430	—

Table Contd...

LF	Particulars	Debit	Credit
	Traveling expenses	2,850	—
	Salaries	33,540	—
	Cash at bank	1,090	—
	Fire wood	1,770	—
	Capital	—	30,000
	Carriage	240	—
	Bad debts	690	—
	Petty expenses	460	—
	Total	1,17,160	1,17,160

7.6 Cash Book

There will be a large number of cash transactions in every business. Examples of cash transactions are cash purchases; cash sales; receipts from debtors; payments to creditors; payments to entry arise in any business, big or small, they are recorded in a 'Cash account book'. Cash book guides the trader to know regularly the bank or cash balance on hand. Cashbook enables the trader to see all the cash transactions recorded in one place in a classified form.

Cashbook is one among the subsidiary book. It is used to record the cash receipts and cash payments. The Ruling of the cashbook is quite different of the rulings of other subsidiary books. Cashbook resembles the ruling of an 'account'. Just like an account, it has two sides, the left hand side and the right hand side. Left hand side of the cash look is known as Debit side, and right hand side of the cashbook is known as Credit side. All cash receipts are recorded on the debit side and all cash payments are recorded on the credit side of the cashbook. The difference between two sides of the cashbook indicates 'balance'. Cashbook always shows a debit balance.

It can be found from the above cashbook ruling that each side of the cashbook is in divided into four columns.

Latest trends

Now a day's most of the modern business houses are maintaining separate books for cash receipts and payments. They are called Receipts book and Payments book.

Dual Purpose

Cashbook resembles the ruling of an 'account'. Cashbook acts as Journal as well as ledger. Hence it is stated that "the cash book is both a book of principal entry i.e. subsidiary Journal and a book of final entry i.e. ledger.

In case of other subsidiary books, every transaction is posted in the subsidiary book and later it will be posted into the ledger. But such procedure is not followed is case of cash book.

Once transactions are posted in the cashbook, need not again be posted in separate cash account in the ledger. *"The cash book thus fulfils the functions of a ledger account and a Journal"*. Cashbook minimizes labour in Journalising as well as in posting of the cash transactions.

7.6.1 Types of Cash Books

There are three kinds of cashbooks,

1. Simple or Single column cashbook.
2. Double column cash book i.e. Cashbook with cash and discount columns, cashbook with Cash and Bank columns.
3. Three column cashbook i.e. cash book with cash. Discount and bank columns.

7.6.2 Simple Cash Book

In the simple cashbook, only transactions pertaining to cash are recorded. Simple cashbook contains only one-amount columns representing cash at office. Opening cash balance plus cash receipts recorded in debit side of the cash book must be equal to the cash payments and closing balance recorded on the credit side.

Illustration No. I

Enter the following transactions in a cashbook and balance it.

1985			Rs.
March	1	Balance on hand	4735
	4	Received from Muralidhar	6000
	5	Goods purchased for cash	2000
	6	Goods sold for cash	1500
	13	Cash sales	400
	18	Paid to Singh	1000
	20	Paid to Sridhar	200
	24	Paid advertisement	100
	26	Remitted to Mohan	400
	28	Draw for personal use	300
	31	Paid office rent	415
	31	Received form Zail singh	400

Cash Book

Date	Particulars	L.F.	Amount	Date	Particulars	L.F.	Amount
			Rs.				Rs.
1985				1985			
Mar				Mar			
1	To balance b/d		4,735	5	By Purchases		2,000
4	To Muralidhar		6,000	18	By Singh a/c		1,000
6	To Sales a/c		1,500	20	By Sridhar a/c		200
13	To Sales a/c		400	21	By Advertise -ment a/c		100
31	To Zail Singh		400	26	By Mohan		400
				28	By Drawings		300
				31	By Rent a/c		415
				31	By Balance c/d		8,620
			13,035				13,035
Apr.							
1	To Balance b/d		8,620				

7.6.3 Double Column Cash Book

(With Cash and Discount Columns)

This cashbook is simply an extension of the simple or ordinary cashbook. Under this method an additional column is provided both on debit side and credit side for recording discount allowed and discount received. The discount column on the debit side of this type of cashbook is meant for recording discount received.

Discount is of two types. 1. Cash discount and 2. Trade discount.

Cash Discount : It is defined as an allowance made by the receiver of cash to the payer to the payer for prompt payment.

Similarly if he purchases goods on credit, his suppliers may be prepared to give some discount or allowance if he makes payment within the time prescribed by the suppliers. So, if the terms of purchase so stipulates he receive cash discount for prompt payment.

It is clear that cash discount allowed by the trader represents loss to the trader; cash discount received by him represents gain to the trader. It is also clear that cash discount allowed or received arises only when cash is received or paid. Since cash received or cash paid recorded in cash book, it will be convenient to record the discount allowed or discount received in the cashbook itself by extending one more column on debit side and credit side. Debit side of the cashbook is used to record discount allowed. Similarly the discount column on the credit side of the cashbook is used to record the discount received.

Trade discount : Trade discount is quite different form cash discount. Trade discount is an allowance made by the manufacturers or wholesale dealers to the retail dealers in the trade, off the catalogue price or Invoice price of goods sold. The main idea behind providing the trade discount is to enable the retail trader to sell the goods at catalogue price by keeping some margin to meet his business expenses and profit. Trade discount is out rightly deducted from the catalogue or list price and the balance is recorded in the books of accounts. Therefore there is no entry made for trade discount in the books of the retailer. Trade discount never appears in the books of account. The amount of trade discount allowed varies according to the nature of the business and nature of the articles.

7.6.4 Three Column Cash Book

(Cash book with Cash, discount and Bank columns)

Before studying the three-column cashbook with cash discount and Bank columns, we must know something about a Bank and Bank transactions. Now a days most of the traders usually opens a current Account with one of the banks in his locally. He deposits his surplus cash with his banker for reasons of safety account from time and can withdrew money by drawing cheques.

What is a Bank : A Bank is an Institution that receives deposits from its customers, repayable on demand by cheques. Banking company is one that does banking business. The bank attracts money on deposits and thereafter lends it to Industries or Trade. Banking regulations Act 1949 defines Banking as "the accepting, for the purpose of lending or Investment, of deposits of money from the public repayable on demand or otherwise and withdraw able by cheque, draft or otherwise.

Functions of the Bank : The main functions of a commercial bank are, (1) Receipt of deposits (2) Granting of loans and advances. In addition to these two primary functions, banks perform a number of other subsidiary functions.

Kinds of Deposits

Bank deposits may take any one of the following forms.

- **(a)** ***Fixed Deposits :*** These are the deposits kept with the bank for a fixed period. They are repayable after the expiry of a fixed period of time. The period ordinarily varies from three months to five years. Banks pay interest on these deposits at different rates depending on the term of the deposit. Bank allows loans on the security of these deposit receipts.
- **(b)** ***Current deposits :*** Current deposits are deposits, which are repayable on demand. These deposits are withdrawable on demand by means of cheques. In case of these deposits, the banker undertakes to honor his customer's cheques so long as the customer has sufficient funds belonging to him with the banker. Every customer has to keep a minimum balance in a current account. There are no restrictions on withdrawals as long as his balance permits such withdrawal. He can deposit and withdraw any number of times. Banks do not allow any interest on current deposits.

(c) ***Saving bank deposits :*** The main object of these deposits is to encourage thrift and habit of saving among the people. These deposits are usually for comparatively small amounts. A customer may deposit money any number of times. But the withdrawal of money is allowed twice a week. In case of more withdrawals than the prescribed limit a service change shall be levied at the scales prevailing for levying service charges on current account. These deposits carry a smaller rate of interest than the fixed deposits.

From of Bank advance

Bank advances may be in the form of loans, overdrafts and cash credits.

1. ***Loans :*** The money so collected by the banks through deposits is lent to producers and traders. Banks may give short-term loans and long-term loans. But generally banks prefer to give short-term loans because their deposits are mostly demand deposits, Loans may be granted with or without securities. Interest is charged on the entire amount of loan granted.
2. ***Overdrafts :*** Banks also extend overdraft facility to customers. A overdraft arrangement means that the bankers permits the customer to overdraw his account up to certain amount i.e. he can take out more money than he has put in his account by means of cheques. The bank charges interest on the amount actually withdrawn.
3. ***Cash Credits :*** These are just like overdrafts. The arrangement here is to allow the customer to borrow up to a certain limit prescribed by the bank against surety bond or securities. Interest is actually charged only on the amount actually borrowed.

7.6.5 Cheques

A customer can withdraw money form his current account by drawing cheques. A cheque is defined as "a bill of exchange drawn on a specified banker and not expressed to be payable otherwise than on demand". In other words it is a bill of exchange drawn on a Banker and payable on demand.

7.6.6 Petty Cash Book

In large business Houses all the cash received is deposited in the Bank and all payments are made by issue of cheques. In such cases it is necessary to leave some cash in the office separately to meet small payments like coolie, charges, carriages, carriage, postage, telegrams, stationery, etc. These payments involve petty amounts. Hence, it cannot be possible to issue cheques for every petty payment. The amount kept for petty payments is known as 'petty cash'. The person who handles the petty cash is called' petty cashier'. The book, in which the receipts and payment of petty cash are recorded, is known as "petty cash book". It must be noted that petty cash book is generally maintained when all cash transactions are passed through bank. However, some business concerns maintain petty cash account even though their cash transactions are not passed through the bank. They appoint petty cashier to look after petty payments in addition to a head cashier or chief cashier. Here the main idea behind appointing petty cashier is to reduce the burden of work of the Head cashier. Head cashier will look after receipts and payments involving big amounts. The petty cash book contains a number of columns to record the cash received periodically and the petty payments under different heads. The petty cash book becomes a necessary subsidiary book in all business concerns.

The petty cash book is maintained just like the cashbook. The advance received by the petty cashier from the Head cashier is recorded on the debit side of the petty cash book. All payments are recorded on the credit side. By balancing the petty cash account, one can know the petty cash on hand lying unspent with the petty cashier on any date.

Analytical petty cash book

Generally, the numbers of petty payments are numerous in large-scale business houses. The appropriate method of recording petty cash payments is to enter them in a petty cash book maintained in a columnar form. Under this method a separate column is provided to record each head of petty expense. A total column is also provided in this method. Every payment is entered in the concerned head of petty expense and in total column. All the payments made are analysed in the columns of petty cash book itself, under the different heads of expenses. Hence it is called Analytical petty cash book. By going through the Analytical petty cash book, one can know easily the total expenditure and the total expense under every head.

7.6.7 Types of petty cash

There are two types of petty cash books based on the pattern of the amount advanced to petty cashier.

1. Fixed advance system of petty cash, and
2. Imprest system of petty cash.

1. ***Fixed advance system of petty cash :*** Under this method the petty cashier is given a fixed sum of advance at the commencement of the period, which may be a week or fortnight or a month. Petty cashier makes payment from this advance. Irrespective of the amount spent by the petty cashier in the previous period, he gets the same amount of fixed advance from the Head cashier.
2. ***Imprest system of petty cash :*** This is considered to be the best system of petty cash book. Imprest means 'Money advanced on loan'. Under this system the management estimates the expenditure roughly for a period of week or month. Head Cashier or Chief Cashier will issue a cheque in favor of petty cashier to the extent of estimated amount to start with. Petty cashier makes payments and records the transactions in the petty cashbook, which has several columns for recording different items of expenditure. At the end of the period say a week or a month the petty cashier balances his book and gets it checked and initialed by the chief cashier as a token of its correctness. The Chief Cashier than advances him the amount, which he spent, so that the original amount of the petty cash with which he started is restored.

6. From the following information prepare cashbook.

Date 2001	Particulars	Amount Rs.
Jun 1	Hari started business	70,000
Jun 2	He deposited the cash in bank	25,000
Jun 3	Goods purchased	20,000
Jun 4	Goods sold	35,000
Jun 5	Furniture purchased	5,000
Jun 6	Goods purchased form Rama	15,000
Jun 10	Salary paid to staff	5,000
Jun 15	Goods sold to Shankar	10,000
Jun 20	Cash paid to Rama	12,000
Jun 22	Cash deposited n Bank	3,000
Jun 25	Cash received from Shankar	7,000
Jun 30	Rent paid	2,500
Jun 30	Telephone expenses paid	1,200
Jun 30	Electricity expenses paid	1,500

Cash Book

Date	Particulars	L.F.	Amount (Rs)	Date	Particulars	L.F.	Amount (Rs)
Jun 1	To Capital a/c		70,000	Jun 2	By Bank a/c		25,000
Jun 4	To Sales a/c		35,000	Jun 3	By Purchases		20,000
Jun 25	To Shankar a/c		7,000	Jun 5	By furniture		5,000
				Jun 10	By salary a/c		5,000
				Jun 20	By Rama a/c		12,000
				Jun 22	By Bank a/c		3,000
				Jun 30	By rent a/c		2,500
				Jun 30	By Telephone Expenses a/c		1,200
				Jun 30	By Electricity Expenses a/c		1,500
					By balance c/d		36,800
	Total		1,12,000	Total			1,12,000
	To balance b/d		36,800				

7. Enter the following transactions in a two-column cash book.

Date 2001	Particulars	Amount Rs.
Sep 1	Cash in hand	10,000
Sep 3	Bought goods for cash	4,500
Sep 5	Paid for wages	5,200
Sep 7	Withdraw form bank for expenses	8,000
Sep 7	Cash paid to younish	2,150
	Discount received	50
Sep 10	Cash sales	15,500
Sep 13	Received cash from Bharat	4,400
	Allowed him discount	100
Sep 15	Purchased stationary from Ram on credit	250
Sep 16	Paid for postage stamps	200
Sep 18	Amount introduced as capital	5,000
Sep 21	Received cash from Raj	7,900
	Allowed him discount	100
Sep 24	Paid cash for traveling expenses	120
Sep 26	Amount paid into bank	2,500
Sep 27	Cash paid to Mukesh	950
	Discount allowed by him	50
Sep 28	Credit purchases form Ali	3,100
Sep 30	Cash purchases	1,500
Sep 30	Paid salaries	2,800
Sep 30	Deposited into bank all cash in excess of	2,000

Two Column Cash Book

Date	Particulars	R.N	Discount	Cash (Rs)	Date	Particulars	V.N.L.F	Discount	Cash (Rs)
Sep 1	To balance b/d			10,000	Sep 3	By purchases			4,500
Sep 7	To Bank a/c			8,000	Sep 5	By wages a/c			5,200
Sep 10	To Sales a/c			15,500	Sep 7	By Younis a/c			2150
Sep 13	To Bharat a/c		100	4,400	Sep16	By Postage			200
Sep 18	To Capital a/c			5,000	Sep24	By Traveling expenses			120
Sep 21	To Raj		100	7,900	Sep26	By Bank a/c			2,500
					Sep27	By Mukesh		50	950
					Sep30	By Purchases			1,500
					Sep30	By Salaries			2,800
					Sep 30	By Bank a/c			28,880
			200	50,800		By balance c/d			2,000
				2000				100	50,800
	To balance b/d								28,880

Table Contd...

7.7 Subsidiary Books

Generally, most of the transactions are of repetitive type in the business (ex: cash receipts, cash payments, credit purchases; credit sales; cash purchases; credit purchases etc.,). Therefore transactions can be classified into different groups according to their nature. Generally transactions are of two types 1. cash transactions 2. Non-cash transactions.

Cash receipts and payments can be grouped into one category whereas credit purchases of goods can be grouped into another category and credit sale of goods is yet another class.

Thus in practice, Journal is sub-divided into several books to save time, labor and establishment cost and they are called subsidiary books or sub-division of Journal.

When cash transactions are more in any business it is very convenient to maintain a separate cashbook to record cash receipts and cash payments. Cash transactions are therefore not entered in the Journal but are directly entered in the Cashbook itself. The Cashbook is therefore a book of original entry in the sense that cash transactions are entered in the cashbook in the first instance in chronological order. A cashbook is therefore an extension of Journal. When Cashbook is maintained there is no need to maintain cash account in the ledger.

In additional to the above books, the Journal is maintained to record all the transactions that cannot be passed through any one of the above books.

Generally the following books in use in any modern business concern of big size.

1. The Cash book to record all cash receipts and payments.
2. The purchases book to record all credit purchases.
3. The sales book to record all credit sales.
4. The Returns outwards book (Purchase returns) to record all goods returned by us tour suppliers.
5. The returns inwards book (Sales returns) to record all good returned to us by our customers.
6. The Bills receivable book to record all bill drawn by us and received by us.
7. The Bills payable book to record all bills drawn by our creditors and accepted by us.
8. Journal proper to record all transactions that cannot be entered in ant one of the above books.

The advantages of sub-division of Journal may be summarized as follows.

1. ***Saving of time and clerical labor :*** Under sub-division of Journal, there is no need to pass Journal entries and write narrations in respect of entries in the special journals. Hence, saves a lot of time, clerical labor and stationery.
2. ***Division of labour :*** The division of Journal into several books, resulting in division of work, ensures more clerks working independently in recording business transactions. Division of labour also gives the advantage specialization leading to efficiency in maintaining of accounts.

3. ***Easy reference :***Since similar transactions are recorded in one place, reference is easier. It is very difficult to go through the entire Journal to locate an entry. But it is easier to go through an subsidiary books.
4. ***Effective Internal check :*** Sub-division of Journal helps the Management to introduce an effective system of Internal checks in the business. Since there are large number of transactions two or three auditors can be appointed at a time to audit the Accounts of the business.
5. ***Up-to-date maintenance of records and books :*** Under this system a good number of clerks can be appointed to handle subsidiary books. Independently it is easy for them to record transactions and furnish any information at any time. In addition this system helps the management to maintain up-to-date record and account books.
6. ***Quick Decisions :*** Sub-division of Journal provides up-to-date information to the Management on any aspect of the business. It helps the management to take quick decisions in the business when occasion demands.

Invoice

When goods are purchased on credit the supplier of goods (Creditor) sends the invoice to the trader either along with the goods or in advance. The invoice which is popularly known as bill, since the invoice gives us details of goods sent by the Creditor, the goods actually received must be checked up with quantities, sizes etc., shown in the invoice. The Invoice itself must be checked to see that the rates charged for the goods supplied are correct (by comparing with original order form) and that the calculations are correct. After thorough checking of invoice, particulars there in must be entered in the Purchase book. Afterwards all invoices must be properly filed and cash invoice is given a consecutive number for easy reference in future.

Discount

Discount is of two types namely cash discount and trade discount.

1. ***Cash Discount :*** It is offered by the Creditor to his debtor for prompt payment. Cash discount is recorded in the Cashbook. This topic is dealt in the chapter on Cashbook.
2. ***Trade discount :*** Trade discount is an allowance or deduction made in catalogue price or Invoice price or list price by the manufacturer or wholesaler to the retailer. The main object of allowing 'trade discount' is to enable the trader to sell the goods to the consumer at list price and still leaving some margin for meeting his trade expenses and his profit. Since trade discount is deducted in the Invoice itself. It does not appear in the books at all. Trade discount is offered to the trader with reference to the time limit within which supplier expects to receive the payment. Entries are to be made in the books of both the supplier as well as retailer on the basis of net amount i.e. Invoice price less discount.

7.7.1 Purchases Returns Book

This book also called 'Returns outwards book or Journal' when the trader purchase goods, he verifies whether they are in good condition and agree with the terms and conditions of the order we placed. If the goods received are defective in quality or damaged in transit or not up to the sample shown at the time of order placing, the trader will return such goods to the supplier. These returns are called as purchases returns, such returns to the suppliers will be entered in a separate book called 'Purchases returns book'. Allowances claimed for breakages, short weight, over-charge etc., also may be dealt with in the same book. This book is also known as 'Returns outwards book' as goods returned are going out of the business. When purchase returns are made to the suppliers, a 'debit note' will be set to them giving reference that their accounts are debited in the books of the trader to the extent of goods returned to them. This is because supplier's account is credited with the whole amount when goods are purchased.

Postings in Purchase Return book

Debit the personal Account of the supplier to whom goods are returned.

Credit the purchase returns account with the periodicals total.

Debit Note

Debit Note is a statement sent by the Purchaser to the seller giving particulars of the goods returned. It indicates the supplier that his account has been debited with the amount stated therein. Debit Notes are prepared in duplicate. Original copy is sent to the supplier to whom goods are returned and the duplicate copy will be retained by the trader for further reference.

7.7.2 Sales Book

This book is also known as "Sales day book", or 'Sales Journal', or 'Sales Register'. Sales book in maintained to record only credit sales of goods in which the trader deals. This book strictly prohibits recording of cash sales of goods and sale of property an assets whether for cash or on credit. Sale of any asset like Building or Machinery is entered in the Journal proper and not in the book. The ruling of the Sales book is similar to that of purchases book. The proforma of sales book is given below.

Date	Particulars	LF	Amount

On the basis of Invoices sent to buyers, the entries are to be made in the Sales book. The name of the person to whom goods are sold is recorded in the particulars column.

Posting form Sales Book

Just like purchases book, sales book is also totaled and closed periodically.

Separate accounts must be opened for every party to whom goods are sold and a sales account.

Debit Customer's account with the individual amount against their names.

Credit sales account with periodical total.

7.7.3 Sales Returns Book

This book is also known as 'Returns inwards book'. Just as we return goods to the suppliers, some times a trader may have to receive back some of the goods he might have sold to customers. Such returns by the customers are recorded in a special Journal meant for that purpose which is called 'Sales Returns Book'. When the customer makes sales returns to the trader, a note will be sent by the trader informing him that his account is credited in the books of the trader to the extent of goods returned by him. This is because of the fact that the customer's account is debited earlier with full amount when goods are sold to him.

Date	Particulars	L.F.	Credit Note Number	Amount Rs.

Just like other Journals, this Journal is also closed periodically and entries therein are posted to the ledger.

Debit sales returns account with the periodical total.

Credit Customer's account who has returned the goods with the individual amount.

Credit Notes

When the seller receives back goods from the Purchaser along with a 'Debit Note' confirming the acceptance of the debit note. In other words this is a statement sent by the seller to the purchaser after the receipt of the goods returned by purchaser. The following is the specimen of a Credit Note' sent by Maruthi Book Depot., Hyderabad, to Gupta Brothers of Visakhapatnam.

Hyderabad –1
25-4-2000

Messrs. Pavan Brothers,
Book Sellers and Distributors,
Visakhapatnam.
Credited by Messers Maruthi Book Depot., Guntur.

By Books returned
5 copies of Biotechnology
@ Rs. 40/- each

7.7.4 Bills Receivable Book

Sd./- Pavan Book Depot.,

When transactions relating to bills are numerous it is a common practice to maintain a separate Bills Receivable and bills payable books. Bills Receivable Book is maintained to record all the bills received from the debtors, by the trader. The following is the proforma of Bills Receivable Book.

Bills Receivable Book

Date	Date of Receipt of Bills	From whom Received	Term of Bills	Due Dare of Bills	Amount Rs.	Remarks

Bills Receivable Book is also, just like other books, periodically totaled and closed by posting. Entries therein are posted to the ledger as under.

Postings from Bills Receivable Book

Debit the bills receivable account with the periodical total shows by the Bills Receivable Books.

Credit the Individual accounts with the amounts of the bills as shown against their names in the Bills Receivable Book.

7.7.5 Journal Proper

Journal proper is used for recording only those transactions which cannot be recorded in any of other subsidiary books. Examples of such transactions are

1. Opening entries.
2. Transfer entries (Transfer from one account to another)
3. Closing entries.
4. Adjusting entries.
5. Entries related to rectification of errors.
6. Entries relating to dishonor of bills or promise nary notes.
7. Credit purchase and sale of assets.
8. Bad debts
9. Withdrawal of good by proprietor for personal use or loss of good by theft, fire etc.

Example : The position of Mr. Kalyan on 31st December 2001 was as follows:

Cash in hand Rs.1500, cashat bank Rs.3000, stock of the goods Rs.5000, Furniture Rs.7000, plant Rs.1500, Sundrydebtors Rs.8000, Sundry creditors Rs.3000,Bank loan (LT)Rs.8000. Record the above balance in the books of Kalyan on first January 2002.

7.8 Trial Balance

Trial balance is a *statement debit and credit balances of various accounts taken out from ledger books as on a particular date.* A trial balance must *agree as on that date.* It shows all delit balances are equal to credit balances. Preparation of Trial balance is an important prerequisite for the preparation of final accounts.

7.8.1 Significance

Trial balance is prepared to ensure that there are no arithmetic errors in the books of accounts. The trial balance must agree, as on a given date i.e., the total of debit balances must be equal to the total of credit balnaces. If it does not agree, that means there are certain arithmetical errors in the books of accounts. However, *mere agreement of a trial balance is not a conclusive proof of accuracy* of the books of accounts. There may be several errors in the books of accounts and still the trial balance may agree. In other words, trial balance cannot reveal all kinds of errors. It can reveal only arithmetical errors. If there are any errors as revealed by trial balance, they should be rectified and final accounts will be prepared only after rectification of errors. In case, the firms is unable to locate and rectify the errors by the date of preparation of final accounts, the difference in trial balance will be placed in account called *suspense account* and it will carried to the balance sheet.

7.8.2 Errors that Cannot be Revealed by the Trial Balance

The following are some of the errors that cannot be revealed by the trial balance:

(a) *Errors of Principle :* If the purchase of an asset, say machinery for Rs. 1,00,000 is posted to purchase account, it is an error of principle. In other words, if an asset is treated by mistake as an expense or vice versa, it is an error of principle.

(b) *Errors of complete omission of a transaction :* If purchase of goods worth Rs. 25,000/- is not recorded in purchases book, it is an error of complete omisssion of a transaction. There is no debit of Rs. 25,000 in purchase account and there is no corresponding credit for Rs. 25,000 in the supplier's account. The trial balance tallies in spite of this error.

(c) Posting on a correct side to a wrong account Instead of debiting Ram's account for Rs. 50,000, if the amount is wrongly debited to Raman's account, it is a case of posting a correct side to a wrong account. As long as there is debit and corresponding credit for theamount, the trial balance agrees.

(d) Recording a transaction in a wrong subsidiary journal : If sale of goods worth Rs. 25,000 to Y is recorded by mistake in purchases book, there will be debit in purchases account for Rs. 25,000 and a coresponding credit in Y's account for the amount and the trial balance agrees. But, the fact is that Y should be debited with Rs. 25,000 and sales should be credited with Rs. 25,000.

(e) Compensating errors one or more errors may compensate the other or several errors and in spite of all these errors, the trial balance may agree accidentally.

7.8.3 Errors that can be Disclosed by Trial Balance

(a) Errors in totalling the trial balance

(b) Posting in one account from the journal and omitting to post another account

(c) Posting to wrong side of account

(d) Totalling the ledger accounts wrongly

(e) Carrying forward to the next page of an account a wrong amount.

Preparation of Trial Balance

For preparing trilal balance, first of all, it should be understood, which are the accounts that goes under debit and credit balances.

7.8.4 Accounts showing debit balances

- Debtors accounts
- Asset accounts such as plant, furniture etc.
- Expenses accounts such as rent paid.
- Losses accounts such as goods destroyed in fire.
- Purchases accounts
- Sales returns account
- Drawings account.

7.8.5 The accounts show credit balances

- Creditors account
- Liabilities account
- Incomes account
- Gains account
- Profits accouns
- Loan account
- Bank overdraft account
- Sales account
- Purchase returns account

- Provision accounts such as provision for doubtful debts, provision for discount on debtors
- Reserves & funds accounts such as General Reserve or Reserve fund, Workmen's Compensation Fund etc.

7.9 Preparation of Final Accounts

It is a preparation of trading account, profit & loss account and balance sheet.

Before preparing final accounts, it is essential to understand the differences between capital and revenue items. Any incorrect allocation of capital and revenue items will disturb the accuracy of the final accounts. For instance, a computer bought for Rs. 40,000 and debited to office expenses account, is a case of error of principle. Asset bought cannot be shown under office expenses account as this amounts to showing capital expenditure as revenue expenditure, which is not correct.

Capital items may be capital expenditure or capital receipt.

7.9.1 Capital expenditure

Capital expenditure refers to that expenditure incurred to acquire a fixed asset used continuously in the business for the purpose of earning revenue. Any amount spent to increase the earning capacity of the asset is also called capital expenditure. The following are the examples of capital expenditure.

(a) cost of plant and machinery, buildings and other fixed assets

(b) cost of installation of such assets

(c) modifying extending or improving an existing fixed asset such as upgrading a production line or a computer

(d) enhance the earning capacity of the asset such as air conditioning an office

(e) acquiring the right to carry on business by paying good will or for patent

Capital expenditure is recorded on the assets side of balance sheet.

7.9.2 Capital receipt

Capital receipt is the amount received in the form of additional capital by issue of shares, loans or debentures or by the sale of fixed assets. Capital receipts are shown in balance sheet.

Revenue items may be revenue expenditure or revenue receipts. Revenue items are recorded in tradin and profit and loss account.

7.9.3 Revenue expenditure

Revenue expenditure refers to that expenditure which is incurred to maintain the earning capacity of the business in the normal course during the current period. In other words, the benefit of the revenue expenditure is utilised in that period itself. The following are the examples for revenue expenditure :

(a) expenditure on rent, wages, salaries, carriage, etc.
(b) interest on loan borrowed to carry out business.
(c) Cost of goods bought for resale.
(d) depreciation of fixed assets.
(e) all expenses incurred in the manufacturing, office, selling, and distribution departments of the business.
(f) loss of stock due to fire or for any other reason.
(g) discounts and allowances.

7.9.4 Deferred revenue expenditure

More often, the business firms spend huge amounts at the time of launching a product or service for research and development, advertising and so on. All this expenditure cannot be charged to the year in which it is incurred. Only a portion of such expenditure is charged every year to profit and loss account. The balance amount of such expenditure is called deferred revenue expenditure, also known as capitalised expenditure, and this is recorded in the balance sheet. Examples of deferred revenue expenditure include: preliminary expenses, underwriting commission, cost of issue bonds, huge advertisedment expenses, investments on research and development and so on.

7.9.5 Revenue receipts

Revenue receipts are the amounts received in the ordinary course of business. Amount received on sale of goods and commission/interest earned are the examples of revenue receipts. Besides, income earned through selling waste paper, packing cases, etc. also constitutes revenue receipt. Revenue receipts are shown in the trading and profit and loss account.

7.9.6 Final Accounts of Sole Proprietor

The process of preparing final accounts of sole proprietor is of two stages : (a) Trading Account and Profit and Loss Account and (b) Balance Sheet.

7.10 Format of Trading

Trading and profit and loss account shows the gross profit (or gross loss) and net profit (or net loss) respectively for the given accounting period. Trading and profit and loss account consists of two parts :

(a) Trading Account (b) Profit and Loss Acccount.

7.10.1 Trading Account

Trading account shows gross profit or gross loss for the end of a given accounting period. Gross profit or gross loss is the excess of sales revenue over the cost of goods sold.

Gross profit = Net sales - Cost of goods sold.

If the cost of goods sold is more than the sales revenue, it results in gross loss.

Items to be considered in trading account are :

(a) Opening stock

(b) purchases less purchase returns (returns outwards)

(c) wages

(d) carriage inwards

(e) fuel and power

(f) sales less sales returns

(g) any other direct expenses such as freight, spent on raw materials

(h) closing stock given as additional information (adjustments)

While preparing trading account for a manufacturing concern, consider only such factory expenses that increase the cost of goods manufactured, such as fuel and power, heating and lighting, etc. In other words, gross profit is arrived at after considering all factory expenses.

The format of trading account is as follows :

Trading Account of Mr. .... for the year ending ....

Dr.					*Cr.*
To opening stock		xxx	By sales	xxx	
			Less : sales returns	xxx	xxx
To Purchases	xxx		By closing stock		xxx
Less : purchase returns	xxx	xxx			
To wages		xxx			
To carriage inwards		xxx			
To fuel and power		xxx			
To direct expenses		xxx			
To gross profit (transferred to profit and loss account)		xxx			
		xxx			xxx

Note : salaries given in trial balance is not considered here. Salaries is office expense and hence it is transferred to profit and loss account. Trading account considers only expenses and receipts at the factory.

7.11 Format of Profit and Loss Account

Profit and Loss Account shows net profit or net loss for the end of a given period.

From the gross profit (or gross loss) transferred from trading account, deduct all expenses relating to office, selling and distribution departments. Add all non-operating income such as commission or rent received, interest received etc.

Profit and loss account considers only revenue expenditure such as those incurred in:

- maintaining the capital asset
- running business from time to time
- selling and distributing the goods of the business they deals in.

The details of expenses and incomes entered in profit and loss account are finished in the following format of profit and loss account: The format shows the accounting treatment also.

Profit and Loss Account of Mr. .... for the year ending....................

Dr			Cr
To salaries	xxx	By gross profit	xxx
To rent	xxx	By discount received	xxx
To insurance	xxx	By commission received	xxx
To carriage outwards	xxx	By reduction in provision for bad debts	xxx
To telephones	xxx	By profit on sale of fixed asset	xxx
To provision for depreciation	xxx		
To bad debts written off xxx			
Add: increase in bad debts xxx	xxx		
To cost of samples	xxx		
To advertising	xxx		
To heating and lighting	xxx		
To interest on loan	xxx		
To discount allowed	xxx		
To net profit transferred to capital account	xxx		
Total	xxx	Total	xxx

To put in this brief,

Net Profit = Gross Profit + Other Income – Expenses.

Here all expenses relating to office, selling and distribution are considered.

7.12 Format of Balance Sheet

Balance sheet is a statement of assets and liabilities of a business as on a given date. It shows a true and fair view of financial position of a business as on a given date.

Balance sheet is a statement. (It is not an account. Hence, it does not have debit side or credit side.) It has two sides: Liabilities side and Assets side. Balance sheet portays accounting equation where in Assets = Equity (owner's equity or capital and creditors' equity or outside liabilities). In other words, under double entry system, assects must always be equal to capital and liabilities.

Balance sheet of Mr.................... as on ....

Liabilities	*Rs*	*Rs*	*Assets*	*Rs*	*Rs*
Long-term liabilities:			**Fixed Assets**		
			Plant and machinery	xxx	xxx
Owner's capital	xxx		*Less:* Provision for	xxx	
Add: net profit from profit			depreciation		
and loss account					xxx
Less: drawings	xxx	xxx			
		xxx	Furniture and fixtures	xxx	
			Less: Provision for	xxx	
			depreciation		xxx
Current Liabilities :			**Current Assects :**		
Sundry creditors		xxx	Stock		xxx
Bills payable		xxx	Sundry debtors		
Bank overdraft			*Less:* provision for bad and	xxx	xxx
			doubtful debts		
Outstanding expenses		xxx	Bills receivables		xxx
			Cash at bank		xxx
			Cash in hand		xxx
			Prepaid expenses		xxx
		xxx	1		xxx

8. Prepare a trading a/c for the year 1995 31st March, from the following particulars.

Particulars	Amount (Rs)
Stock of goods on 1-4-1994	2,00,000
Stock of goods on 31-3-1995	4,50,000
Purchases – cash	3,90,000
Credit	8,25,000
Sales – cash	5,30,000
Credit	11,00,000
Returns to suppliers	25,000
Returns by costomers	30,000
Goods withdrawn by James or personal use	30,000
Goods distributed as free samples during the year	4,500
Duty and clearing charges	60,000

Solution :

Trading account of Mr. James for the year ended 31st March, 1995

Particulars	Rs.	Rs.	Particulars	Rs.	Rs.
To Opening stock		2,00,000	By sales-cash	5,30,000	
To purchases-cash	3,90,000		Credit	11,00,000	
Credit	8,25,000				
	12,15,000			16,30,000	
Less:			Less:		
Returns	25000		Returns by customers	30,000	16,00,000
Goods for personal	30000		By closing stock		4,50,000
Goods used for sample	4500				
	59,500	11,55,500			
To duty and clearing charges		60,000			
To gross profit c/d		8,34,500			
		20,50,000			20,50,000

9. From the following balances extracted at the close of year ended 31st March 1996, prepare profit and loss account.

Particulars	Amount (Rs)
Gross profit	50,000
Carriage outward	3,500
Salaries	6,000
Rent	1,000
Fire Insurance Premium	800
Bad debts	2,000
Commission received	1,500
Discount (Dr)	500
Apprentice premium (Cr)	2,000
Printing & Stationary	300
Rates & Taxes	350
Traveling expenses	500
Discount allowed by creditors	1,000
Sundry trade expenses	300

Solution :

Profit and loss a/c for the year ended 31st March 1996

Particulars	Amount (Rs)	Particulars	Amount (Rs)
To Carriage outward a/c	3500	By gross profit b/d	50000
To salaries a/c	6000	By apprentice premium a/c	2000
To rent a/c	1000	By Discount by creditors a/c	1000
To fire insurance premium a/c	800	By Commission a/c	1500
To Bad debts a/c	2000		
To Discount a/c	500		
To Printing and stationary a/c	300		
To Rent and taxes a/c	350		
To Traveling expenses a/c	500		
To Sundry trade expenses a/c	300		
To Net profit (transferred to capital a/c)	29,250		
	54,500		54,500

10. The trial balance of Chandu on 31-12-1996 revealed the following balances prepare balance sheet.

Debit Balances	Rs.	Credit Balances	Rs.
Sundry debtors	64000	Sales	2,65,000
Plant & machinery	1,54,000	Capital	1,00,000
Purchases	68000	Purchase returns	1275
Sales returns	1000	Discount received	800
Opening stock	30000	Creditors	25000
Discount allowed	350		
Bank charges	75		
Furniture	45,000		
Salaries	6800		
Wages	10000		
Carriage inwards	750		
Carriage outwards	1200		
Rates, rents, taxes	2000		
Advertisements	2000		
Cash at bank	6900		
	3,92,075		3,92,075

Adjustments

Closing stock 35,000

Notes : Closing stock given in the adjustment should be posted two times

(a) On credit side of trading a/c

(b) On the assets side of balance sheet.

Solution:

Trading & of Mr. Chandu for the year ended 31-Dec-1996

Debit	Rs.	Credit	Rs.
To opening stock	30,000	By sales 2,65,000	
To Purchases 68,000		(-) returns 1,000	2,64,000
(-) returns 1,275	66,725	By closing stock	35,000
To wages	10,000		
To Carriage inwards	750		
To Gross profit c/d	1,91,525		
	2,99,000		2,99,000

Table Contd...

Profit & Loss of Mr. Chandu for the year ended 31st Dec.1996.

Debit	Rs.	Credit	Rs.
To discount allowed	350	By gross profit b/d	1,91,525
To Bank charges	75	By discount received	800
To salaries	6,800		
To carriage outwards	1,200		
To rent, rate, taxes	2,000		
To advertisement	2,000		
To net profit	1,79,900		
	1,92,325		1,92,325

Balance Sheet as at 31-12-1996

Liabilities	Rs.	Rs.	Assets.	Rs.	Rs.
Capital	1,00,000		Sundry debtors		64,000
+ Net profit	1,79,900	2,79,900	Closing stock		1,54,000
Creditors		25,000	Furniture		45,000
			Plant and machinery		6,900
			Cash at bank		35,000
		3,04,900			3,04,900

12. From the following trial balance taken from the books of Ramana and company. Prepare trading and profit loss account for the year ended 31-12-2000 and a balance sheet as on that date.

Particulars	Debit	Credit
Drawing and capital	12,000	80,000
Opening stock	12,000	—
Investments	30,600	—
Salaries	12,000	—
Carriage	3,000	—
Returns	6,000	2600
Purchases & sales	1,20,000	1,60,000
Debtors & creditors	60,000	—
Discount allowed	2,200	—
Cash	16,400	—
Wages	28,000	—
Reserve for doubtful debts	—	2,000
Bank overdraft	—	25,000
Loans	2,400	10,000
	3,04,600	3,04,600

Adjustments

1. Closing stock was valued Rs. 1,20,000.
2. Wages & salaries were outstanding by Rs. 10,000 & Rs. 6,000.
3. Appreciate investments by 10%.
4. Maintain reserve for doubtful debts at the rate of 5% per anum.

Solution

Trading and profit loss a/c of Ramana & co. for the year ended 31st Dec.2000.

Particulars	Rs.	Rs.	Particulars	Rs.	Rs.
To opening stock		12,000	By sales	1,60,000	
To purchases	1,20,000		(-) returns	6,000	1,54,000
(-) returns	2,600	1,17,400	By closing stock		1,20,000
To carriage		3,000			
To wages	28,000				
(-) Outstanding wages	10,000	38,000			
To gross profit c/d		1,03,600			
		2,74,000			2,74,000
To salaries	12,000		By gross profit b/d		1,03,600
(+) Outstanding salaries	6,000	18,000	By appreciation on investments		3,060
To Doubtful debts		3,000	By reserve for doubtful debts		2,000
			(given in trail balance)		
To Net profit		85,460			
		1,08,660			1,08660

Balance sheet of Ramana & co as on 31st Dec.2000.

Capital	80,000		investments	30,600	
(+) Net profit	85,460		(+) Depreciation on investments	3,060	
	1,65,460				33,660
(-) Drawings	12,000	1,53,460	Loans (Dr)		2400
Outstanding salaries		6,000	Debtors	60,000	
Loans (Cr)		10,000	(-) Doubtful debtors	3,000	57,000
Creditors	25,000		Cash		16,400
Bank overdraft		25,000	Closing stock		1,20,000
		2,29,460			

Important Problems

1. Prepare Journal entries in the books of Rao & Co., from the following transactions.

Date 2001	Particulars	Amount Rs.
Apr 1	Started business with capital	1,00,000
Apr 5	Paid into bank	50,000
Apr 8	Purchased goods for cash	15,000
Apr 9	Paid to Shyam	5,000
Apr 9	Discounted allowed by him	1,000
Apr 10	Cash sales	5,000
Apr 11	Sold to Krishna for cash	1,500
Apr 12	Purchased goods from Shyam	2,500
Apr 13	Paid wages to workers	10,000
Apr 20	Received from Pankaj allowed him discount Rs.50	2,000
Apr 21	Withdrawn form bank	4,000
Apr 23	Paid Shyam by cheque	3,000
Apr 30	Withdrawn for personal use	1,000

Solution :

Journal entries in the Book of R90 & co.

Date 2000	Particulars		L.F.	Debit Rs.	Credit Rs.
Apr. 1	Cash a/c	Dr.		50,000	
	To Capital a/c				50,000
	(Being business started with capital)				
5	Bank a/c	Dr.		50,000	
	To Cash a/c				50,000
	(Being cash paid into bank)				
8	Purchases a/c	Dr.		15,000	
	To Cash account				15,000
	(Being goods Purchased for cash)				
9	Shyam a/c	Dr.		6,000	
	To Cash a/c				5,000
	To Discount received a/c				1,000
	(Being cash paid to Shyam a/c)				
10	Cash a/c	Dr.		5,000	
	To Sales a/c				5,000
	(Being goods sold for cash)				

Table Contd...

Date 2000	Particulars		L.F.	Debit Rs.	Credit Rs.
11	Cash a/c	Dr.		15,000	
	To Sales a/c				15,000
	(Being goods sold for cash)				
12	Purchases a/c	Dr.		2,500	
	To Shyam a/c				2,500
	(Being goods purchased from Shyam)				
13	Wages a/c	Dr.		10,000	
	To Cash a/c				10,000
	(Being Wages paid)				
20	Cash a/c	Dr.		2,000	
	Discount allowed a/c			50	
	To Pankaj a/c				2,050
	(Being cash received from Pankaj)				
21	Cash a/c	Dr.		4,000	
	To Bank a/c				4,000
	(Being cash withdrawn form bank)				
23	Shyam a/c	Dr.		3,000	
	To Bank a/c				3,000
	(Being with drawn for personal use)				
30	Drawings a/c	Dr.		1,000	
	To Bank a/c				1,000
	(Being withdrawn for personal use)				

2. Journalise the following transactions done in year 2001.

Date 2001	Particulars	Amount Rs.
Nov 1	Commenced business with cash	15,000
Nov 2	Paid into bank	8,000
Nov 3	Bought goods for cash	5,00
Nov 4	Bought furniture for office use by cheque	5,00
Nov 10	Withdrawn form bank for office use	900
Nov 13	Goods sold to Paul	1,000
Nov 15	Bought goods form Ram	1,000
Nov 18	Paid trade expenses	500
Nov 19	Received cash from Paul & allowed discount of Rs. 10	500
Nov 25	Paid wages	100
Nov 28	Paid Ram in full settlement	700
Nov 30	Interest on capital paid	990
Nov 30	paid rent	300

Solution :

Date 2000	Particulars	L.F.	Debit Rs.	Credit Rs.
Nov. 1	Cash a/c Dr.		15,000	
	To Capital a/c			15,000
	(Being business started with capital)			
2	Bank a/c Dr.		8,000	
	To Cash a/c			8,000
	(Being cash paid into bank)			
3	Purchases a/c Dr.		500	
	To Cash account			500
	(Being goods Purchased for cash)			
4	Furniture a/c Dr.		500	
	To Bank a/c			500
	(Being cash paid to Ram & Discount a/c)			
10	Cash a/c Dr.		900	
	To Bank a/c			900
	(Being cash withdrawn form bank for office)			
13	Paul a/c Dr.		1000	
	To Sales a/c			1000
	(Being goods sold to Paul on credit)			
15	Purchases a/c Dr.		1000	
	To Ram a/c			1000
	(Being goods purchased form Ram on credit)			
18	Trade expenses a/c Dr.		500	
	To Cash a/c			500
	(Being trade expenses paid in cash)			
19	Cash a/c Dr.		500	
	Discount allowed a/c		10	
	To Paul a/c			510
	(Being cash received from Paul)			
25	Wages a/c Dr.		100	
	To Cash a/c			100
	(Being Wages paid in cash)			
28	Ram a/c Dr.		1000	
	To Cash a/c			990
	To Discount received a/c			10
	(Being cash paid to Ram and discount received)			
30	Interest on capital a/c Dr.		700	
	To Cash a/c			700
	(Being interest on capital paid in cash)			

Date 2000	Particulars		L.F.	Debit Rs.	Credit Rs.
30	Rent a/c	Dr.		300	
	To Cash a/c				300
	(Being rent paid)				

3. Pass necessary journal entries for the following transactions and post them in appropriate ledger accounts of Srinivas in the year 1998.

Date	Particular
Mar 1	Started business with Rs. 2,50,000 in the bank and Rs. 40,000 with cash.
Mar 1	Bought shop fitting Rs. 40,000 and Vans Rs. 50,000 both paid by cheque.
Mar 2	Paid rent by cheque Rs. 5,000
Mar 3	Bought goods for resale on credit from Zaheer & co Rs. 50,500
Mar 5	Cash sales Rs. 5,000
Mar 8	Paid wages of assistant in cash Rs. 1,500
Mar 10	Paid insurance by cheque Rs. 500
Mar 12	Cash sales Rs. 8,500
Mar 15	Paid wages of assistant in cash Rs. 1,000
Mar 17	Paid Zaheer & co Rs. 35,000 by cheque
Mar 19	Bought goods for resale on credit from Rao & Co. Rs. 30,000
Mar 19	Cash sales Rs. 8,000
Mar 22	Paid wages of assistant in cash Rs. 1,500
Mar 24	Bought stationary paid in cash Rs. 1,000
Mar 25	Cash sales Rs. 15,000
Mar 27	Paid Rao & Co. Rs. 14,500 by cheque
Mar 29	Paid wages of assistant in cash Rs. 2,000
Mar 31	Paid Rs. 20,000 into the bank.

Solution :

Date 2000	Particulars		L.F.	Debit Rs.	Credit Rs.
Mar.1	Bank a/c	Dr.		2,50,000	
	Cash a/c	Dr.		40,000	
	To Capital a/c				2,90,000
	(Being business started with capital)				
1	Furniture & fitting a/c	Dr.		40,000	
	Van a/c			50,000	
	To Bank a/c				90,000
	(Being the purchase of fitting and van)				

Table Contd...

Date 2000	Particulars		L.F.	Debit Rs.	Credit Rs.
2	Rent a/c	Dr.		5,000	
	To Bank account				5,000
	(Being rent paid by cheque)				
3	Purchases a/c	Dr.		50,500	
	To Zaheer & Co. a/c				50,500
	(Being Goods purchased on credit)				
5	Cash a/c	Dr.		5,000	
	To Sales a/c				5,000
	(Being Goods sold for cash)				
8	Wages a/c	Dr.		1,500	
	To Cash a/c				1,500
	(Being wages paid to assistant)				
10	Insurance a/c	Dr.		500	
	To Bank a/c				500
	(Being insurance paid by cheque)				
12	Cash a/c	Dr.		8,500	
	To Sales a/c				8,500
	(Being goods sold for cash)				
15	Wages a/c	Dr.		1,000	
	To Cash a/c				1,000
	(Being Wages paid in cash)				
17	Zaheer & Co. a/c	Dr.		35,000	
	To Bank a/c				35,000
	(Being paid by cheque)				
Mar19	Purchase a/c	Dr.		30,000	
	To Rao & Co a/c				30,000
	(Being goods purchased on credit)				
19	Cash a/c	Dr.		8,000	
	To Sales a/c				8,000
	(Being goods sold for cash)				

Table Contd...

Date 2000	Particulars		L.F.	Debit Rs.	Credit Rs.
22	Wages a/c	Dr.		1,500	
	To Cash account				1,500
	(Being wages paid to assistant)				
24	Stationary a/c	Dr.		1,000	
	To Cash a/c				1,000
	(Being purchases of stationary)				
25	Cash a/c	Dr.		15,000	
	To Sales a/c				15,000
	(Being goods sold for cash)				
27	Rao & Co. a/c	Dr.		14,500	
	To Bank a/c				14,500
	(Being paid by cheque)				
29	Wages a/c	Dr.		2,000	
	To Cash a/c				2,000
	(Being wages to assistant paid in cash)				
31	Bank a/c	Dr.		20,000	
	To Cash a/c				20,000
	(Being Cash paid into bank)				

Ledger Accounts in the Books of Srinivas

Dr.		Cash Account					Cr.
Date	**Particulars**	**L.F.**	**Amount (Rs)**	**Date**	**Particulars**	**L.F.**	**Amount (Rs)**
Mar 1	To Capital		40,000	Mar 8	By Wages a/c		1,500
Mar 5	To Sales a/c		5,000	Mar 15	By Wages a/c		1,000
Mar 12	To sales a/c		8,500	Mar 22	By Wages a/c		1,500
Mar 19	To Sales a/c		8,000	Mar 24	By stationary		1,000
Mar 25	To sales a/c		15,000	Mar 29	By Wages a/c		2,000
				Mar 31	By Bank a/c		20,000
				Mar 31	By Balance c/d		49,500
	Total		76,500		Total		76,500
Apr. 1	To balance b/d		49,500				

Table Contd...

Dr.			Bank Account				Cr.
Date	**Particulars**	**L.F.**	**Amount (Rs)**	**Date**	**Particulars**	**L.F.**	**Amount (Rs)**
Mar 1	To capital a/c		2,50,000	Mar 1	By furniture & fittings a/c		40,000
Mar 31	To cash a/c		20,000		By van a/c		50,000
				Mar 2	By rent a/c		5,000
				Mar 10	By insurance a/c	500	
				Mar 17	By Zaheer & co		35,000
				Mar 27	By Rao & Co a/c	14,500	
				Mar 31	By balance c/d		1,25,000
	Total		2,70,000		Total		2,70,000
Apr. 1	To balance b/d		1,25,000				

Dr.			Capital a/c				Cr.
Date	**Particulars**	**L.F.**	**Amount (Rs)**	**Date**	**Particulars**	**L.F.**	**Amount (Rs)**
Mar 31	To balance c/d		2,90,000	Mar 1	By bank a/c		2,50,000
				Mar 1	By cash a/c		40,000
	Total		2,90,000		Total		2,90,000
				Mar 2	By balance b/d		2,90,000

Dr.			Furniture Account				Cr.
Date	**Particulars**	**L.F.**	**Amount (Rs)**	**Date**	**Particulars**	**L.F.**	**Amount (Rs)**
Mar. 1	To Bank a/c		40,000	Mar 31	By Balance c/d		40,000
	Total		40,000				40,000
Mar 1	To balance b/d		40,000				

Dr.			Van Account				Cr.
Date	**Particulars**	**L.F.**	**Amount (Rs)**	**Date**	**Particulars**	**L.F.**	**Amount (Rs)**
Mar. 1	To Bank a/c		50,000	Mar 31	By balance c/d		50,000
	Total		50,000	Total			50,000
Mar.1	To balance b/d		50,000				

Table Contd...

Dr.			Rent a/c				Cr.
Date	Particulars	L.F.	Amount (Rs)	Date	Particulars	L.F.	Amount (Rs)
Mar. 2	To Bank a/c		5,000	Mar 31	By balance c/d		5,000
	Total		5,000		Total		5,000
	To balance b/d		5,000				

Dr.			Purchase a/c				Cr.
Date	Particulars	L.F.	Amount (Rs)	Date	Particulars	L.F.	Amount (Rs)
Mar. 3	To Zaheer a/c		50,500	Mar 31	By balance c/d		80,500
Mar19	To Rao & Co. a/c 30,000						
	Total		80,500		Total		80,500
	To balance b/d		80,500				

Dr.			Sales a/c				Cr.
Date	Particulars	L.F.	Amount (Rs)	Date	Particulars	L.F.	Amount (Rs)
	To Balance c/d		36,500	Mar 5	By Cash a/c		5,000
				Mar 12	By cash a/c		8,500
				Mar 19	By cash a/c		8,000
				Mar 25	By cash a/c		15,000
	Total		36,500		Total		36,500
					By balance b/d		36,500

Dr.			Wages a/c				Cr.
Date	Particulars	L.F.	Amount (Rs)	Date	Particulars	L.F.	Amount (Rs)
Mar 8	To cash a/c		1,500	Mar 5	By Balance c/d		6,000
Mar15	To cash a/c		1,000				
Mar22	To cash a/c		1,500				
Mar29	To cash a/c		2,000				
	Total		6,000		Total		6,000
	To balance b/d		6,000				

Table Contd...

Dr.			Zaheer & a/c				Cr.
Date	**Particulars**	**L.F.**	**Amount (Rs)**	**Date**	**Particulars**	**L.F.**	**Amount (Rs)**
Mar15	To Returns a/c		60,000	Jan 5	By Purchases a/c		50,500
Mar15	To Bank a/c		35,000		By balance c/d		44,500
Total			95,000		Total		95,000
To balance b/d			44,500				

Dr.			Insurnace & a/c				Cr.
Date	**Particulars**	**L.F.**	**Amount (Rs)**	**Date**	**Particulars**	**L.F.**	**Amount (Rs)**
Mar 10	To Bank a/c		500		By Balance c/d		500
	Total		500		Total		500
	To balance b/d		500				

Dr.			Rents outwards & a/c				Cr.
Date	**Particulars**	**L.F.**	**Amount (Rs)**	**Date**	**Particulars**	**L.F.**	**Amount (Rs)**
Mar15	To balance c/d		60,000	Mar 15	By Zaheer & C		60,000
	Total		60,000		Total		60,000
	By balance b/d		60,000				

Dr.			Rao & Co., a/c				Cr.
Date	**Particulars**	**L.F.**	**Amount (Rs)**	**Date**	**Particulars**	**L.F.**	**Amount (Rs)**
Mar15	To bank a/c		14,500	Mar 19	By Purchases		30,000
	To balance c/d		15,500				
	Total		30,000	Total	30,000		
	By balance b/d		15,500				
Mar 24	To cash a/c		1,000	Mar 15	By balance c/d		1,000
	Total		1,000		Total		1,000
	To balance b/d		1,000				

Table Contd...

4. Prepare a trial balance for the month ending 31st August 2001

	Rs.
Cash a/c	50,500
Madhu capital a/c	30,000
Interest from bank	3,000
Discount (credit)	250
Sales	35,000
David a/c	3,000
Purchase returns a/c	500
Bank a/c	10,500
Rent a/c	2,500
Salaries a/c	500
Entertainment expenses	150
Purchase a/c	2,000
Sales returns a/c	300

Solution :

LF	Particulars	Debit	Credit
	Cash a/c	50,500	—
	Madhu capital a/c	—	30,000
	Interest form bank	—	3,000
	Discount	—	250
	Sales	—	35,000
	David a/c	3,000	—
	Purchase returns a/c	—	500
	Bank a/c	10,000	—
	Rent a/c	2,500	—
	Salaries a/c	500	—
	Entertainment expenses	150	—
	Purchase a/c	2,000	—
	Sales returns	100	—
		68,750	68,750

5. Prepare trial balance as on 31st Dec 1998.

Purchases	43,000
Sales	72,500
Insurance premium	510
Drawings	6280

Plant and machinery	4500
Commission paid	1070
Opening stock	11,200
Repairs	880
Returns inwards (sales returns)	1,000
Discount allowed	1,150
Rent paid	3,000
Returns outwards (purchase returns)	400
Investments	2,500
Creditors	14,260
Debtors	1,430
Traveling expenses	2,850
Salaries	33,540
Cash at bank	1,090
Fire wood	1,770
Capital	30,000
Carriage	240
Bad debts	690
Petty expenses	460

Solution:

LF	Particulars	Debit	Credit
	Purchases	43,000	—
	Sales	—	72,500
	Insurance premium	510	—
	Drawings	6,280	—
	Plant and machinery	4,500	—
	Commission paid	1,070	—
	Opening stock	11,200	—
	Repairs	880	—
	Return in wards	1,000	—
	Discount allowed	1,150	—
	Rent paid	3,000	—
	Return outwards	—	400
	Investments	2,500	—
	Creditors	—	14,260
	Debtors	1,430	—

Table Contd...

LF	Particulars	Debit	Credit
	Traveling expenses	2,850	—
	Salaries	33,540	—
	Cash at bank	1,090	—
	Fire wood	1,770	—
	Capital	—	30,000
	Carriage	240	—
	Bad debts	690	—
	Petty expenses	460	—
		1,17,160	1,17,160

3. From the following information prepare cashbook.

Date 2001	Particulars	Amount Rs.
Jun 1	Hari started business	70,000
Jun 2	He deposited the cash in bank	25,000
Jun 3	Goods purchased	20,000
Jun 4	Goods sold	35,000
Jun 5	Furniture purchased	5,000
Jun 6	Goods purchased form Rama	15,000
Jun 10	Salary paid to staff	5,000
Jun 15	Goods sold to Shankar	10,000
Jun 20	Cash paid to Rama	12,000
Jun 22	Cash deposited n Bank	3,000
Jun 25	Cash received from Shankar	7,000
Jun 30	Rent paid	2,500
Jun 30	Telephone expenses paid	1,200
Jun 30	Electricity expenses paid	1,500

Cash Book

Date	Particulars	L.F.	Amount (Rs)	Date	Particulars	L.F.	Amount (Rs)
Jun 1	To Capital a/c		70,000	Jun 2	By Bank a/c		25,000
Jun 4	To Sales a/c		35,000	Jun 3	By Purchases		20,000
Jun 25	To Shankar a/c		7,000	Jun 5	By furniture		5,000
				Jun 10	By salary a/c		5,000
				Jun 20	By Rama a/c		12,000
				Jun 22	By Bank a/c		3,000

Table Contd...

Date	Particulars	L.F.	Amount (Rs)	Date	Particulars	L.F.	Amount (Rs)
				Jun 30	By rent a/c		2,500
				Jun 30	By Telephone Expenses a/c		1,200
				Jun 30	By Electricity Expenses a/c		1,500
					By balance c/d		36,800
	Total		1,12,000		Total		1,12,000
	To balance b/d		36,800				

3. Enter the following transactions in a two-column cashbook.

Date 2001	Particulars	Amount Rs.
Sep 1	Cash in hand	10,000
Sep 3	Bought goods for cash	4,500
Sep 5	Paid for wages	5,200
Sep 7	Withdraw form bank for expenses	8,000
Sep 7	Cash paid to younish	2,150
	Discount received	50
Sep 10	Cash sales	15,500
Sep 13	Received cash from Bharat	4,400
	Allowed him discount	100
Sep 15	Purchased stationary from Ram on credit	250
Sep 16	Paid for postage stamps	200
Sep 18	Amount introduced as capital	5,000
Sep 21	Received cash from Raj	7,900
	Allowed him discount	100
Sep 24	Paid cash for traveling expenses	120
Sep 26	Amount paid into bank	2,500
Sep 27	Cash paid to Mukesh	950
	Discount allowed by him	50
Sep 28	Credit purchases form Ali	3,100
Sep 30	Cash purchases	1,500
Sep 30	Paid salaries	2,800
Sep 30	Deposited into bank all cash in excess of	2,000

Two Column Cash Book

Date	Particulars	R.N	Discount	Cash	Date	Particulars	V.N.L.F	Discount	Cash
Sep 1	To balance b/d			10,000	Sep 3	By purchases			4,500
Sep 7	To Bank a/c			8,000	Sep 5	By wages a/c			5,200
Sep 10	To Sales a/c			15,500	Sep 7	By Younis a/c		50	2,150
Sep 13	To Bharat a/c		100	4,400	Sep 16	By Postage			200
Sep 18	To Capital a/c			5,000	Sep 24	By Traveling expenses			120
Sep 21	To Raj		100	7,900	Sep 26	By Bank a/c			2,500
					Sep 27	By Mukesh		50	950
					Sep 30	By Purchases			1,500
					Sep 30	By Salaries			2,800
					Sep30	By Bank a/c			28,880
						By balance c/d			2,000
				50,800					
	To balance b/d			28,880					

8. Prepare a trading a/c for the year 1995 31st March, from the following particulars.

Particulars	Amount
Stock of goods on 1-4-1994	2,00,000
Stock of goods on 31-3-1995	4,50,000
Purchases – cash	3,90,000
Credit	8,25,000
Sales – cash	5,30,000
Credit	11,00,000
Returns to suppliers	25,000
Returns by costumers	30,000
Goods withdrawn by James or personal use	30,000
Goods distributed as free samples during the year	4,500
Duty and clearing charges	60,000

Solution

Trading account of Mr. James for the year ended 31st March, 1995

Particulars	Rs.	Rs.	Particulars	Rs.	Rs.
To Opening stock		2,00,000	By sales-cash	5,30,000	
To purchases-cash	3,90,000		Credit	11,00,000	
Credit	8,25,000				
	12,15,000			16,30,000	

Table Contd...

Particulars	Rs.	Rs.	Particulars	Rs.	Rs.
Less:			Less:		
Returns	2,500		Returns by costumers	30,000	16,00,000
Goods for personal	30,000		By closing stock		4,50,000
Goods used for sample	4,500				
	59,500	11,55,500			
To duty and clearing charges		60,000			
To gross profit c/d		14,15,500			
		20,50,000			20,50,000

9. From the following balances extracted at the close of year ended 31st March 1996, prepare profit and loss account.

Particulars	Amount
Gross profit	50,000
Carriage outward	3,500
Salaries	6,000
Rent	1,000
Fire Insurance Premium	800
Bad debts	2,000
Commission received	1,500
Discount (Dr)	500
Apprentice premium (Cr)	2,000
Printing & Stationary	300
Rates & Taxes	350
Traveling expenses	500
Discount allowed by creditors	1,000
Sundry trade expenses	300

Solution:

Profit and loss a/c for the year ended 31st March 1996

Particulars	Amount	Particulars	Amount
To Carriage outward a/c	3500	By gross profit b/d	50000
To salaries a/c	6000	By Apprentice premium a/c	2000
To rent a/c	1000	By Discount by creditors a/c	1000
To fire insurance premium a/c	800	By Commission a/c	1500
To Bad debts a/c	2000		
To Discount a/c	500		

Table Contd...

Particulars	Amount	Particulars	Amount
To Printing and stationary a/c	300		
To Rent and taxes a/c	350		
To Traveling expenses a/c	500		
To Sundry trade expenses a/c	300		
To Net profit (transferred to capital a/c)	32,050		
	54,500		54,500

10. The trail balance of Chandu on 31-12-1996 revealed the following balances. Prepare balance sheet.

Debit Balances	Rs.	Credit Balances	Rs.
Sundry debtors	64000	Sales	2,65,000
Plant & machinery	1,54,000	Capital	1,00,000
Purchases	68000	Purchase returns	1275
Sales returns	1000	Discount received	800
Opening stock	30000	Creditors	25000
Discount allowed	350	Bank charges	75
Furniture	45,000	Salaries	6800
Wages	10000	Carriage inwards	750
Carriage outwards	1200	Rates, rents, taxes	2000
Advertisements	2000	Cash at bank	6900
	3,92,075		3,92,075

Adjustments

Closing stock 35,000

Notes : Closing stock given in the adjustment should be posted two times

(a) On credit side of trading a/c

(b) On the assets side of balance sheet.

Solution :

Trading a/c of Mr. Chandu for the year ended 31-12-1996

Debit	Rs.	Credit	Rs.
To opening stock	30,000	By sales	2,65,000
To Purchases 68,000		(-) returns 1,000	2,64,000
(-) returns 1,275	62,725	By closing stock	35,000
To wages	10,000		
To Carriage inwards	750		
To Gross profit c/d	1,91,525		
	2,99,000		2,99,000

Table Contd...

Profit and Loss a/c of Mr. Chandu for the year ended 31st Dec.1996.

Debit	Rs.	Credit	Rs.
To discount allowed	350	By gross profit b/d	1,91,525
To Bank charges	75	By discount received	800
To salaries	6,800		
To carriage outwards	1,200		
To rent, rate, taxes	2,000		
To advertisement	2,000		
To net profit	1,79,900		
	1,92,325		1,92,325

Balance Sheet of Mr. Chandu as on 31-12-1996

Liabilities	Rs.	Rs.	Assets	Rs.	Rs.
Capital	1,00,000		Sundry debtors		64,000
+ Net profit	1,79,900	2,79,900	Plant and machinery		1,54,000
Credit		25,000	Furniture		45,000
			Cash at bank		6,900
			Closing stock		35,000
		3,04,900			3,04,900

11. From the following trial balance taken from the books of Ramana and company. Prepare trading and profit loss account for the year ended 31-12-2000 and a balance sheet as on that date.

Particulars	Debit	Credit
Drawing and capital	12,000	80,000
Opening stock	12,000	—
Investments	30,600	—
Salaries	12,000	—
Carriage	3,000	—
Returns	6,000	—
Purchases& sales	1,20,000	—
Debtors & creditors	60,000	—
Discount allowed	2,200	—
Cash	16,400	—
Wages	28,000	—
Reserve for doubtful debts	—	2,000
Bank overdraft	—	25,000
Loans	2,400	10,000
	3,04,600	3,04,600

Adjustments:

1. Closing stock was valued Rs. 1,20,000.
2. Wages & salaries were outstanding by Rs. 10,000 & Rs. 6,000.
3. Appreciate investments by 10%.
4. Maintain reserve for doubtful debts at the rate of 5% per anum.

Solution :

Trading and profit loss a/c for the year ended.

Dr.					Cr.
Particulars	**Rs.**	**Rs.**	**Particulars**	**Rs.**	**Rs.**
To opening stock		12,000	By sales	1,60,000	
To purchases	1,20,000		(-) returns	6,000	1,54,000
(-) returns	2,600	1,17,400	By closing stock		1,20,000
To carriage		3,000			
To wages	28,000				
(-) outstanding wages	10,000	38000			

Summary

1. ***Accounting:*** Accounting may be defined as the process of identifying, measuring, recording and communicating the economic events of an organisation to interested users of the information.
2. ***Objective of Accounting:*** The primary objectives of accounting can be stated as
    1. To maintain records of business
    2. Calculation of profit or loss
    3. Depiction of financial position
    4. To make information available to various groups and users.
3. ***Users of accounting information:*** The users can be divided into two broad groups (i) Internal users (ii) External users
4. ***Internal users:*** Internal users are the persons who are interested to know about the firms earning capacity. These are the persons who are directly interested in results of the business. Owners are interested to know the rate of return on capital employed, the long-term solvency of the firm and the rate of dividends. They include management, owners and employees.
5. ***External Users:*** External users include potential investors, creditor, Financial institutions, Government, Tax authorities, Regulatory Agencies, Consumers, labour unions, Trade Associations, Stock Exchange, Researches and others. Investors on the basis of accounting information, decide about buying, holding or selling investments in a business organisation.
6. ***Accounting process:*** Accounting process involves is nothing but identifying, measuring, recording, classifying, summarising, analysing and communicating the business transactions or economic events in a systematic manner.
7. ***Accounting principles:*** According to AICPA accounting principle means a general law or rule adopted on proposed as a guide to action, a settled ground or basis of conduct or practice. Accounting principles can broadly classified into two categories.

    1. Accounting concepts 2. Accounting Conventions
8. ***Accounting concepts:*** Accounting is a system evolved to achieve a set of objectives. In order to achieve the goals, we need a set of rules or guidelines. These guidelines are termed as Basic Accounting concepts. The term concepts refers to an idea or thought. These are the fundamental ideas or basic assumptions underlying the Theory and Practice of financial accounting.

9. (a) ***Business entity Concept:*** All the transactions are recorded in the books of business and not in the books of the proprietor. The Proprietor is also treated as a creditor for the business. When he contributes capital he is treated as person who has invested his amount in the business.

Effects

(i) financial position of the business can be easily found.

(ii) Earning capacity of business can be easily ascertained.

10. (b) ***Going Concern Concept:*** This concept relates with the long life of the business. This helps other business undertakings to make contracts with specific business unit for business dealings in future.

Effects

(i) Working life of asset is taken into consideration for writing of depreciation because of this concept.

11. ***Cost Concept:*** This concept explains an asset is recorded at its cost in the books of account, i.e., the price which is paid at the time of acquiring it. In balance sheet, these assets appear not at cost price every year, but depreciation is deducted and they appear at the amount which is cost less depreciation under this concept.

Effects

(i) Under this concept market price is ignored. Balance sheet indicates financial position on cost but not expired cost basis.

(ii) This concept is only for fixed assets are not affected by it.

12. ***Accounting period concept:*** Each and every business wants to know the results of his investment and efforts after a certain period. Generally on year period is regarded as an ideal for this purpose., it may be quarterly, half years or 2 years also. From taxation point of view one year period is necessary as income tax is payable every year.

Effects

(i) Financial Position and earning capacity of one year may be compared with another year.

(ii) These companies help the management planning and increasing the efficiency of business.

13. ***Dual Aspect concept:*** Under this concept, every transaction has got a two fold aspect.

(i) Receiving of benefit and

(ii) Giving of equivalent benefit.

When a firm acquires an asset (receiving of the benefit), it must have to pay cash (giving of the benefit). According to this concept, two accounts are to be passed in the books of accounts, one for receiving the benefit and the other of the giving the benefit.

Effects

(i) Financial position and earning capacity of one year may be compared with another year.

(ii) These comparisions help the management planning and increasing the efficiency of business.

14. ***Dual Aspect Concept:*** Under this concept, every transaction has got a two fold aspect.

(i) Receiving of benefit

(ii) Giving of equivalent benefit for a instance, when a firm acquires an asset (receiving of the benefit), it must have to pay cash (giving of the benefit).

Effects

(i) This concept is of great help in indicating the true position of the business.

(ii) This concept helps in detecting the errors of employees and in having strict control over them.

(iii) The accounting equation i.e., Assets = Equities (or liabilities + Capital) is based on this concept.

15. Matching Concept

The process of relating costs to revenue is called "Matching Process". Expenses which are incurred during a particular accounting period for earning the revenue of the related price are to be considered.

Effects

(i) Proprietor can easily know about his profit or loss.

(ii) On the basis of this concept, he can make efforts to create economy, increasing efficiency and increasing his income.

16. ***Realisation Concept:*** Every business unit spends money to purchase goods or to manufacture goods for sale. Sale of goods either for cash or on credit is essential to make earning.

17. ***Convention of disclosure:*** Accounting records and statements should be honest and materially informative, exclusion of material facts makes them incomplete and unreliable. Financial Statements must convey all significant economic information relating to the entity. Therefore care should be taken to disclose all material information while making accountancy record.

18. ***Convention of Materiality:*** Materiality means relative importance, whether a matter should be disclosed or not in the financial statements depends on its materiality i.e., whether it is material or not. According to this convention, accounting record should be made at all material facts.

19. ***Convention of Consistency:*** The most advantage of this convention is that is facilitates comparision of one year's accounts with other years. Continuance of one practice in number of years indicated consistency. Adopting of same practice over and over again is an old convention.

20. ***Convention of Conservatism:*** Future is uncertain though an estimate may be made about future events, no one can guess future with perfect certainity in business. Every sincere business man makes an estimate of future losses and than some provision for it is made as provision for bad debts. Business man mostly ignore the items of future profits. This tendency is termed as conservatism.

21. ***Branches of Accounting:*** The three branches of Accounting are (i) Financial Accounting (ii) Cost Accounting (iii) Management Accounting

    (a) Monitor the business activities

    (b) Calculate profit or loss for a given period

    (c) fulfill legal obligations.

    (d) show financial position for a given period.

    (e) Communicate the information to the interested parties.

22. ***Double Entry Book-Keeping:*** The object of book-keeping is to keep a complete record of all transactions that take place in business. The double entry book-keeping refers to a system of accounting in which every transaction effects atleast two accounts. In this, the amount of every transaction is written twice, once as debit and again as credit.

    Every business transaction having two aspects one will be treated as debit and other is credit. The debit and credit will be decided on the basis of nature of the aspect. Each aspect may related to either of the following 3 types of accounts.

    (i) Personal accounts

    (ii) Real accounts (RA)

    (iii) Nominal accounts (NA)

23. ***Rules for Debiting and crediting:*** The rules of debit and credit depend on the nature of an account. If aspect related to persons, personal accounts rule, if assets real account rule and if expenses or incomes nominal account rules are applicable.

24. ***Personal Accounts:*** Personal account deals with persons. These include natural persons, artificial persons or legal persons and representative personal accounts. When an account represents certain person or persons. Then it is called representative personal

25. ***Real Accounts:*** Real account deals with Assets. These includes tangible assets. E.g. : Land, Buildings, Apartments, Machinary, etc., which can be seen and touched and intangible assets like good will, Trade Marks etc., which can not be seen but can be measured.

26. ***Nominal Accounts:*** Nominal Accounts are those accounts which are in name only. They are simple used to define the nature of transactions. All expenses like Eg : Rent, wages, salary, Transportation etc,. and all incomes like discount received, rent received, commission received etc.

27. ***Journal:*** Journal is the book of entries in which business transactions are originally recorded in chronological order. Since every transaction is recorded first in the Journal it is also called the book of first entry.

28. ***Advantage of Journal:*** Journal is used for the following reasons.
    (i) It shows all necessary information regarding a transactions.
    (ii) it provides an explanation of the transaction
    (iii) it provides a datewise record of all the transactions.
    (iv) it helps to locate and prevent errors.

29. ***Ruling of a Journal:*** A Journal is generally kept on a columnar basis, it has the following five columns.

    (i) date (ii) particulars (iii) Ledger folio (v) amount (credit) (vi) amount (debit)

30. ***Balancing the Ledger Accounts:*** The balance is an accounting term which means the difference between two sides of an account. The following steps are followed for balancing the accounts.
    (i) On a rough sheet of paper take the total of the two sides of the account concerned.
    (ii) Compute the difference of the total of two sides.
    (iii) If the debit side total is more put the difference on the credit side amount column by writing the words in particular column "By Balanced". If the credit side total is more, put the difference on the debit side amount column by writing the words in particular column to balance c/d.
    (iv) After putting the difference in the appropriate side of the account, add both the sides of the account draw a thin line, above and below the total.
    (v) Bring down the debit balance on the debit side by writing the words in particular column " To Balance b/d" is credit balance on the credit side "By balance b/d".

31. ***Trial Balance:*** Trial balance may be defined as a statement of debit and credit totals or balances extracted from the various accounts in the ledger with a view to test the arithmetical accuracy of the books. The trial balance forms a connecting link between ledger accounts and the final accounts. If the trial balance does not agree, it shows that there are some errors which must be detected and rectified if the correct final accounts are to be prepared.

Than the credit side, the difference is put in the debit column of the trial balance and if the credit side is bigger, the difference is written in the credit column of the trial balance.

32. ***Trading Account:*** This account is prepared to know the trading results of the business i.e., how much gross profit the business has earned from buying and selling during a particular period. The difference between the sales and cost of goods sold is gross profit.

33. ***Profit and Loss Account:*** This account is prepared to calculate the net profit of the business. There are certain items of incomes and expenses of the business which must be taken into consideration for calculating net profit of the business.

34. ***Balance Sheet:*** It is final stage of preparation of final accounts. The recording of transactions starts from the Journal and end with the preparation of balance sheet. It is a statement prepared with a view to measure the financial position of a business on a certain fixed date. A Balance sheet is also described as a statement showing the sources and application of capital.

Essay Questions

1. Explain briefly Accounting Principles and Accounting conventions.
2. What do you understand by Double Entry Book keeping?
3. Explain the objectives of accounting and its role in business. Also explain the uses of accounting.
4. "Every debit must have a corresponding credit". Explain.
5. What is meany by Journal? What are the sub divisions of Journal?
6. Define ledger? Explain its importance in accounting process?
7. Give the various types of subsidiary books?
8. Wha is trial balance? Explain the objectives in preparing it.
9. What is Trading? Profit and loss account? State the contents?
10. Discuss the head and importance of a balance sheet.
11. Explain briefly accounting concepts and conventions.
12. How do you say that balancesheet is the status report of a business?
13. Should balance sheet always balance?
14. "Accounting records are affected to a great extent by the personal judgement of the accountant". Explain by giving examples.
15. Do you agree that enterprises should have to adopt uniform accounting practices? why?

Short Questions

1. What do you mean by accounting? What are its divisions?
2. What is a transaction. How does it differ from an event?
3. What is book keeping?
4. Why is recording of transactions necessary?
5. What distinguishes book keeping from accounting?
6. What are the functional branches of accounting?
7. Describe briefly accounting conventions.
8. What do you understand by generally accepted accounting principles?
9. What language does business use to record transactions?
10. Explain the terms debit and credit.
11. What is the logic behind debting one aspect and crediting another?
12. What is the advantage of double entry book-keeping over single entry?
13. Give the rules for debit and credit of the three classifications of aspects.
14. What does Journalising mean?
15. Where will you take the balance of subsidary books?
16. Describe a cash book with cash, bank and discount columns.
17. What do you mean by LF?
18. What is petty cash book?
19. What is meant by a leader account?
20. What computer packages are available for ledger rising?
21. How do you balance a ledger account?
22. What do you understand by trial balance?
23. Why should trial balance tally?
24. What are final accounts. Why are they prepared?
25. What is trading account. Why it is prepared?
26. What is profit and loss appropriation account?
27. What do you understand by term balancesheet?

CHAPTER 8

Financial Analysis Through Ratios

8.1 Introduction

An absolute figure does not convey anything unless it is related with the other relevant figure. Magnitude of current liabilities of a company does not tell anything about solvency position of the company. It is only when it is related with current assets figures of the same company an idea about the solvency position of the company can be had. Ratios make a humble attempt in this direction.

Ratios are signigficant both in vertical and horizontal analysis. Ratios help the analyst to form a judgement whether performance of the corporation at a point of time is good, questionable or poor. Likewise, use if ratios in horizontal analysis indicates whether the financial conditions of the corporation is improving or deteriorating and whether the cost, profitability of efficiency is showing an upward or downward trend.

Finanacial ratios are meaningful to judge finanacial condition and profitability performance of the corpotation only when there is comparision. In fact, analysis of ratio involves two types of comparison. First, a comparison of present ratio with past and expected future ratios for the same corporation. When financial ratios for several preceding years are computed, the analyst can determine the composition of change and whether there has been an improvement or deterioration in the financial position of the corporation over the period of time. The second method of comparison involves comparing the ratios of the company with those of similar type of company or with industry average at the same point of time. Such a comparison would provide considerable insight into the relative finanacial condition and performance of the company.

8.2 Meaning of Ratio Analysis

The most important task of a financial manager is to interpret the financial information in such a manner, that it can be well-understood by the people, who are not well-versed in financial information figures. The technique, by which it is so done, known as "Ratio Analysis".

'Ratio' is a relationship between two or more variable expressed in,

1. Percentage 2. Rate 3. Proportion

Ratio analysis is an important technique of financial analysis. It depicts the efficiency or short-fall of the organization in the form of trend analysis.

Different ratios appeal to different people. Management, having the task of running a business efficiency, will be interested in all ratios. A supplier of goods on credit will be particularly interested in liquidity ratios, which indicate the ability of the business to pay its bills. Existing and future shareholders will be interested in investment ratios which indicate the level of return that can be expected on an investment in the business. Major customers, intent on having a continuing source of supply, will be interested in the financial stability as revealed by the capital structure, liquidity and profitability ratios. Debenture and loan stock holders will be interested in the ability of a business to pay interest, and ultimately to repay the capital. A banker, giving only short-term loans, will be interested mainly in the liquidity of the business, and its ability to repay those loans.

The overall advantages of ratios is that they enable valid comparisons to be made between business of varying size and in different indusries.

All the problems of a business can't be solved by ratio analysis. It will merely give a general indication of a trend at the same time spotlighting any divergence normality. This knowledge, however, should enable management to correct whatever may be wrong in business.

8.2.1 Steps in Ratio Analysis

1. Collection of information which are relevant from the financial statements and then to calculate different ratios accordingly.
2. Comparison of computed ratios of the same organization or with the industry ratios.
3. Interpretation, drawing of inference and report-writing.

8.3 Functional Classification of Ratios

All the ratios discussed previous can be classified on the basis of their functions as follows.

1. Liquidity Ratios :
   - (a) Current ratio
   - (b) Acid test ratio
2. Solvency Ratios :
   - (a) Current ratio
   - (b) Acid test ratio
   - (c) Equity ratio
   - (d) Debt ratio
   - (e) Debt-equity ratio
   - (f) Net income to debt service ratio

3. Profitability Ratios :
   - (a) Gross profit ratio
   - (b) Net profit ratio
   - (c) Return on equity
   - (d) Return on investment
   - (e) Return on net worth

4. Activity Ratios :
   - (a) Inventory turnover
   - (b) Debtors turnover
   - (c) Fixed assets turnover
   - (d) Working capital turnover

5. Leverage ratio :
   - (a) Debt ratio
   - (b) Net income to debt service ratio
   - (c) Debt equity ratio
   - (d) Proprietary ratio

6. Financial ratios :
   - (a) Fixed assets ratio
   - (b) Capital gearing ratio
   - (c) Debt-equity ratio
   - (d) Current ratio
   - (e) Liquidity ratio

The classification given above would help students to work out problems which do not specify the individual ratios to be worked out but the student is asked to calculate a particular groupd such as solvency ratios, leverage ratios, etc.

8.4 Objectives of Particular Ratio Analysis

The table given below would also help students to calculate the required ratios in a given problem :

Objective of Analysis	Ratios to be Computed
1. Short term fincial solvency	(a) Current ratio
	(b) Liquidity ratio
2. Long term financial solvency	(a) Equity or proprietary ratio
	(b) Debt ratio
	(c) Debt equity ratio
	(d) Shareholders equity to total equity ratio
3. Immediate solvency	(a) Liquidity ratio
	(b) Return on investment
4. Overall efficiency	(a) Operating ratio
	(b) Assests turnover and other turnover ratios
	(c) Return on proprietors equity
	(d) Earnings per share
5. Profitability in relation to sales	(a) Gross profit ratio
	(b) Net profit ratio

6. Profitability in relation to investment	(a)	Return on investment
	(b)	Return on proprietor's equity
	(c)	Earnings per share
7. Over-trading or under-trading	(a)	Proprietory ratio
	(b)	Current ratio
	(c)	Stock turnover ratio
8. Trading on equity	(a)	Capital gearing ratio
9. Over-capitalization and Under-capitalization	(a)	Current ratio
10. Operating efficiency	(a)	Operating ratio
	(b)	Expense ratios

8.5 Advantages of Ratio Analysis

Ratio analysis is a very important and useful tool for financial analysis. It serves many purposes and is helpful not only for internal management but also or prospective investors, creditors and other outsiders. The follwoing are the important uses (advantages) of ratio analysis.

1. It is an important and useful tool to check upon the efficiency with which the working capital is being used (managed) in a business enterprise. Efficient management of working capital.
2. It helps the management of business concern in evaluating its finanacial position and efficieny of performance.
3. It serves as a sort of health test of a business firm, because with the help of this analysis finance, managers can determine whether the firm is financially healthy or not.
4. A ratio analysis covering a number of past accounting (financial) periods clearly shows the trend of changes in the business position that is whether the trend in financial position, income postion etc is upward, or downward or static. The progress or downfall of a business concern is clearly indicated by this analysis.
5. It helps in making financial estimates for the future (that is in finanacial forecasting)
6. It helps the task of managerial control to a great extent.
7. It helps the credit suppliers and investors in evluating a business firm as a desirable debtor or as potential investment outlet.
8. With the help of this analysis ideal (standard) ratios can be established and these can be used for the purpose of comparison of a firm's progress and performance.
9. This analysis communicates important information regarding financial strength and standing, earning capacity, debt (borrowing) capacity, liquiditiy position capacity to

meet fixed commitments (charges, solvency, capital gearing, working capital management, future prospects, etc., of a business concern.

10. This analysis may be employed for the purpose of comparing the working result and efficiency of performance of a business enterprise with that of other enterprises engaged in the same industry (Inter-firm-comparison).
11. It helps the managment or a business concern to discharge their basic functions of planning, coordinating, controlling etc.
12. It serves as an instrument for testing management efficiency.
13. It sometimes provides a useful tool for decisions on certain policy matters.

8.6 Limitations of Ratio Analysis

1. Accounting ratios (Calculated under the system of ratio analysis) will be correct only if the accounting data (figures), on which they are based, are correct.
2. It is mainly a historical analysis or an analysis of the past financial data.
3. In regard to profits of a business concern, ratio analysis may in certain circumstanes be misleading.
4. Continuous changes in price levels (or purchasing power of money) seriously affect the validity or comparison of accounting ratios calculated for different accounting (financial) periods and make such comparisons very difficult.
5. Comparisons become difficult also on account of difference in the definition of several finanacial (accounting) terms like gross proft, operating profit, net profit etc., and on account of a considerable diversity in practice as regards their measurement.
6. The validity of comparison is also seriously affected by window dressing in the basic finanacial statements and by differences in accounting methods used by different business concerns.
7. A single ratio will not be able to convey much information.
8. This analysis gives only a part of the total information required for proper decision making.
9. Ratio analysis should not be taken as substitute for sound judgement.
10. It should not be overlooked that business problem cannot be solved mechanically through ratio analysis or other types of finanacial analysis.

8.7 Advantages to Management

1. Ratio analysis simplifies the understanding of financial statement.
2. Ratio carries out inter relation ship among various financial figures.
3. Ratios contribute significantly towards effective planning and fore casting.
4. Ratios facilitate inter firm and intra firm comparison.

5. Ratios serve as effective control techniques.
6. Ratio provides the particular information needed of a particular person.

8.8 Significance and Purpose of Ratio Analysis

Ratio analysis is useful to internal and external people of the business enterprises. The following are the people benfited by ratio analysis 1. an investor 2. suppliers 3. employers 4. bankers and 5. lenders 6. management 7. regulatory authorities 8. different agencies.

8.8.1 Managerial uses

Ratio analysis helps to financial managers in many ways. Particularly it helps in (a) decision making (b) financial forecasting and planning (c) communication (d) coordination (e) control (f) other uses of budgetry control and standard costing.

8.8.2 General Classification of ratio analysis

Ratio analysis can be classified under following heads 1. Traditional classification 2. Financial classification 3. Usage of ratios 4. Nature of ratio at a point of time in relation to which ratio are calculated.

8.9 General Classification of Ratios

1. **Liquidity ratios** or short-term financial ratios.
2. **Activity ratio** or efficiency ratios (current asset management)
3. **Solvency ratio** or analysis of long term (financial position).
4. **Profitability ratio** or analysis of financial position.
5. **Overall ratio** or analysis of industrial position.
6. **Leverage ratios** or analysis capital structures

1. ***Liquidity ratios :***
   (a) Current Ratio = Current assets / current liabilities
   (b) Quick or Acid test or Liquidity Ratio = Liquid or Quick assets / Current assets
   (c) Absolute ratio liquid = Absolute liquid Assets / Current Assets.
2. ***Activity ratios :***
   (a) Stock Turnover Ratio = Cost of goods sold/ Average Inventory cost
   (b) Debtors Turnover Ratio = Net credit annual Sales / Average trade debtors
   (c) Average collection period = Total trade debtors / Sales per day or 365/DTR
   (d) Creditors turnover ratio = Net credit annual purchases / Average trade creditors
   (e) Working Capital Turnover Ratio = Cost of Sales / Net Working Capital

3. ***Solvency ratio :***

   (a) Debt equity ratio = Debt / Equity

   (b) Funded debt to total Capitalisation ratio = Funded Debt / Total Capitalization

   (c) Long-term debt to shareholders funds = Long = term debt / Share holders Funds

   (d) Solvency ratio = Total liabilities to outsiders / Total asset

   (e) Fixed Assets to Net worth = Fixed Assets (after depreciation) / Shareholders fund

   (f) Current assets to proprietor funds = Current assets / Shareholders funds

   (g) Debt coverage ratio = Net Profit before Interest and Taxes / Fixed Interest.

4. ***Profitability ratio :***

   (a) Gross profit ratio = (Gross profit / Net sales) × 100

   (b) Net profit ratio = (Net profit / Net sales) × 100

   (c) Operating ratio = (Operating cost / Net sales) × 100

   (d) Expenses ratio = (Concerned expenses / Net sales) × 100

   (e) Operating Profit Ratio = (Operating profit / Net sales) × 100.

5. ***Overall profitability ratio :***

   (a) Return on investment = (Net profit before interest and tax / Share holders funds)

   (b) Return on Equity Capital Ratio = (Net profit after interest and taxes/paid up equity)

   (c) Earning per share ratio = (Net profit after interest and taxes-Preference debt)/ Number of equity shares.

   (d) Return on net capital Employed = (Adjusted Net profit / Net capital Employed) × 100

   (e) Dividend Yield Ratio = (Dividend on Equity share / Earning per share) × 100.

6. ***Leverage ratios :***

   (a) Capital Gearing ratio = (Equity share capital + Reserves and surpluses)/ (Preference Capital + Longterm debt)

   (b) Financial Leverage = (Earnings before Interest and Taxes) / (Earnings before Interest and Taxes – Interest + Preferred Dividend)

   (c) Operating Leverage = Contribution / Earning before interest and taxes

Problem 1

Calculate current ratio for the given balance sheet.

Liabilities	Amount (Rs)	Assets	Amount (Rs)
Share capital	2,00,000	Machinery 4,00,000	
Reserves & Surplus	1,50,000	(-) Accumulated	
		depreciation (-) 60,000	3,40,000
12% Debentures	1,00,000	Investment	1,50,000
Term loans	60,000	Stock	1,20,000
Short – term loans	1,20,000	Sundry debtors 5,00,000	
		(-) Bad debts 3,75,000	1,25,000
Sundry creditors	1,80,000	Loans and advances	30,000
Provision for taxation	75,000	Cash at bank.	1,20,000
	8,85,000		8,85,000

Solution :

Current assets and current liabilities are

Current Liabilities	Amount (Rs)	Current Assets	Amount (Rs)
Short – term loans	1,20,000	Stock	1,20,000
Sundry creditors	1,80,000	Sundry debtors	1,25,000
Provision for taxation	75,000	Loans and advances	30,000
		Cash at bank	1,20,000
	3,75,000		3,75,000

$$\text{Current ratio} = \frac{\text{Current assets}}{\text{Current liabilities}} = \frac{3,95,000}{3,75,000}$$

$$= 1.053$$

Problem 2

Calculate quick ratio for the above examples balance sheet.

Solution :

Current assets = 3,95,000

(-) Stock = 1,20,000

Quick assets 2,75,000

Current liabilities = 3,75,000

$$\text{Quick ratio} = \frac{\text{Quick assets}}{\text{Current liabilities}}$$

$$= \frac{2,75,000}{3,75,000}$$

$$= 0.733 \text{ times}$$

Problem 3

For Goodwill Trading Company Ltd., model quick assets and current liabilities are :

Quick assets :

Loans and advances	Rs. 6,00,000
Investment	Rs. 2,00,000
Sundry debtors	Rs. 10,00,000
Cash at bank	Rs. 5,00,000
Total	Rs. 23,00,000

Current liabilities :

Bank overdraft	Rs. 8,00,000
Outstanding expenses	Rs. 50,000
Bills payable	Rs. 1,50,000
Total	Rs. 10,00,000

Solution :

$$\text{Quick ratio} = \frac{\text{Quick assets}}{\text{Current liabilities}}$$

$$= \frac{23,00,000}{10,00,000}$$

$$= 2.3 \text{ times}$$

Problem 4

From the following information, calculate the absolute quick ratio.

Quick assets :

Sundry debtors	8,00,000
Cash at bank	5,20,000
Investment (short term marketable securities)	2,10,000
Loans and advances	3,00,000

Current liabilities :

Bills payable	1,70,000
Sundry creditors	5,00,000
Bank overdraft	2,50,000
	9,20,000

Solution :

Cash at bank	5,20,000
Marketable securities	2,10,000
	7,30,000

$$\text{Absolute quick ratio} = \frac{\text{absolute quick assets}}{\text{current liabilities}} = \frac{7,30,000}{9,20,000}$$

$$= 0.79 \text{ times}$$

Problem 5

The profit of a company after tax and interest is Rs. 3,50,000. Provision for taxation is Rs. 5,00,000. Payment of interest is Rs. 2,50,000. Find interest coverage ratio.

Solution :

Profit after tax and interest		Rs. 3,50,000
(+) Provision for taxation	5,00,000	
Interest payment	2,50,000	
		Rs. 7,50,000
Profit before interest and tax		Rs. 11,00,000

$$\text{Interest coverage ratio} = \frac{\text{Profit before interest and tax}}{\text{Interest}}$$

$$= \frac{11,00,000}{2,50,000}$$

$$= 4.4 \text{ times}$$

Problem 6

For a trading company, interest obligation is Rs. 2,60,000 and profit before interest and tax is Rs. 8,40,000. Find interest coverage ratio.

Solution :

$$\text{Interest coverage ratio} = \frac{8,40,000}{2,60,000}$$

$$= 3.23 \text{ times}$$

Problem 7

The summarized balance sheet of Pavani Ltd., is as follows : Find debt equity ratio.

Liabilities	Amount	Assets	Amount
Share capital	5,00,000	Machinery	3,50,000
Reserves & Surplus	50,000	Preliminary expenses	1,00,000
12% Debentures	3,00,000	Stock	2,00,000
Term loans	60,000	Sundry debtors	1,10,000
Short – term loans	1,50,000	Loans and advances	3,00,000
		Profit & loss a/c (accumulated) up to last year 2,50,000	
Sundry creditors	2,00,000	(-) Profits for current year 50,000	2,00,000
	12,60,000		12,60,000

Solution :

Equity :

Share capital	Rs. 5,00,000	
Reserve and surplus	Rs. 50,000	
		5,50,000
(-) Accumulated losses	Rs. 2,00,000	
(-) Preliminary expenses	Rs. 1,00,000	3,00,000
Equity of owner's fund =		2,50,000

Debt :

12% Debentures	Rs. 3,00,000
Terms loans	60,000
	3,60,000

$$\text{Debt – equity ratio} = \frac{\text{debt}}{\text{equity}}$$

$$= \frac{3,60,000}{2,50,000}$$

= 1.44 times

Problem 8

Equity and debt of Jyothi Ltd., is given below calculate debt equity ratio.

Equity :

Share capital	20,00,000
Capital reserve	15,000
Revenue reserve	20,000
	20,35,000

Debt :

Secured loans	10,00,500
Fixed deposits	5,00,000
	15,00,500

Solution :

$$\text{Debt equity ratio} = \frac{\text{debt}}{\text{equity}}$$

$$= \frac{15,00,500}{20,35,000}$$

$$= 0.737$$

Problem 9

For the above problem, find debt to total funds ratio.

Solution :

Total funds = Debt + Equity

= 15,00,500 + 20,35,000

= 35,35,500

$$\text{Debt to total funds ratio} = \frac{\text{Debt}}{\text{Total funds}}$$

$$= \frac{15,00,500}{35,35,500}$$

$$= 0.424$$

Problem 10

For Laxmi Ltd., debt and equity are given below. Find debt – equity ratio and debt to total fund ratio.

Debt :

Secured loans	10,00,000
Public deposits	1,40,000
	11,40,000

Equity :

Capital reserve	5,00,000
Revenue reserve	2,00,000
Share capital	25,00,000
	32,00,000

Solution :

Debt – equity ratio = debt/equity

$$= \frac{11,40,000}{32,00,000}$$

$$= 0.35625$$

$$\text{Debt} + \text{Equity} = 11,40,000 + 32,00,000$$

$$= 43,40,000$$

$$\text{Debt to total fund ratio} = \frac{\text{Debt}}{\text{Debt} + \text{Equity}}$$

$$= \frac{11,40,000}{43,40,000}$$

$$= 0.262$$

Problem 11

For a private company calculate capital turnover ratio using the following information.

Equity	5,00,000
Debt	8,00,000
Sales	10,00,000

Solution :

Equity	5,00,000
(+) Debt	8,00,000
Capital employed	13,00,000

$$\text{Capital turnover ratio} = \frac{\text{Sales}}{\text{Capital employed}}$$

$$= \frac{10,00,000}{13,00,000}$$

$$= 0.769$$

Problem 12

Calculate capital turnover ratio for the following information of a company

Fixed assets	20,00,000
Current assets	12,00,000
Current liabilities	7,00,000
Sales	25,50,000

Solution :

Fixed assets	20,00,000	
Current assets	12,00,000	32,00,000
(-) Current liabilities	7,00,000	7,00,000
Capital employed		25,00,000

$$\text{Capital turnover ratio} = \frac{25,50,000}{25,00,000}$$

$$= 1.02$$

Problem 13

Calculate fixed assets turnover ratio for the given information.

Sales	10,00,000
Fixed assets	7,50,000

Solution :

$$\text{Fixed assets turn over ratio} = \frac{10,00,000}{7,50,000}$$

$$= 1.33$$

Problem 14

Sales and fixed assets of Bhagya Ltd., is given as follows.

Sales	35,00,000
Fixed assets	15,00,000

Find fixed assets turn over ratio.

Solution :

$$\text{Fixed assets turn over ratio} = \frac{35,00,000}{15,00,000}$$

$$= 2.33$$

Problem 15

Using the information of Priya Co. Ltd., Calculate working capital turn over ratio.

Current assets	10,50,500
Current liabilities	3,10,000
Sales	15,00,000

Solution :

Current assets	10,50,500
(-) Current liabilities	3,10,000
Net working capital	7,40,000

$$\text{Working capital turn over ratio} = \frac{\text{Sales}}{\text{Net working capital}}$$

$$= \frac{15,00,000}{7,40,000}$$

$$= 2.0256$$

Problem 16

For Good Will Trading Ltd., calculate working capital turn over ratio.

Sales	60,00,000
Net working capital	33,50,000

Solution :

$$\text{Working capital turnover ratio} = \frac{60,00,000}{33,50,000}$$

$$= 1.791$$

Problem 17

Particulars	Rs.	Particulars	Rs.
Opening stock	20,000	Sales	83,000
Purchases	50,000	Closing stock	30,000
Carriage inward	3,000		
Wages	10,000		
Gross Profit	30,000		
	1,13,000		1,13,000

Calculate stock turnover ratio.

Solution :

Sales	83,000
Gross profit	30,000
Cost of goods sold	53,000

$$\text{Average stock} = \frac{\text{Opening stock} + \text{closing stock}}{2}$$

$$= \frac{20,000 + 30,000}{2}$$

$$= 25,000$$

$$\text{Stock turn over ratio} = \frac{\text{Cost of goods sold}}{\text{Average stock}}$$

$$= \frac{53,000}{25,000}$$

$$= 2.12$$

Problem 18

Calculate stock turn over ratio from the given information.

Sales	50,00,000
Gross profit	15,50,000
Opening stock	10,25,000
Closing stock	6,55,000

Solution :

Sales	50,00,000
(-) Gross profit	15,50,000
Cost of goods sold	34,50,000

$$\text{Average stock} = \frac{\text{Opening stock} + \text{Closing stock}}{2}$$

$$= \frac{10,25,000 + 6,55,000}{2}$$

$$= \text{Rs. } 8,40,000$$

$$\text{Stock turn over ratio} = \frac{34,50,000}{8,40,000} = 4.107$$

Problem 19

From the following information, calculate debtors turn over ratio.

Sales for the year 2002

Cash	60,000
Credit	75,500

Opening balances

Sundry debtors	30,000
Bills receivable	10,000

Closing balances

Sundry debtors	25,500
Bills receivable	20,000

Solution :

Opening sundry debtors	30,000	
(+) Bills receivable	10,000	40,000
Closing sundry debtors	25,500	
(+) Bills receivable	20,000	45,500
		85,500

$$\text{Average debtors} = \frac{85,500}{2} = 42,750$$

$$\text{Debtors turn over ratio} = \frac{\text{Credit sales}}{\text{Average debtors}}$$

$$= \frac{75,500}{42,750}$$

$$= 1.766$$

Problem 20

For Pavani Ltd., calculate debtors turn over ratio from the flowing information.

Sundry debtors at beginning	20,00,000
Sundry debtors at end	12,50,000
Sales	25,50,250

Solution :

Sundry debtors at beginning	20,00,000	
Sundry debtors at end	12,50,000	
		32,50,000

$$\text{Average debtors} = \frac{32,50,000}{2} = 16,25,000$$

$$\text{Debtors turn over ratio} = \frac{25,50,250}{16,25,000} = 1.569$$

Problem 21

Given information about Mouli enterprises calculate gross profit ratio.

Sales	2,25,000	
(-) sales returns	25,000	2,00,000
Opening stock		15,000
Closing stock		10,000
Purchases	1,40,000	

(-) purchases returns	25,000	1,15,000
Wages		35,000
Other manufacturing expenses		20,000

Solution :

Cost of goods sold :

Opening stock	15,000
(+) Purchases	1,15,000
(+) Wages	35,000
(+) Other manufacturing expenses	20,000
	1,85,000
(-) Closing stock	10,000
Cost of goods sold	1,75,000

Gross profit :

Sales	2,00,000
(-) Cost of goods sold	1,75,000
Gross profit	25,000

$$\text{Gross profit ratio} = \frac{\text{Gross profit}}{\text{Sales}} \times 100$$

Sales

$$= \frac{25,000}{2,00,000} \times 100$$

$$= 12.5\%$$

Problem 22

For Swapna. Co. Ltd., calculate gross profit ratio for the following information.

Sales	75,25,500
Gross profit	50,00,000

Solution:

$$\text{Gross profit} = 50,00,000$$

$$\text{Gross profit ratio} = \frac{50,00,000}{75,25,500} \times 100$$

$$= 66.44\%$$

Problem 23

From the following information, calculate net profit ratio.

Sales	2,50,000
Cost of production	1,20,000
Administrative expenses	10,500
Selling & distribution expenses	5,000
Interest	2,000
Tax	3,000

Solution:

Sales	2,50,000
Cost of production	1,20,000
Gross profit	1,30,000
(-) Administrative expenses	10,500
(-) Selling & distribution expenses	5,000
	15,500
Net profit before interest & tax	1,14,500

Net profit ratio $= \dfrac{1,14,500}{2,50,000} \times 100$

$= 0.458 \text{ x } 100$

$= 45.8\%$

Problem 24

Find the net profit for the following information.

Net profit 15,75,000

Sales 50,00,000

Solution:

Sales $= \dfrac{\text{Net profit}}{\text{Sales}} \times 100$

$= \dfrac{15,75,000}{50,00,000} \times 100$

$= 31.5\%$

Problem 25

From problem 23 net profits can be calculated as

Solution:

Gross profit		1,30,000
(-) Administrative expenses	10,500	
(-) Selling & distribution expenses	5,000	15,500
Net profit before tax & interest		1,14,500
(-) Interest payment		2,000
Net profit before tax		1,12,500
(-) Tax		3,000
Net profit after tax		1,09,500

Net Profit after tax

$$\text{Net profit ratio} = \frac{\text{Net Profit after tax}}{\text{Sales}} \times 100$$

$$= \frac{1,09,500}{2,50,000} \times 100$$

$$= 43.8\%$$

Problem 26

For a trading company, calculate net profit ratio from the following data.

Net profit after interest & tax	10,80,255
Sales	70,00,000

Solution:

$$\text{Net profit ratio} = \frac{10,80,255}{70,00,000} \times 100$$

$$= 15.43\%$$

Problem 27

From the following information, calculate return on investment.

Owner's fund or equity	2,50,000
Long – term loans	3,60,000
Profit before interest & tax	30,000

Solution:

Owner' fund	2,50,000
Long-term loans	3,60,000
Capital employed	6,10,000

$$\text{Return on investment} = \frac{\text{Profit before interest \& tax}}{\text{Capital employed}} \times 100$$

$$= \frac{30,000}{6,10,000} \times 100$$

$$= 4.9\%$$

Problem 28

From the given information of Eswari enterprises, find return on investment for that company

Profit before interest and tax	8,80,100
Capital employed	15,00,000

Solution:

$$\text{Return on investment} = \frac{8,80,100}{15,00,000} \times 100$$

$$= 58.6\%$$

Problem 29

Using the information, calculate return on equity

Equity	5,00,000		
Profit before interest & tax	50,000		
(-) Interest	10,000		
Profit before tax		40,000	
(-) Income tax			15,000
Profit after interest and tax			25,000

$$\text{Return on equity} = \frac{\text{Profit after interest \& tax}}{\text{Equity}} \times 100$$

$$= \frac{25,000}{5,00,000} \times 100$$

$$= 5\%$$

Problem 30

Calculate return on equity for Rao & Bros. Company using the following information.

Equity	25,50,250
Profit	19,00,500
Interest on loans	2,55,000
Income tax	8,10,000

Solution:

Profit	19,00,500
(-) Interest	2,55,000
Profit before tax	16,45,500
(-) Income tax	8,10,000

$$\text{Return on equity} = \frac{8{,}35{,}500}{25{,}50{,}250} \times 100$$

$$= 32.76\%.$$

Summary

1. *Ratio Analysis:* Ratio is an expression of one number in relation to another. Ratio analysis facilitates the presentation of the information of financial statements in simplified, concise and summarized form. Ratios are expressed in three ways.
   a. Quotient obtained by dividing one value by the other. The unit os expression is known as 'times'.
   b. Quotient obtained is multiplied by hundred. The unit expression is known as 'percentage'.
   c. Ratio is also expressed as a proportion.
2. *Use and Significance of Ratio analysis:* It is one of the most powerful tools of financial analysis. It is with the help of ratios that the financial statements can be analysed more clearly and decisions made from such analysis. The use of ratios is not confined to financial managers only. With the use of ratio analysis we can measure the financial condition of a firm and can point out whether the condition is strong.
3. Two basis approaches of analysis are (a) *Horizontal analysis* (b) *Vertical analysis.*
4. The process of establishing relation between two quantitative figures and interpreting the result for helping in decision-making is called ratio analysis.
5. *Ratio* is an expression of one number in relation to another.
6. Ratios can be grouped into four types.
7. The liquidity ratios assess the capacity of the company to repay its short-term liability.
8. Current ratio $= \dfrac{\text{Current assets}}{\text{Current liabilities}}$.
9. Quick ratio is also known as acid test ratio.
10. Quick ratio $= \dfrac{\text{Quick assets}}{\text{Current liabilities}}$.
11. The acceptable norm for absolute quick ratio is 50%
12. Satisfactory condition for quick ratio is 1:1.

13. Absolute quick ratio = $\frac{\text{Absolute quick assets}}{\text{Current liabilities}}$.

14. Interest coverage ratio is also known as *times interest earned or times interest covered.*

15. Debt – equity ratio = $\frac{\text{Debit}}{\text{Equity}}$.

16. Generally debt to total funds ratio is 67% or 0.67:1.

17. Activity or efficiency ratio is the other name for turn over ratio.

18. Managerial efficiency can be tested using capital turn over ratio.

19. Fixed assets turn over ratio = $\frac{\text{Sales}}{\text{Fixed assets}}$.

20. *Working capital turn over* ratio indicates numbers of times the net working capital is converted into sales.

21. Stock turn over ratio is also known as *inventory turn over* ratio.

22. Debtors turn over ratio = $\frac{\text{Credit sales}}{\text{Average debtors}}$.

23. Receivables turn over ratio is alternative name for debtors turn over ratio.

24. Debtors collection period = $\frac{\text{365 days or 12 months}}{\text{Debtors turn over ratio}}$

25. *Profitability* ratio measures the profit earning capacity of an enterprise.

26. Gross profit ratio is also called as Gross profit margin.

27. Net profit ratio = $\frac{\text{Net profit}}{\text{Sales}} \times 100$.

28. Operating profit = Net sales – Operating cost

29. The ideal current ratio is 2:1.

30. Short-term solvency is known by *liquidity* ratio.

31. Total funds = Debt + equity.

32. Debt – equity ratio is also called *Owner's funds*.

Essay Questions

1. What are the Ratios used for analysis of Industrial position ?
2. What are the classification of Ratio Analysis ?
3. What is a 'ratio'? State the importance of Ratio Analysis ?
4. Classify the ratios and explain uses of each group.
5. Explain briefly Analysis vs interpretation.
6. How do you compute Return on Investment ?
7. How do you define Managerial Ability Based on Ratio Analysis ?
8. Explain elaborately Functional classfication of Ratio analysis.
9. Define Ratio, What are the objectives of Ratio analysis ?
10. What are the advantages are limitations of Ratio analysis ?
11. What are the advantages to Management ?
12. Compare and contrast leveraged ratios and solvency ratios.

Short Questions

1. Explain briefly Ratio Analysis and its role.
2. What is the significance of Ratio Analysis ?
3. What are the limitations of Ratio Analysis ?
4. What are the advantages of Ratio Analysis ?
5. Explain briefly Liquidity ratios.
6. Explain briefly Activity ratios.
7. Explain briefly Solvency ratios.
8. Explain briefly Profitability ratios.
9. Explain briefly Average ratios.
10. Explain briefly Debt-Equity ratio.
11. Explain briefly Profit turnover ratios.
12. Differentiate Quick ratio as well as absolute quick ratio.

Multiple Choice Questions

1. Income – elasticity of demand is expressed as

 a. $\dfrac{\text{Percentage change in quantity demanded}}{\text{Percentage change in income}}$

 b. $\dfrac{\text{Change in income}}{100 \times \text{change in quantity demanded}}$

 c. $\dfrac{\text{Percentage change in income}}{\text{Change in quantity demanded}}$

 d. $\dfrac{\text{Change in quantity demanded}}{100 \times \text{change in income}}$

2. "Ceteris paribus" Term is related to

 a. Monetary theory
 b. Law of demand
 c. General equilibrium theory
 d. All of the above.

3. If the income elasticity of demand is greater than one the commodity is

 a. A non-related good.
 b. A necessity
 c. An inferior good
 d. A luxury good

4. Extension and contraction of demand are the result of
   a. Change in price
   b. Change in consumers income
   c. Change in taste
   d. Change in advertisement
5. The demand curve for a commodity always moves
   a. Upward from right to left
   b. Downward from right to left
   c. Parallel to horizontal axis
   d. Downward from left to right.
6. If the amounts of two commodities purchased both increase or decrease when the price of one changes, the cross elasticity of demand between them is:
   a. One
   b. Negative
   c. Positive
   d. Zero
7. Which of the following. Statements are correct or most nearly correct?
   a. A commodity will have value if it is wanted by somebody.
   b. A commodity will have value only if it is scarce relative to demand.
   c. The value of a commodity depends upon its price.
   d. The value of a commodity entirely depends upon the demand for it.
8. Demand has reference to
   a. A given period and price
   b. A given period of time
   c. A given price
   d. None of these
9. A demand schedule is shown as
   a. A result of increase in the size of the family
   b. A result of change in taste
   c. A function of price alone
   d. A result of change in income
10. Demand for a good is elastic if
    a. As a result of rise in price, total expenduture on the good decreases.
    b. A price fall produces a decrease in total expenditure on that good.
    c. A price fall produces a less than proportionate rise in the quantity demanded
    d. Demand for that good decreases when price falls.
11. For old products, which type of demand forecasting is suitable
    a. Sample survey method
    b. Delphi method
    c. Complete enumeration method
    d. Trend method

12. If the quantity demanded of a commodity is plotted against the price of a substitute goods, the demand curve is expected to be.

    a. Vertical b. Positively sloped

    c. Horizontal d. negatively sloped

13. Demand for elasticity is

    a. Perfectly inelastic b. Relatively Elastic

    c. Relatively inelastic d. perfectly inelastic

14. Of the following commodities which has the lowest elasticity of demand

    a. Car b. Low

    c. Tea d. Houses

15. Cross elasticity of demand between petrol and car is

    a. Negative b. Low

    c. Zero d. High

16. Price elasticity of demand is best defined as:

    a. The change in cost when output is increased by one unit

    b. Change in the taste of consumers at different prices

    c. The responsiveness of demand to a change in supply.

    d. The rate of response of demand to a change in supply.

17. The exceptions to the Law of demand are

    a. Applicable to individual demand curves

    b. Applicable to individual consumers

    c. Result of wrong understanding of the law

    d. Genuine and real.

18. Cross-elasticity of demand between two perfect substitutes will be

    a. Low b. Very high

    c. Infinity d. Very low

19. Suppose your income increases by 20 percent and demand for commodity increases by 10 percent then the income elasticity of demand is

    a. Infinity b. Negative

    c. Zero d. Positive

20. One common definition of a luxury good is a good with an income elasticity of

    a. Less than one but more than zero b. Greater than

    c. Equal to one d. none of these

21. A straight line, downward sloping demand curves implies that, as price falls, the elasticity of demand.

    a. Is zero b. Remains same

    c. Decreases d. Increases

22. Other things being equal a decreased in demand can be caused by

    a. A rises in the price of the commodity

    b. A rise in the income of the consumer

    c. A falls in the price of the commodity

    d. A rise in the price of substitute

23. Elasticity of demand can be measured in the following way

    a. $\frac{\text{Percentage of change in demand}}{\text{Percentage of change in price}}$

    b. $\frac{\text{Change in demand}}{\text{Change in price}}$

    c. % Change in price / % Change in supply

    d. $\frac{\text{\% Change in demand}}{\text{\% Change in price}}$

24. A demand curve which is horizontal and parallel to the axis represents

    a. Relatively inelastic demand b. Relatively elastic demand

    c. Infinitely elastic demand d. Infinitely inelastic demand

25. The law of Demand which

    a. Can be completely discarded

    b. Has numerous exceptions and therefore not helpful

    c. Cannot be verified and therefore unrealistic

    d. Is of fundamental importance and ideal to broad conclusions.

26. If two goods are complements, this means that a rise in the price of one commodity will induce
    a. No shift in demand for the other commodity.
    b. A downward shift in demand for the other commodity.
    c. An upward shift in demand for the other commodity.
    d. A rise in price of the other commodity.
27. The law of Demand which
    a. Can be completely discarded
    b. Has numerous exceptions and therefore not helpful
    c. Cannot be verified and therefore unrealistic
    d. Is of fundamental importance and ideal to broad conclusions.
28. Which of the following is the odd one out among the methods of measuring elasticity of demand?
    a. Point method
    b. Arc method
    c. Percentage method
    d. None of these
29. Which of the following is a cause of a movement along ht demand curve?
    a. Improvement in Technology
    b. Change in price of a complementary good
    c. Change in price of the commodity
    d. Change in price of a substitute good
30. The term demand in economics means
    a. Ability of a society to buy all that is available in the market at a given time.
    b. Desire of an individual to buy a certain amount of a good or service.
    c. Ability of an individual to buy a certain amount of a good or service.
    d. Both b and c.
31. The devaluation of currency would increased the export earnings only when the demand for the nations exports in the foreign market is
    a. Elastic
    b. Inelastic
    c. Perfectly elastic
    d. unitary elastic

32. With an increase in income, a consumer is expected to buy more of

    a. All kinds of goods b. Normal goods.

    c. Inferior goods d. Geffen goods

33. Ceteris paribus (other things being equal), the quantity demanded of a commodity falls as its price rises. This fact is known as

    a. Decreased in demand b. Extension of demand

    c. Contraction of demand d. Increased in demand

34. In measuring price elasticity

    a. Price and quantity both are dependent variable

    b. Price and quantity both are independent variable

    c. Price is an independent variable and quantity is a dependent variable

    d. Price is a dependent variable and quantity is an independent variable

35. Which equations suitable where the income elasticity demand is concerned

    a. $\frac{\text{Changc in income}}{100 \times \text{change in quantity demanded}}$

    b. $\frac{\text{Percentage change in income}}{\text{Change in quantity demanded}}$

    c. $\frac{\text{Percentage change in quantity demanded}}{\text{Percentage change in income}}$

    d. None of these

36. To get more revenue, a finance minister must tax a commodity.

    a. With elastic demand b. With unit elasticity

    c. With more than unit elasticity d. With inelastic demand

37. There is increase in demand when

    a. less is demanded at the same price

    b. more is demanded at a lower price

    c. less is demanded at a higher price

    d. None of these

38. Micro-economic theory study how an economy determine

    a. the price of goods
    b. the price of services
    c. Cross elasticity
    d. Arc elasticity

39. The term "consumer goods" is used by economists to refer to

    a. goods produced for consumers in a free market only
    b. goods, other than free goods, whose use directly satisfies consumer's wants
    c. goods produced by consumers in return for a wage
    d. goods which are used by consumers in order to earn their living

40. Which of the following is not an economic problem?

    a. deciding between extra paid work and extra leisure
    b. deciding between different ways of spending leisure time
    c. deciding on the level and form of personal saving
    d. deciding between expenditure on one good and another

41. Economics

    a. contains a valid core of theory applicable to all economic systems
    b. is normative
    c. is concerned only with capitalism
    d. predicts the near future but not the far future

42. Two goods have to be consumed simultaneously are

    a. identical
    b. complementary
    c. substitutes
    d. none of these

43. When with a change in price the total outlay on a commodity remains constant, it is a case of

    a. perfect elasticity
    b. perfect inelasticity
    c. unit elasticity
    d. zero elasticity

44. The price elasticity of demand for a good A is minus 2. What is the change in price that will induce a 10% fall in the quantity demanded?

    a. –20%
    b. 5%
    c. +20%
    d. +2%

45. Market demand is

a. the sum of all individual demands

b. demand at prevailing average prices

c. ability to pay the price asked

d. demand in a perfectly free market

46. Which of the following is the method of measuring elasticity of demand when changes in price of a commodity is substantial?

a. percentage method b. point method

c. arc method d. none of these

47. The greater the percentage of income spent on a commodity

a. the greater its elasticity is likely to be

b. the weaker its elasticity is like to be

c. the unchanged its elasticity is likely to be

d. nothing can be said

48. $\frac{q1-q}{q1+q}\times\frac{p1-p}{p1+p}$ is to find out (Where p,p1 : Initial and final prices; q,q1 : demands at the above prices)

a. Point elasticity b. Percentage elasticity

c. Cross elasticity d. Arc elasticity

49. Cross elasticity of demand is measured as

a. Percentage change in quantity demanded of commodity 'X' divided by Percentage change in price of commodity 'Y'.

b. Percentage change in the quantity of a commodity demanded divided by the Percentage change in the price of that commodity.

c. Percentage change in quantity demanded of commodity 'X' divided by Percentage change in quantity demanded of commodity 'Y'.

d. None of these.

50. In economics production may be defined as an act of

a. Creating utility b. earning profit

c. Producing machine d. Providing services

51. The production function describes the
    a. Economic relationship between input and output.
    b. Technological relationship between input and output.
    c. Mathematical relationship between input and output.
    d. (a) and (b)
52. The production function relates:
    a. Wages to output
    b. Cost to input
    c. Inputs to output
    d. Costs to output
53. Which of the stage is relevant for affirm which aims at maximum economic efficiency?
    (a) Stage III
    b. Stage II
    c. Stage I
    d. Stage I and Stage II
54. Stage II production begins where the AP of labor begins to decline:
    a. Never
    b. Zero
    c. Always
    d. Any of the above:
55. When the AP of labor is positive but declining the MP of labor could be
    a. Declining
    b. Zero
    c. Negative
    d. Any of the above:
56. In short run the Law of variable proportions is also known as the:
    a. Law of increasing returns
    b. Law of diminishing returns
    c. Law of constant returns
    d. Law of return to scale.
57. Which of the following statements is correct with regard to law of variable proportion?
    a. The average and marginal product of the variable factor will eventually become constant
    b. The average and marginal product of the variable factor will eventually decreases
    c. The average and marginal product of the constant factor will eventually decreased
    d. The average and total product of the variable factor will eventually decrease
58. Regarding the law of variable proportions, all inputs are free to vary "It is":
    a. Absolutely wrong
    b. Wrong, and one input is fixed while the other is free to vary
    c. Correct and the two inputs are not perfect complements
    d. A and b are correct

59. The marginal product is:
    a. The extra input obtained form employing an additional unit of a factor
    b. The extra output obtained form employing an additional unit of a factor
    c. The extra profit obtained form employing an additional unit of a factor.
    d. The extra loss suffered form employing and additional unit of a factor.
60. Odd one out of the following:
    a. The AFC curve   b. The AVC curve
    c. The MC   d. The AC curve
61. The economies and diseconomies of large scale production is determined by:]
    a. The long run MCC   b. The short run ACC
    c. The normal long run ACC   d. The normal long run TCC
62. In the long run:
    a. price is equal to maximum average total cost
    b. price is greater than average total cost
    c. price is equal to minimum average total cost
    d. price is equal to minimum average cost
63. When the output produced is maximum for the given level of inputs the firms achieve:
    a. Technical efficiency   b. Technological efficiency
    c. Production efficiency   d. Maximum profit
64. When the output of a firm is increasing its average fixed cost
    a. Decline and then rises   b. Decline continuously
    c. Decline in a constant nature   d. Rise continuously.
65. Increasing returns to scale can be explained in terms
    a. External diseconomies and internal economies.
    b. External and internal economies.
    c. External internal diseconomies.
    d. External diseconomies and internal economies
66. "Marketing economies may be on the buying or selling side of a business" This Statement is
    a. Correct   b. Correct but not complete
    c. Neither complete nor correct   d. None of these.

67. The external diseconomies of scale experienced by a firm include the
    a. Supply of suitable skilled labour in the area
    b. Growth of firms processing its waste materials
    c. Development of Research Unit Servicing the industry
    d. None of these
68. If there is a fixed factor and variable factor the law should be:
    a. Law of variable proportion
    b. Law of increasing return to scale
    c. Law of diminishing marginal utility
    d. Law of Equi-marginal utility.
69. When the average product is above the marginal product means.
    a. Average product is increasing
    b. Average product is decreasing
    c. Average product remains constant
    d. Average product shows high profit.
70. The marginal product curve is above the average product curve when the average product is:
    a. Decreasing b. Increasing
    c. Becomes constant d. None of the above
71. Implicit cost may be considered as
    a. Social cost b. Imputed cost
    c. Private cost d. Variable cost
72. Which of the following is not correct in connection with variable cost?
    a. It can be referred to as the prime cost
    b. It can be referred to as the direct cost
    c. It can be referred to as sunk cost
    d. It can be referred to as avoidable cost.
73. Average fixed cost can be obtained through
    a. AFC = TFC/total units b. AFC = FC/variable cost
    c. AFC = TC/FC d. AFC = TFC/TQ

74. The average variable cost is the difference of
    a. AVC and TC
    b. AFC and TFC
    c. A VC and MC
    d. AFC and ATC
75. Marginal Cost is:
    a. The additional cost of producing an extra unit of input.
    b. The additional cost of production
    c. The additional cost producing an extra unit of output
    d. a) or b)
76. A firm's variable costs purely depends on:
    a. Firm's input
    b. Firm's raw materials
    c. Firm's output
    d. Firm's investment
77. The average profit an be obtained while taking the difference between
    a. AC and AR
    b. AR and TR
    c. AC and TR
    d. TC and TR
78. Which of the following cost is closely related to Marginal cost
    a. Fixed cost
    b. Implicit cost
    c. Indirect cost
    d. Variable cost
79. Which of the following is correct in connection with variable cost?
    a. Paying the manager of the factory
    b. Paying the labourers
    c. Paying for heavy machines
    d. Paying for the building
80. Odd one out
    a. Fixed cost
    b. Direct cost
    c. Variable cost
    d. Avoidable cost
81. The general average cost curve, is also known as
    a. Total cost curve
    b. Average total cost curve
    c. Total marginal cost curve
    d. Average fixed cost curve
82. The operating costs can be included in:
    a. Fixed cost
    b. Opportunity cost
    c. Variable cost
    d. Implicit cost

83. An example for book cost is

a. raw material
b. building
c. furniture
d. depreciation

84. Cost which don't involve any expenditure is called.

a. sunk cost
b. shut down cost
c. avoidable cost
d. out of pocket cost

85. Fixed costs which have to be incurred even if production of an undertaking are discontinued temporarily are called

a. sunk cost
b. shut down cost
c. avoidable cost
d. out of pocket cost

86. Costs which have been incurred and are irrelevant in a particular situation are called

a. sunk cost
b. shut down cost
c. abnormal cost
d. unavoidable cost

87. The costs which are partly fixed and partly variable are called

a. fixed cost
b. variable cost
c. semi-variable cost
d. imputed cost

88. Interest on owned money capital is an

a. Implicit cost
b. Fixed cost
c. Explicit cost
d. Explicit cost of production.

89. The technical relationship between input as a variable factor and the resulting output. Is the definition of?

a. Law of increasing returns
b. Law of diminishing returns.
c. Law of return to sale
d. Law of decreasing return to scale.

90. Which of the following tend the MC curve to rise up?

a. Law of increasing returns to scale
b. External diseconomies
c. Law of variable proportion
d. Law of diminishing returns to scale.

91. Alternative cost are also known as

a. Opportunity cost
b. Direct cost
c. Fixed cost
d. Variable costs

92. Which of the followings statement is correct? Fixed costs are:

    a. Those costs which do not decrease as output increases

    b. Those costs which do not increase as output increases

    c. Those costs which do not increases as output decreases

    d. a) and b) only.

93. The marginal cost curve first decreases and then increases as:

    a. The input increases form Zero upwards

    b. The output increases from middle not from zero

    c. The input increases form zero upwards.

    d. The output increases form zero upwards.

94. The sum of total cost and total variable cost is equal to:

    a. Total marginal cost b. Total variable cost

    c. Sunk cost d. Total cost in the short run

95. Book costs are also called as

    a. fixed cost b. variable cost

    c. imputed cost d. explicit cost

96. Out of pocket cost are also called as

    a. fixed cost b. variable cost

    c. imputed cost d. explicit cost

97. Calculate explicit cost form the given data

    Land owned : Rs. 2000

    Family labour Rs. 1000

    Labour hired Rs. 2000

    Material purchase Rs. 5000

    Machine purchase Rs. 4500

    a. 11,500 b. 5,000

    c. 10,000 d. 3,000

98. Calculate explicit cost from the given data

Land owned : Rs. 2000

Family labour Rs. 1000

Labour hired Rs. 2000

Material purchase Rs. 5000

Machine purchase Rs. 4500

a. 11,500 b. 3,000

c. 10,000 d. 5,000

99. When variable cost decreases the Break Even Point

a. Increases b. decreases

c. Remains same d. in determinate

100. Under perfect Competition the number of firms:

a. Are many b. Is limited

c. Are so many d. Are many but limited.

101. Which of the following statement is correct?

i. One of the essential conditions of perfect Competition is product differentiation.

ii. One of the essential conditions of perfect Competition is only one price prevails for identical goods at any one time.

iii. An individual demand curve and market demand curve coincide each other in a monopolist market.

iv. A commodity will have value only if it is scare relative to demand.

a. ii) and iii) b. i) and ii)

c. i) and iii) d. i) and iv)

102. Pure oligopoly means:

a. A few firms produce a homogeneous product.

b. A few industries produce a homogeneous product.

c. A few firms produce a heterogeneous product.

d. A few firms produce differentiated and identical product.

103. Degree of control over the price of its product by monopoly is

a. Very small b. Very large

c. Negligible d. a) or c)

104. Agriculture products an example of:

a. Perfectly competitive model b. Imperfectly Competitive model.

c. Monopoly model d. Oligopoly model.

105. Under Perfect Competition the price of product:

a. Can be controlled b. Can't be controlled

c. Control within certain limit d. None of the above

106. A market firm implies that two firms are known as:

a. Oligopoly b. Oligopsony

c. Duopsoy d. Duopoly

107. Only one price for identical goods at any one time, is the essential condition of:

a. Monopoly b. Monopolistic competition

c. Perfect competition d. Monopsony

108. For maximizing profit in the short run, the condition is:

a. AR=AC b. MR = MC

c. MR = AR d. MC = AC

109. An entrepreneur will stay in business in the long run as long as he meets:

a. All costs of production b. Fixed costs of production

c. Variable costs of production d. None of these

110. Monopolistic competition constitutes

a. Single firm production close substitutes

b. Many firms producing close substitutes

c. Few firms producing differentiated products of close substitutes

d. None of these.

111. Under perfect competition : Which equation is true?

i. MC = P ii. MC>P

iii. MC<P iv. None of these

a. I) and iii) only b. iv) only

c. I) only d. iii) only

112. Under perfect competition a firm can produce with

a. An optimum plant b. An optimum output

c. Maximum profit d. Identical products at low cost.

113. A situation in which the number of competing firms is relatively small is known as

a. Monopoly
b. Perfect Competition
c. Monopolistic competition
d. Oligopoly

114. The firms are under severs pressure to keep their costs low, a situation characterized by

a. Perfect competition
b. Duopoly competition
c. Monopoly competition
d. Monopolistic competition

115. Cigarette industries are closely related to

a. Perfectly competition
b. Imperfectly competitive model
c. Monopolistic market
d. Oligopolistic market

116. A single seller of a particular product in a particular town or city means

a. Monopsony
b. Perfect competition
c. Monopoly
d. Monopolistic competition

117 There is a single seller of a commodity which has no close substitutes

a. Pure oligopoly
b. Pure monopoly
c. Monopoly
d. Duopoly

118 Price control is one of the monopoly regulations which is post advantageous for:

a. The producer
b. The consumer
c. The government
d. The seller

119. In differentiated oligopoly, firms are producing:

a. Close substitutes and not identical goods
b. Some identical goods
c. Differentiated and identical goods
d. Close substitutes and identical goods

120. Which of the following is an example of perfect competition?

a. Indian railways
b. Doordarshan
c. Computer hardware industry
d. Agriculture industry

121. Which of the following is not a characteristic of monopoly?

a. Only one producer
b. Firm is active price marker
c. Product differentiation
d. Large profit margins

122. Monopolistic competition means

a. Large number of firms producing
b. Differentiated of advertising
c. Brand loyalty
d. All of the above

123. Which of the following is / are example of monopolistic competition

a. Toothpaste industry
b. Television sets
c. Soap & detergents
d. All of the above

124. Oligopolistic competition means

a. Supply is concentrated in few hands
b. high profit margins
c. Advertisement
d. all of the above

125. The main difference between the oligopolistic market and that of monopolistic competition is that under oligopoly

a. there are few sellers, each with a sizable proportion of the market.
b. There is no competition through advertising
c. There is a product differentiation
d. The firms will earn super-normal profits

126. Which of the following assumption is correct in connection with oligopoly

a. if an oligopolies increase his price his rivals will follow
b. if an oligopolist increase his price his rivals will not follow
c. if an oligopolist increase his price his rivals will lower their price
d. if an oligopolist increase his price his rivals will not react

127. When in a market the number of buyers is very large and the number of sellers is very small, it is known as

a. monopoly
b. oligopoly
c. imperfect competition
d. perfect competition

128. Price discrimination is under taken with aim of

a. increasing sales maximizing profits
b. reducing sales and raising prices
c. minimizing cost & maximizing revenue
d. serving the market with earning of profits

129. Dumping means selling at
   a. a higher price in home market and lower price in foreign market
   b. a lower price in home market and higher price in foreign market
   c. the same price in the home and the foreign markets
   d. a lower price in home market and different prices in foreign markets

130. Monopoly power is high when
   a. there are no close substitutes
   b. there are no competitions
   c. there is only one seller of a product
   d. all the above

131. Monopolist can fix
   a. both price and output
   b. either price or output
   c. neither price nor output
   d. none of the above

132. The retailed trade, in general provides an example of
   a. perfect competition
   b. monopolistic competition
   c. oligopoly
   d. monopoly

133. Monopsony is a form of market organization in which there is a
   a. single seller of an output
   b. single seller of an input
   c. single buyer of an input
   d. single buyer of an output

134. The AR curve and industry demand cure are same
   a. in case of monopoly
   b. in case of oligopoly
   c. in case of perfect competition
   d. monopolistic competition

135. Bilateral monopoly means
   a. two rival sellers only
   b. two rival buyers only
   c. a monopoly seller buying his input from many suppliers
   d. a monopolist facing a monoponist

136. Price discrimination is possible
   a. only under monopoly situation
   b. under any market form
   c. only under monopolistic competition
   d. only under perfect competition

137. "It can sell as much as it wants at the market price" is related to

a. perfect competition b. monopoly

c. oligopoly d. monopsony

138. The loss or decrease in the value of assets is called as

a. Depreciation b. Appreciation

c. Realization d. Outstanding

139. Opening stock plus purchases plus direct expenses for

a. Sales a/c b. Profit and Loss a/c

c. Capital d. Net profit

140. ____________ cycle is required for estimation of working capital.

a. gross working capital b. working capital

c. money d. business

141. Net working capital is the difference between ________________

a. fixed assets and current assets b. current assets and current liabilities

c. current assets and fixed liabilities d. current liabilities and fixed assets

142. Long Term Investment of funds is called ________________

a. capital b. net working capital

c. gross working capital d. capital budgeting

143. Plough back funds is ________________ source of Fund

a. long term b. internal

c. preference share d. equity share

144. ______________ holders have preference over dividends.

a. debenture b. preference share

c. preference share d. equity share

145. ____________ shares are traded on stock exchange if they are listed

a. equity b. public deposits

c. debenture d. bonds

146. Value printed on share is called ________________

a. equity b. premium

c. preference d. face value

147. Dividends are fixed in the case of ___________________

a. debenture b. equity

c. preference d. public deposit

148. Example for internal sources of funds ___________

a. Ploughing back fund b. bank loans more than one year

c. shares d. debentures

149. Raising capital for long term from general public is called ______________

a. ploughing-back b. trade credit

c. equity d. public deposits

150. Interest is paid on loan and dividend is paid for ___________________

a. debenture b. public deposits

c. bank loan d. equity share

151. ______________ payment is legal obligation

a. interest b. dividend

c. bonus d. loan

152. Expand DCF ______________

a. Discounted Cash Flow method b. Dividend Cash Fund

c. Debenture Cash Fund d. Debtor Cash Fund

153. Expand NPV _________________

a. Net Positive Value b. Net Preference Value

c. Net Present Value d. a) or b)

154. ___________________ methods of capital budgeting do not consider Present Value of Money concept.

a. Net present value b. Payback period

c. Profitability index d. Internal rate return

155. _________________ table we see for present value if there are constant cash flows.

a. Annuity b. Present

c. Compound Interest d. Simple Interest

156. A rate at which Profitability Index (PI) = 1 and net present value (NPV) = 0 is called ________________

a. Payback period b. internal rate of return

c. Net prate of return d. accounting rate of return

157. Present value calculation is reciprocal of ________________ calculation.

a. Simple interest b. compound interest

c. Annuity table d. payback period

158. Allocation of funds to various projects through capital budgeting is called ____________

a. Capital rationing b. capital expenditure

c. Capital receipt d. revenue expenditure

159. Formula for net present value ________________

a. Present value of cash outflows / present value of cash inflow

b. Present value of cash inflows/ present value of cash outflow

c. Present value of cash inflows less present value of cash outflow

d. Present value of cash outflow plus present value of cash inflow

160. The book in which all transactions are recorded in Chronological order is called

a. Journal b. Ledger

c. Trial Balance d. Balance sheet

161. ________________ is a book of prime or original entry.

a. Ledger b. Single Entry Book Keeping

c. Journalizing d. posting

162. The process of recording transactions in journal is called ________________

a. Journal b. Ledger

c. Trial balance d. Balance sheet

163. In case of personal accounts receiver's account is ________________

a. Debited b. Credited

c. Posted d. Journalized

164. In case of personal account giver's account should be ________________

a. Debited b. Credited

c. Posted d. Journalized

165. In case of real accounts Debit is given to ________________

a. What comes in
b. What comes in
c. What goes out
d. The giver

166. In case of real accounts Credit is given to ________________

a. What goes out
b. What comes in
c. The receiver
d. The giver

167. Expenses and losses should be ________________ in journal

a. Credited
b. Debited
c. Not to be considered in Journal
d. Appear both in Debit and Credit based on the nature of item

168. While passing journal entries accounts dealing with incomes and gain should be ____________

a. Credited
b. Debited
c. Not to be considered in Journal
d. Appear both in Debit and Credit based on the nature of item

169. Cash purchases from Deepak should be credited to ______________

a. Purchase Account
b. Cash Account
c. Deepak Account
d. Goods Account

170. Cash purchased of goods from Sunil should be debited ____________

a. Purchase account
b. cash account
c. Sunil account
d. Drawings account

171. A credit sale of goods to Ram should be debited to ____________

a. Ram account
b. Sales account
c. Credit account
d. Cash account

172. Purchase of Furniture for cash from Mr. X should be debited to ____________

a. Furniture account
b. Purchase account
c. Cash account
d. Mr. X account

173. A sale of goods to Varma for cash should be debited to ________________

a. Goods account
b. Cash account
c. Sales account
d. Varma account

174. Withdrawal of cash form business by the Proprietor should be debited to

a. Proprietor account
b. Cash account
c. Sales account
d. Drawing account

175. Withdrawal of goods form business by the Proprietor should be credited to

a. Proprietor account
b. Cash account
c. Bank account
d. Goods account

176. What is the rule of normalization in case of real accounts?

a. Debit: What comes in
b. Debit: Expenses and Losses
c. Debit: The Receiver
Credit: The giver
d. Credit: What goes out
Credit: The receiver

177. What is the rule of normalization in case of personal accounts?

a. Debit: What comes in
b. Debit: Expenses and Losses
c. Debit: The Receiver
Credit: The giver
d. Credit: What goes out
Credit: The receiver

178. What is the rule of normalization in case of nominal accounts?

a. Debit: What comes in
b. Debit: Expenses and Losses
c. Debit: The Receiver
Credit: The giver
d. Credit: What goes out
Credit: The receiver

179. Name the Main book of Accounts in which all accounts are kept

a. Sales Book
b. Cash Book
c. Ledger
d. Purchase Book

180. Managerial economics is close to

a. Micro economics
b. Macro economics
c. assertive
d. Theory of Wages and Employment

181. Integration of economic theory with business practice is called

a. Managerial economics
b. Economics
c. Macro economics
d. Micro Economics

182. Which of the following is NOT a problem of business?

a. optimisation of inputs b. minimisation of costs

c. maximisation of revenue d. increased property tax collections

183. Who said that economics is the study of nature and uses of national wealth?

a. Paul A. Samuelson b. Prof. Lionel Robbins

c. Adam Smith d. Alfred Marshal

184. "Economics is the study of scarce resources and unlimited wants". Who said this?

a. Paul A. Sameulson b. Prof. Lionel Robbins

c. Adam Smith d. Alfred Marshal

185. Which of the following cannot be verified by looking at the facts?

a. positive statement b. prescriptive actions

c. normative statement d. welfare statement

186. Which of the following is not covered by Managerial Economics?

a. price-output decision b. profit related decision

c. investment decision d. foreign direct investment (FDI) decision

187. Which one of these is not a recent government measure to strengthen the economy?

a. Globalisation b. Encouraging mergers and acquisitions

c. Strengthening MRTP Act d. Restrictive trade practices

188. The pre-requisite for rational decision-making is

a. logical analysis of one's choices without error

b. consistency between goals and choices

c. rigidly defined choices

d. choices not involving any trade-offs

189. Which of the following is a normative statement?

a. Reducing inequality should be a major priority for mixed economies

b. Reducing inequality would be a major priority for mixed economics

c. Reducing inequality could be a major priority for mixed economics

d. Reducing inequality might be a major priority for mixed eonomies.

190. Economic goods are scarce resources because they

a. are limited in supply to satisfy society requirements

b. are limited to man made goods

c. cannot be increased in terms of supply

d. are important to satisfy human needs

191. Which of the following indicates micro approach from national perspective?

a. lock out in a factory
b. per capita income of the country
c. total investments in India
d. total employment in the country

192. Gopal: Rains are very poor this year.

Karuna: Seeds available in the market are also unreliable.

Madan: Fertilisers presently available with the dealer is also in quality.

Radha : we ought to be selective while we purchase.

In this conversation, who makes a normative statement?

a. Gopal
b. Karuna
c. Madan
d. Radha

193. Which of the following is the technical relationship that reveals the maximum amount of output capable of being produced by each and every set of inputs?

a. Cobb-Douglas production function
b. Production function
c. Theory of production
d. Economies of scale

194. With which of the following is the production function more concerned?

a. financial aspects
b. technological aspects
c. physical aspects
d. economic aspects

195. Which of the following is defined at a given stage of technical knowledge?

a. Theory of Production
b. Production Function
c. Law of Diminishing Returns
d. Law of Constant Returns

196. The Law of Returns is also called

a. Law of Fixed Proportions
b. Law of Variable Proportions
c. Law of Constant Returns
d. Law of Increasing Returns

197. The Law of Returns states that when at least one factor of production is fixed and when others are varied, the total output in the initial stages will .... at an increasing rate, and after reaching certain level of output, the total output will .... at declining rate.

    a. increase, decrease
    b. decrease, increase
    c. decrease, decrease
    d. increase, increase

198. In the short run, it is assumed that capital is a .... factor input and labour is a .... input.

    a. variable, variable
    b. fixed, fixed
    c. variable, fixed
    d. fixed, variable

199. Isoquants are also called

    a. isoproduct curves
    b. isocost curves
    c. price indifference curve
    d. indifference curve

200. Which of the following is not a feature of an isoquant?

    a. downward sloping
    b. convex to origin
    c. one intersecting the other isoquant
    d. do not touch axes

ANSWERS

1. b	2. d	3. b	4. a	5. c	6. a	7. d
8. b	9. a	10. a	11. a	12. d	13. b	14. b
15. b	16. a	17. c	18. a	19. c	20. d	21. b
22. d	23. d	24. a	25. c	26. b	27. d	28. d
29. c	30. d	31. a	32. b	33. d	34. c	35. e
36. c	37. c	38. d	39. d	40. d	41. d	42. d
43. b	44. b	45. a	46. b	47. c	48. b	49. a
50. a	51. b	52. c	53. c	54. b	55. d	56. b
57. b	58 b	59. b	60. c	61. b	62. b	63. b
64. b	65. a	66. d	67. a	68. b	69. b	70. a
71. b	72. c	73. c	74. d	75. c	76. c	77. a
78. d	79. b	80. a	81. b	82. c	83. a	84. b
85. d	86. d	87. c	88. b	89. a	90. c	91. a
92. b	93. d	94. d	95. c	96. d	97. a	98. d
99. b	100. a	101. a	102. a	103. b	104. a	105. b
106. d	107. c	108. b	109. c	110. d	111. c	112. a
113. d	114. d	115. d	116. c	117. b	118. b	119. a
120. a	121. c	122. b	123. d	124. a	125. a	126. a
127. b	128. b	129. a	130. a	131. d	132. b	133. b
134. c	135. a	136. d	137. a	138. a	139. b	140. b
141. b	142. d	143. b	144. b	145. a	146. d	147. c
148. a	149. c	150. d	151. a	152. a	153. c	154. b
155.a	156. b	157. b	158. a	159. c	160. a	161. a
162. c	163. a	164. b	165. a	166. a	167. b	168. a
169. b	170. a	171. a	172. a	173. b	174. d	175. d
176. a	177. c	178. b	179. c	180. a	181. a	182. d
183. c	184 d	185. c	186. 5	187. c	188. d	189. a
190. a	191. a	192. d	193. d	194. c	195. b	196. d
197. d	198. d	199. a	200. c			

Index

L

M

N

O

P

R

S

U

V

W